T0351122

Crypto Millionaires

Blockchain, *the key to the world of cryptocurrencies*—a phrase that sounds like a promise of wealth. But what exactly is Blockchain? Unfortunately, in most books, articles, and discussions, it is either explained in a way that's hard to understand or oversimplified with unnecessary emotional baggage, presented either technically or ideologically. Some see Blockchain as a savior from greedy bankers, while others view it as a tool for building cryptocurrencies that undermine central banks. Which image is closer to reality? The story of Blockchain is not just a tale of mathematical experiments. It's primarily a story of the age-old attempt to record human activities and the value that flows from them. This time, however, the goal is to make it accessible to everyone on equal terms.

This book delves into the evolution and technical intricacies of Blockchain technology, steering clear of the common focus on mere cryptocurrency speculation. It clarifies complex concepts and underscores Blockchain's capacity to revolutionize industries and empower individuals globally, thereby demystifying the technology and making its profound potential accessible to everyone.

Mateusz Mach is the founder of Nextrope, a leading software company in the Blockchain industry, which specializes in Blockchain implementations for enterprise clients and governments. At the age of 17, he developed Five App, the world's first messenger designed for the deaf community. He is an alumnus of New York University Abu Dhabi and a finalist in the *Forbes* Europe 30 Under 30 ranking as well as the New Europe 100 list, coordinated by Google and the *Financial Times*.

Crypto Millionaires
Blockchain: A Chance for All?

Mateusz Mach

CRC Press
Taylor & Francis Group
Boca Raton London New York

CRC Press is an imprint of the
Taylor & Francis Group, an **informa** business

Designed cover image: © Mateusz Mach and Karolina Stasica

First edition published 2025
by CRC Press
2385 NW Executive Center Drive, Suite 320, Boca Raton FL 33431

and by CRC Press
4 Park Square, Milton Park, Abingdon, Oxon, OX14 4RN

CRC Press is an imprint of Taylor & Francis Group, LLC

© 2025 Mateusz Mach

Library of Congress Cataloging-in-Publication Data
Names: Mach, Mateusz, author.
Title: Crypto millionaires : blockchain: a chance for all? / Mateusz Mach.
Description: First edition. | Boca Raton, FL : CRC Press, 2025.
Identifiers: LCCN 2024001523 (print) | LCCN 2024001524 (ebook) |
ISBN 9781032621418 (hbk) | ISBN 9781032621432 (pbk) |
ISBN 9781032621456 (ebk)
Subjects: LCSH: Cryptocurrencies. | Blockchains (Databases) | Millionaires.
Classification: LCC HG1710.3 .M24 2025 (print) | LCC
HG1710.3 (ebook) | DDC 332.4/048--dc23/eng/20240412
LC record available at https://lccn.loc.gov/2024001523
LC ebook record available at https://lccn.loc.gov/2024001524

ISBN: 978-1-032-62141-8 (hbk)
ISBN: 978-1-032-62143-2 (pbk)
ISBN: 978-1-032-62145-6 (ebk)

DOI: 10.1201/9781032621456

Typeset in Sabon
by SPi Technologies India Pvt Ltd (Straive)

For my mom,
so that you finally understand exactly what I do :)

"If we want things to stay as they are, things will have to change."
—*Giuseppe Tomasi di Lampedusa*

Contents

Acknowledgments

I would like to express my heartfelt gratitude to Michał Andrzejewski, with whom I collaborated both at my software house, Nextrope, and in this book project. I met Michał back at NYU, as we studied Economics as classmates. Our passionate discussions about Technology and Finance sparked many of the curiosities I then explored and finally shared in this book. His unwavering support and invaluable contributions played a pivotal role in shaping *Crypto Millionaires*. Michał not only provided meticulous editing but also offered critical economic, financial, sociological, and historical insights that enriched the narrative and depth of this exploration into the Blockchain riches.

A special thanks is also extended to the talented translators Agata Kóska and Karolina Stasica, whose dedication and linguistic prowess ensured that the essence of my message, originally penned in Polish for the first edition, was faithfully conveyed to a broader audience. Their commitment to preserving the integrity of the content in multiple languages has made this book accessible to a global readership.

Running Nextrope, a company devoted to delivering cutting-edge solutions in Web 3.0, Blockchain, and the Metaverse, has been a journey of continuous learning and innovation. This book is a reflection of the experiences, lessons, and stories gathered along this exciting path.

To all those who shared their tales of success and hardship, thank you for contributing to the rich tapestry of *Crypto Millionaires*. Your stories serve as both inspiration and cautionary tales, offering readers a glimpse into the diverse landscapes of cryptocurrency entrepreneurship.

Finally, to the readers, I extend my sincere gratitude. Your interest in exploring the world of Blockchain technology is not just a journey through these pages but an invitation to embark on your own path toward becoming a cryptocurrency entrepreneur. In a world that constantly evolves, may this book be a guide and a source of motivation as you navigate the exciting and dynamic realm of crypto.

Happy reading and best of luck on your entrepreneurial endeavors!

Introduction

Panta rhei. That's Greek for "everything flows." Everything moves and evolves. The only constant in the world is change. And Blockchain technology is no different.

When I developed my first Blockchain project, I was at college—at New York University, to be more precise. At that point, I was devoting a significant portion of my time to typical student life at a top-tier university. I was attending lectures. Not to make it nerdy, I was following only those academic discussions that really sparked my interest. Majoring in Economics and having already a solid tech and entrepreneurial background from my earlier projects, I naturally picked up all the little arguments between famous professors on how cryptocurrencies were a bubble that would have soon disappeared as a worthless gimmick for not-so-economically sound teens.

The time has passed, proving wrong all the ex-cathedra rules preached by the academic antagonists of this story. "Thou shalt not bullshit"—one could have commanded those critics who had not seen the potential of the Blockchain in its earliest days.

For sure it makes for a funny story, the irony of some academics not wrapping their heads around crypto soon enough. Yet it has some broader implications. It illustrates the phenomenon of spontaneous embracement of decentralization that you cannot ignore if you want your opinion to matter in the economic and financial world.

As I write this introduction in March 2024, reflecting on the journey of writing this book throughout 2023, there was never a shadow of doubt in my mind that cryptocurrencies were bound to become a key part of the economy. I was particularly convinced that instruments based on Bitcoin, would gain recognition as legitimate financial tools. Now, I am thrilled to announce that the market has officially entered a bullish phase. For the first time since 2021, Bitcoin has shattered its previous all-time high (ATH).

The term "crypto winter" describes a downturn in the cryptocurrency market, characterized by declining prices and investor skepticism. However, this challenging phase did not signify the end for cryptocurrencies. Rather, it was a period of intense consolidation and maturation. During the crypto winter, the industry witnessed significant advancements. Developers and

DOI: 10.1201/9781032621456-1

companies focused on innovation, improving Blockchain technology, enhancing security, and refining user experiences. That era saw the emergence of platforms and applications that extended Blockchain's utility beyond just financial speculation.

Simultaneously, regulatory bodies around the world began to provide clearer guidelines for digital currencies. This period also acted as a natural selection process, where only projects with genuine utility and strong fundamentals survived. This helped clean up the market, setting the stage for a healthier ecosystem.

The early months of 2024 marked a significant turnaround when U.S. Securities and Exchange Commission approved Bitcoin Exchange-Traded Funds (ETFs), offering a regulated and accessible way for investors to engage with Bitcoin. This was viewed as a critical step toward integrating digital currencies into the broader financial landscape.

Additionally, the crypto community's excitement about the upcoming Bitcoin halving event, which will cut the reward for mining new blocks in half, has significantly contributed to the overall optimism. Historically, these halving events have served as pivotal moments for Bitcoin, often leading to substantial price increases. Interestingly, this cycle witnessed Bitcoin reaching a new all-time high even before the halving took place, deviating from past patterns where peak values were observed post-halving. This shift underscores growing confidence in Bitcoin and a faster mainstream acceptance of cryptocurrencies.

Simultaneously, the evolution from the "crypto winter" to a bullish market highlights the industry's resilience and its cyclical nature. It suggests a mature and sustainable path forward for digital currencies. This growth is mirrored in the broader business landscape.

Leading global corporations are now integrating decentralized databases and distributed ledger technology (DLT) into their daily operations. Commercial banks are offering products based on cryptocurrencies. Crypto companies are either already listed on stock exchanges or gearing up for spectacular initial public offerings. Just a few years ago, such developments would have been unthinkable. Cryptocurrencies used to be either combated or shoved into the financial world's shadows. The way the tables have turned is, in my estimation, the most definitive proof that we are in the middle of a business and economic revolution.

Every turning point in history presents enormous opportunities, not just for societies but especially for the Bold and the Brave. Take the American industrialists at the turn of the 19th and 20th centuries or the great innovators of Silicon Valley in the 1970s and 1980s, history is full of examples. Joseph Schumpeter, a renowned Austrian economist, coined the term that captures their role perfectly—"creative destruction." Schumpeter's idea relies on replacing old, outdated methods of human endeavor with newer, more efficient, and more refined ones.[1] Entrepreneurs are the ones pushing the world forward. They receive rewards for their efforts and the risks taken from the market—which actually is the whole society.

The benefits of the widespread adoption of cryptocurrencies and Blockchain technology wonderfully reflect the principle of "creative destruction." It's the entrepreneurs from the Blockchain industry who are pushing the boundaries of the often archaic rules of the financial sector. The current status quo, although convenient for banks and governments, has its downsides: financial exclusion, unfair fees, and unjustified business practices. Cryptocurrencies and other Blockchain applications bring hope that this status quo can be broken. The only question that remains is: "Who is to accomplish this?"

Technological innovations are brought to life by people. Ethereum, for instance, has a team of developers with Vitalik Buterin as its most renowned figure. Bitcoin (BTC) is associated with Satoshi Nakamoto, whoever that may be. The Winklevoss twins, Harvard graduates portrayed in the film *The Social Network*, founded The Gemini Exchange. Numerous smaller projects owe their existence to entrepreneurs in the crypto industry, often unknown by name. They remain anonymous either by deliberate choice or because their success is so modest that it's barely noticeable even to cryptocurrency geeks. Those individuals often come from diverse backgrounds—some are programmers, others business specialists. They represent a wide spectrum of temperaments—from introverted nerds to outgoing personalities who shine at banquets or give colorful interviews in industry media. However, the entire community of entrepreneurs mentioned here shares a common denominator: the status of crypto millionaires.

This book isn't about the people who've made fortunes in the world of crypto. It is about the world they've shaped. Don't expect tabloid gossip about the luxury lives of crypto millionaires. My intention is not to hand out shallow stories about entrepreneurs who've struck gold in the Blockchain industry. It isn't a compendium of trivia about those featured on the *Forbes* list. Instead, I want to offer you something far more significant—a deep dive into the reality of their business: the crypto industry, where the most promising, hardworking, and ambitious individuals can become millionaires.

And let's get this straight: this book isn't a get-rich-quick manual. It won't turn you into a crypto tycoon overnight just because you've scanned through it and picked up a couple of handy business tips. I don't believe in easy fixes. I've learned the hard way that business success comes down to consistent tough work, not sheer luck. It applies to every sector, including Blockchain technology.

In the process of writing this book, I've aimed to find the right balance between various perspectives on the crypto industry. I found previous publications on the subject unsatisfying—they either presented Blockchain too technically, too academically, or too idealistically. If a programmer wrote a book on Blockchain, they might dive straight into the syntax of Solidity without any preamble. If an academic economist tackled the subject, you'd be left decoding pseudo-intellectual jargon like "exogenous factors in modeling decentralized network effects" (wtf?!). And if an entrepreneurial influencer and motivational speaker took a shot, you'd end up with another self-help guide, possibly touting tokenization as the ultimate solution for securing multi-million dollar business development financing. And let me tell you, all those approaches are misleading.

Blockchain, often wrapped in super technical terms or oversimplified stories, gets a lot of dramatic talk. Some say it's key to freeing us from the clutches of greedy bankers; others see it as just a technology for digitally producing digital coins that central banks don't cherish that much. But let's be real, that kind of chat doesn't help anyone understand what's going on. That's not a discussion, it's bullshit.

Really, the story of Blockchain is more than just a bunch of experiments in cryptography. It's about the timeless human effort to keep track of our actions and the value that comes from them. What we're seeing now is different from the old ways of finance and business. This time around, it's with a ledger that's supposed to be open and fair for everyone. But is it really like that? Within this book, I will explore that topic together with you.

NOTE

1 https://www.redalyc.org/journal/5863/586364185007/html/

Chapter 1

Blockchain—from a Florentine monk to the anonymous cryptographer

1.1 MONEY, TRADE, AND THE PSYCHOLOGY OF WEALTH

Money. It's a fundamental yet intuitive medium of value exchange, so intuitive that it often requires no extensive formal education to master the art of moneymaking. Consider individuals like Robert Kiyosaki or Richard Branson, with dyslexia affecting the latter. Take Kiyosaki, for instance. He is known for his rather unconventional view on formal education, stating, "In the real world, the smartest people are people who make mistakes and learn. In school, the smartest don't make mistakes."[1] His point is that learning from failures can lead to expertise in making correct financial decisions. It's all about understanding the intuition of money.

Schools often focus on theoretical knowledge and template thinking, which doesn't necessarily align with how business operates. Business demands a unique mindset—one that's focused on understanding people's needs, problem-solving, and innovative thinking. These skills aren't typically learned in a classroom. It's worthwhile to consider the argument that many millionaires—not necessarily the "crypto" ones—accumulated their wealth not through academic achievements but through perseverance, strategic approaches, and logical thinking skills. But what about on a larger scale: does this apply to whole societies? Does having a solid, universal education mean more wealth for everyone? And what happens when we add another dimension to this analysis: time? Let's unravel these questions.

To really understand how wealth piles up in new financial systems, we need to hit the rewind button—way back, about 4,500 years. Let's travel to one of my favorite regions in the world—the Levant countries in the Arab part of the Mediterranean Sea. Fast forward to today, and you'll find Lebanon, Syria, and Israel. But back in the day, it was the heart of the Phoenician civilization. Due to the challenging, mountainous terrain, it was impossible to build an advanced network of land roads. So, the Phoenicians built port cities and laid the foundation of their wealth on trade. They knew how to play their cards—they worked around the challenging geography

DOI: 10.1201/9781032621456-2

and traded valuable goods, meeting human needs. But the question is, was that enough to pile up wealth? Let's see.

Do you know who gets the credit for inventing money? The Phoenicians. Niklas Arvidsson, a Swedish economist and innovation analyst, makes an interesting point in his book *Building a Cashless Society*. He talks about money not just as a tool but as a social contract—a game-changer in human history. Arvidsson points out that the key feature of currency-based exchange is its functionality, namely: the trust in future payback.

Here's how it works:

> In a true barter economy, transactions must be made by exchanging goods and services in real-time, except that mutual trust can allow exchanges to be independent of time. I can give you 100 kilograms of wheat if I trust that in two months, you'll give me 50 kilograms of corn. But money is even better; it finalizes the transaction immediately, not in two months. Money is a necessary condition for trade, which stimulates specialization, further trade, and the entire cyclical mechanism. Our modern economy is built on trust, and money is one of its most important foundations.[2]

So, the history of wealth is essentially a tale of value exchange, trade, human needs, and aspirations. Money was created with two main goals:

1. To simplify trade by setting a standard rate for goods-to-money exchange.
2. To let people profit from the exchange on the spot and save it for later, basically trading today's consumption for tomorrow.

Money perfectly fulfilled those tasks, playing a purely functional role. But what sparked those needs? Psychology or, to be more specific, human self-interest. As Adam Smith, the father of modern economics, put it:

> It is not from the benevolence of the butcher, the brewer, or the baker, that we expect our dinner, but from their regard to their interest. We address ourselves, not to their humanity but to their self-love, and never talk to them of our necessities but of their advantages.[3]

So, economics shows us how looking out for number one can work out well for everyone.

1.2 AGAINST SOCIAL STAGNATION

Now, let's travel back to about 4,000 years ago when the Phoenicians invented money. Since then, the Mediterranean region alone has seen at least four empires, hundreds of new rulers, and even three world religions come up. Each of these new social constructs brought significant shifts in people's lives. You might think that the politics and power struggles of those times, happening in distant courts, didn't affect them. Not at all.

Every time a new ruler came to power, they brought in their way of handling money and set limits on business activities. People who were creative and ambitious had to deal with not just these earthly, profane rules, but also religious ones. Imagine this: during the Middle Ages, the Catholic Church controlled a lot of what Europeans did and made a lot of money doing it. They followed the Bible very strictly, which led them to ban things that we'd see as financial services now. Back then, they called it usury. Lending money and earning interest on loans was banned.

> If any of your brothers becomes poor and are unable to support themselves among you, help them as you would a foreigner and stranger, so they can continue to live among you... You must not lend them money at interest.[4]

Those rules, originally crafted thousands of years ago by anonymous authors to protect the poor and vulnerable, ended up stunting economic growth and wealth creation.

Simultaneously, the Church was reigning over a social structure known as feudalism. Society was made up of people who were practically seen as servants rather than free individuals. Everyone was slotted into different social classes and owed specific duties to their ruler and the Church. One such duty was serfdom, which meant working for a landowner. Imagine being offered this deal today:

> I'm the boss—the landowner. You get to work on my land. Two days a week, you work for free. The rest of the time, you can gather grain, but don't forget to set aside a 10% cut for the Church.

Alongside serfdom, the ban on lending money at interest was another unfair component of that story. From the time of the Phoenicians, nearly 2,500 years ago, progress in money mechanisms hit a brick wall. The Church and monarchs, who were the rule-makers, banned lending money at interest due to religious and ideological reasons. So, money couldn't reach its full potential as a tool in people's hands, as history would later reveal. In feudal Europe, money had two basic roles:

1. as a medium of exchange,
2. as a means to accumulate capital.

These are financially safe activities, but they don't bring high yields. Imagine managing your own budget and giving up buying an apartment on credit or, for the risk-takers, giving up trading on the stock market with leverage or trading crypto. Let's think outside the box. Way back then, were some people smarter, bolder, ready to take greater risks—just like there are today? People who wanted more than just getting by, who dreamed of becoming rich, even if it ruffled the feathers of rulers and priests? History tells us that these people did exist. Thanks to them, we live in a world far richer than the one our ancestors knew.

1.3 THE MOST IMPORTANT ITALIAN INVENTION

According to global statistics, Italy is culturally the richest destination in the world. No other country has as many UNESCO heritage sites as Italy, a total of 58 entities.[5] Every tourist has heard about Italy's eminent architects, painters, and other artists. School curricula teach us about Alessandro Volta's discovery of electricity and Guglielmo Marconi's invention of the radio. However, there is something often overlooked. Something that is maybe even more significant—accounting and finance.

1.3.1 Financial engineering

Italy was once the center of global finance. It may be shocking to many of you accustomed to the picturesque images of Cinque Terre and the historic center of Florence. I'm taking you on a quick journey to medieval cities in northern Italy.

Our story begins in Venice, home to a highly influential group of merchants for centuries. They profited from overseas trade, and their business model dictated the state organization of the Venetian Republic. It was an open state that stood out on the map of Europe, which was generally closed and intolerant. As the main port on the Adriatic, Venice conducted advanced trade with the Byzantine Empire and the Islamic world. Venetian merchants made a lot of profit from this. At the height of its power and wealth, the Venetian Republic had 36,000 sailors who operated 3,300 ships and dominated Mediterranean trade. Prominent Venetian families competed with each other to build the most magnificent palace and support the most talented artists. However, it wasn't just about aesthetics but primarily about ambition and the pursuit of wealth. Such simple human motivations dictated the political and social choices of the Venetian elite.

In medieval Europe, everyone was pretty much under the Pope's rule. He was not only a religious leader but also greatly influenced political and economic life. However, the Venetians, even though they were officially Catholics, were known for their loose approach toward religious rules. This allowed them to bypass the Church's restrictions on usury and lending money. In the 13th century, they created a system of maritime trade credit (*prestito maritimo*), which on paper was a form of profit-sharing. In reality, though, it was about financing in the form of granted credit. Venetian merchants formed a special-purpose company (*colleganza*), set up specifically for a trade journey. This company combined donors (today we would say: shareholders) and traders (managers).[6]

The advantage for borrowers was that they could freely dispose of the money and weren't subject to any top–down controls. The silent partner contributed about three-fourths of the invested capital, and the active partner carried out the trading journey—the rest. The purpose and division of tasks and shares were agreed in writing before departure. This was no different from today's process of registering a company—writing a statute and having it accepted by the shareholder's meeting.

Now, here's something interesting. In the conservative reality of medieval Europe, the active partner had an opportunity to reinvest their profits while on their trade journey. In this way, the risks were divided between the company's participants or shareholders. With the division of financial and managerial risk, each risk could be better managed. As a result, specialized merchants focused on "delivering" cheap and good items, and expedition founders—on organizing financing. This whole setup opened up an exciting possibility—the accumulation of capital. These trading companies were later established not just for individual expeditions but for dozens of them. It's like creating a chain of successful businesses. This led to the creation of economies of scale and even greater wealth was born. The Church couldn't "stick to anything" because, on paper, loans were used to finance trade expeditions, not to earn usury—that is, credit interest.

Venetians were the ones who sold treasury bonds or reverse mortgage papers (a *fondo perduto*). But like every other system, they had a significant problem—geographical constraints. The Venetian Republic didn't have natural resources, and their main source of production was salt mining. Venice derived considerable profits from maritime trade, but the global financial system wasn't integrated enough to talk about international financial operations. Over time, Venice began to lose the competition with other Italian cities. Over the years, it specialized in two areas: overseas trade and construction. These areas generated large revenues but also considerable costs. Therefore, the final margins of Venetian merchants ceased to impress. There were, after all, more profitable ways of making money. The great fortunes that arose from overseas trade and real estate investment were simply unsustainable. For this reason, Venice was losing more and more clearly in the competition for the title of leader in this European wealth ranking each year. Medieval Europe understood that the most profitable form of activity was finance.

Let's rewind the story again, this time to 600 years ago. Every ruler issued their own currency. In Venice, these were ducats and lire. The image of the prince (doge) on the coin was a guarantee of its value. But what happens when you go abroad? For all people, their local ruler was the only important one. All others were either strangers struck on a piece of strange metal or well-known enemies. For this reason, in foreign trade, there was a parallel monetary system, in which coins were made of a specific precious metal: gold or silver. Local coins were exchangeable for these "international" ones, which allowed local rulers to speculate.

The system of dual currencies—one in the local circulation and the other in foreign—was very unstable. Can you imagine using two currencies parallelly for a long time? It completely destabilized the public finances of cities dependent on trade—especially Venice. Here's a noteworthy example. Once, Venetian financiers loaned money to the African king of Mali, Kankan Mansa Musa, to fulfill his religious duties of Islam and go on a pilgrimage to Mecca. Musa was considered the richest man in the world. Some sources estimate his fortune at the equivalent of today's $400 billion.[7] It's estimated that the king of Mali was technically able to donate even 18 tons of gold to Muslim's Holy City.[8] Up to 10 tons could have been borrowed from Venetian bankers. When the African king repaid his obligation to the Venetians, the exchange rate of precious metals (silver and gold) fell from 1:20 in 1340 to 1:11 in 1342.[9] This meant that for one gold coin, you could buy 20 silver ones, and two years later—only 11. This meant a decrease in the purchasing power of gold by as much as 45%! Imagine that! Silver was sharply rising in price, and gold was becoming cheaper. But as we know, what goes up must come down. The following years brought a reversal of this trend and a return to speculative madness.

1.3.2 The art of accounting

Imagine running a business in the face of significant fluctuations. It's like trying to navigate a ship in a stormy weather. You can't plan effectively. Without the ability to predict, you can't make informed economic decisions. Let's face it, we all want to be *homo oeconomicus*—a rational individual making sound economic choices, right? But how can you make well-reasoned decisions without proper knowledge of the economic situation?

Now, in the rapidly changing reality caused by monetary shocks in northern Italy, modern accounting was born. Introducing clear, uniform rules of economic accounting allowed the monitoring of production and trade activities. How did that come about? Well, now, we're moving to Tuscany. Just as the Church was the source of problems and unjustified restrictions in our last story, this time, the ideas of a Florentine monk pushed forward the progress of finance. And the whole of humanity toward further progress.

Accounting had to be born shortly after the invention of money. There were at least two reasons for it. First, the profits from trade, accumulated in the form of money, had to be recorded somewhere. You had to "stand on the firm ground." Knowing how much wealth you have; how much you can spend on your own entertainment; how much to invest, and how much to save safely. From this need, a simple system of single-entry bookkeeping was born. In such a form, a list of all transactions was kept without complicated accounts and classifications. For example, a merchant who imported expensive spices to Venice had to keep three simple registers: how much he bought the goods for, how much he sold them for, and what costs he incurred for the sea voyage. At the end of a given period—after the trip or at the end of the year—such a merchant summed up how much money he had earned or lost.

To truly grasp the value of this activity, let's consider a key indicator: the trading rates of Venice's primary commodity, salt. The numbers paint a vivid picture. Venetian merchants typically acquired salt for a mere 1 ducat per ton. When the salt left Venice, the state collected tax (at a variable rate). Finally, after shipment to the customer, the selling price was about 33 ducats per ton.[10] That means their net margin was as high as 85%. It was a masterclass in maximizing returns, a testament to the shrewdness and efficiency of Venetian trade practices.

However, there was another reason that made accounting even more important than just informing people about the wealth they were accumulating. Accounting stopped being a private matter or a personal summary of the state of money possessed. Financial books became a public matter. With economic activity protected by the state, there was a duty to pay taxes. For example, in the Venetian Republic, even 30% of the doge's (duke's) income came from the duty imposed on the trade of saltstone.[11] This money was used to pay for magnificent public utility buildings. And these were large expenses. The main attraction of Venice is the Basilica of St. Mark, not without reason called the Golden Church (*Chiesa d'Oro*). Built 800 years ago, from the beginning it was supposed to be a symbol of Venetian power, wealth, and splendor.[12] Large tax revenues were needed for such investments. However, taxpayers wanted to pay as little as possible so that a larger part of the profit from trade remained in their treasuries. For both sides, accounting was an excellent tool to manipulate their declared incomes and the resulting tax obligations.

The second reason for the colossal social and economic significance of accounting, even in its simple or even primitive form of single entries, was the need to assess creditworthiness. To finance joint expenses (including wars or investments in public utility buildings), the Venetians managing the Republic created a system of treasury bonds (*imprestiti*).[13] As spending increased, the government of the Republic borrowed money from wealthy families at a fixed rate. This form of financing was attractive to both parties in the transaction: the government received a large injection of cash, and wealthy Venetians invested in a safe asset with low risk. After all, it was the Venetian government that declared to have borrowed money and had obliged itself to repay. *Imprestiti* worked on the principle of "bearer" bonds; they could be sold and bought on the "second-hand" market. Venice was way ahead of its time, with a developed financial market where debt securities were traded over 700 years ago. Can you believe that?

Debt and related financial operations, especially speculation, are a very delicate subject. The operation of a system based on debt operations is associated with great mutual trust. All parties of this complex economic system "agree" that debts will be repaid. Therefore, more funds can be borrowed, and existing ones traded on financial markets.

Where does this trust come from? From creditworthiness. All participants in the system must be sure that everyone on board the ship marked "Debt" has a life jacket with them. You can't let in people whose financial situation doesn't allow them to incur debt. That, however, works both ways. First, bond buyers are sure that the issuer (that is, the Venetian doge) is solvent. On the one hand, the state authorizes bankers to offer Venetian bonds on credit to the general public, intending to raise their demand. On the other hand, it's crucial to avoid letting the poor become indebted, enticed by the allure of earning interest from these bonds. A creditworthiness assessment is nothing more than a risk assessment, after getting acquainted with the financial situation of both parties to the transaction. For this reason, to enable wealthy residents to participate more effectively in common burdens, especially in conducting war, the *estimo* was introduced. *Estimo* was a universal valuation of the wealth of a Venetian citizen. For security reasons, no one was allowed to invest in Venetian bonds more than the amount indicated in the *estimo*. But there was a small catch.

Estimo, like any accounting operation, was a simplified image of reality. While it is possible to assess the value of "large" assets, at some point challenges begin. Can you accurately value someone's jewelry? Art? Ships, each in a different technical condition? Like any accounting document, the *estimo* was inaccurate and imperfect. For this reason, the share of bonds in the assets of subscribers could significantly exceed 100%. Isn't it strange? Only seemingly, because the assets were declared by the subscribers themselves. Probably increasingly less in the real amount.

Did that system collapse? History seems to barely mention it. Over time, Venice lost its leading position among European ports. The plague epidemic of 1347–1351, which caused the death of one-third of Europe's population, contributed significantly to this. Venice was its main victim. Apart from this event, the Venetian business model was never hit by a crash. Venice experienced rather gradual stagnation, due to which it finally lost in the race of financial innovations. Why could the Venetian business model be maintained for so long? Perhaps the profits of the Republic were so large that they compensated for the risk resulting from imperfect accounting systems. And yet the currency fluctuations in northern Italy were so large that those little "creative accounting" tricks and dodgy deals probably slid by just fine for the Venetians—ironic for a city surrounded by water, huh?

Venetian merchants were recording their transactions in a single-entry system. Think of this system as a one-dimensional line where monetary transactions have a set value. Depending on the type of accounting book, these values can represent costs, profits, or sum of assets. However, what's missing in this approach is the most crucial aspect of accounting: the meaning of money in trade relations. In a single-entry system, monetary values of obligations only have nominal values. They're just numbers that on their own can't reflect the importance of obligations and values in human relationships.

Leaving Venice behind, we travel through Italy to Tuscany. This region marks a significant chapter in the evolution of finance. The story from Florence will help you to understand the advancement made by Italian accountants. They introduced a two-dimensional form of accounting. Transactions had not just a mathematical value but also a specific meaning in relations between people. Since we're talking about relations, there must be two sides to the transaction: the seller and the buyer, the lender and the borrower, the creditor and the debtor. And if there are two sides, there must be two ledgers. This revolutionary shift from a collection of separate ledgers to a unified, dual-sided system meant that every transaction was split into two complementary parts. Both sides of the equation had to match. At the end of the accounting period, the debtor had to repay his creditor, and the buyer—the producer. While it might seem almost trivial from our perspective, adding one column to the accounting register was one of the most significant breakthroughs in global economic history.

This monumental change was brought about by Luca Pacioli, often dubbed the father of accounting. Pacioli was a Franciscan monk and a mathematician—a perfect example of an educated man of his era. He lived in the second half of the 15th century in Florence—a time of social and economic development for the city. Today, we would say that Florence was a hub of innovation for all of Europe. Pacioli himself closely collaborated with Leonardo da Vinci.[14] Few know that Pacioli taught him mathematics. Is there any better testament to the genius of the Florentine monk than being the tutor of the master?

In 1494, Pacioli penned down his ideas for a new accounting system. We owe him the most basic concepts used in accounting and business. Pacioli described his theory of double entry using the Latin words *debere* (to owe) and *credere* (to trust). This is where our terms *debit* and *credit* come from— as two sides of a closed accounting transaction.

Pacioli also created specific, but flexible rules that universally allowed for the keeping of all accounting books and transaction registers. He outlined these rules in his most important work, *Summa de arithmetica, geometria, proportioni et proportionalita* (*About arithmetic, geometry, proportions and proportionality*):

> All creditors must join the book from your right hand and all debtors from your left hand. All items, placed in the Book must be double that is if you make a creditor, you must make a debtor;
>
> Every gamble, debit or credit must contain three things: the date of the transaction, the amount, and the reason;
>
> The day the debt and credit are written down must be the same.

> The book has to be kept with the same coin, but all coins present can be indicated in batches: ducats, florins, skuds, etc. You must end the book with the coin used at the beginning of the book.[15]

Making a table in the form of a "T" and converting the currency rate is only half the effort of an accountant. Following Pacioli's rules is only a way of recording transactions. After all, that's what accounting is all about: using words and numbers as simply as possible to accurately describe the financial decisions people have made. This was the genius of Pacioli, that he created universal rules to describe a reality that was becoming increasingly complex every year due to relationships between people and continuous technical progress. The double-entry system was, therefore, a revolution that pushed the economy toward a previously unknown stability and development. This accounting system has been used for 529 years, and it's still used today. Isn't that something?

1.3.3 Banking

Let's stick to the same era, the 15th century. However, we're moving from Florence a mere 80 kilometers to another city in Tuscany, a place that gifted the world with the most fundamental institution of the financial sector: institutionalized banks. We're shifting to Siena, whose city council (the *Magistratura*) founded a financial society, which today we can confidently call the oldest bank in the world. It's the Banca Monte dei Paschi di Siena (MPS). It operates to this day, continuously since 1472.[16]

The MPS bank was established as a type of association called monte di pietà, which literally translates to "mountain of compassion." In Renaissance Europe, these were financial institutions aimed at providing low-interest loans to people in difficult financial situations. Their main job was to help people who were struggling with money by giving them loans at low interest. It's kind of like what we call CSR (Corporate Social Responsibility) today, but with a historical twist. They had gathered money from people willing to help; however, they didn't just hand it out without restrictions. Instead, they made a deal with those who got the money: they needed to work and pay back the loan, but the terms were easier and kinder. It was more than just giving away money—it was about helping people in a way that made them responsible and gave them a chance to get back on their feet.

However, the business model of MPS quickly began to change. MPS activities expanded beyond the poorest social classes. In particular, landowners needed the capital provided by the bank. Thus, MPS started offering much higher-interest land credit.[17]

Don't think, however, that MPS was the very first bank in history. Financial services have been around since ancient times. What distinguished the MPS bank from earlier examples, like those in Venice, was its exceptionally stable structure. In the past, particularly in Venice, financial services were set up for specific business projects unrelated to the finance sector itself. However, in the case of MPS, the organization's business model was focused entirely on finance. It wasn't the prince or Venetian merchants who organized a special-purpose company for a war or trade expedition and provided its financing. It was the social elite organizing a specialized business that could finance literally any other economic activity.

In that way, the bankers of Siena specialized their business in a newly emerging niche: banking services. According to economic rules, when a business specializes, it works better and uses its resources (like time, money, and people) more effectively. Consequently, through specialization, an institution like a bank MPS could achieve greater profits than an association of merchants who only spent part of their time on finance. By focusing solely on financial services, the founders of MPS created a financial empire that has been operating continuously to this day—for 549 years.

The MPS bank functioned as a commercial bank as we know it today. In this business model, a bank generates profit by providing capital and earning interest on the loans granted. The interest could be reinvested in a new project and thus increase the bank's asset account. The increasing capital accumulated by the bank provided funds for granting ever-larger loans to more and more clients. The model was based on compound interest. The exponentially growing capital allowed for a continuous increase in the value and volume of loans. The more loans were granted, the greater the profits accumulated—this is how this new banking machine worked, and it was accelerating more and more.

To understand how powerful and almost indestructible a business arose with the establishment of the MPS bank, suppose the following situation. Imagine that you belong to the social and business elite in Tuscany. All of your projects are going great, and you have a stable profit of 1,000 florins a year.[18] Let's assume that, converted to today's dollar value, it's $500,000. Imagine that you have been invited to invest in the MPS bank along with the other 19 influential residents with the same wealth as yours. There are 20 of you co-founders in total, so you establish a bank with a share capital of $10 million. For the start, you launch a credit action for only 9% of the collected funds. The remaining 91% is placed in the bank's treasury as a security deposit. You agree that whatever the bank earns, it will pay you in the form of dividends at the rate of one-fourth of the income due to you. The remaining three-fourths of the funds the bank will deploy to further investments in the next year.

Let's summarize all these data in Table 1.1.

During the first year of operation, $27,000 is returned to the bank's cashier, which is immediately reinvested in new loans. For the 20 bank co-founders, $6,750 is left to be divided, that is, $338 per investor. This value is the income per share—and due to the MPS business model, this value is constantly growing (Figure 1.1).

Table 1.1 Hypothetical profitability calculations for a historical MPS bank

Data	Values
Number of shares (number of co-founders)	20
Value of a single share in the bank	1,000 florins = $500,000
Share capital of the bank	$10,000,000
Bank's capital-to-asset ratio	9%
Scale of lending in the first year of operations	$900,000
Interest rate on loans	4%
Bank's profit from interest rate on loans granted in the first year of operations	$36,000 (scale of lending x%)
Percentage of retained earnings (unpaid dividends)	75%

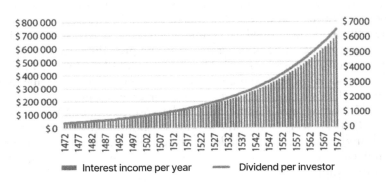

Figure 1.1 Hypothetical performance of MPS bank in its first 100 years of operation.

Your business, thriving on the concept of compound interest, isn't just growing; it's expanding at an exponential rate. This isn't a straight-line increase but a rapid multiplication of growth. Consequently, the bank sees a significant rise in its revenues year after year. This makes the business model exceptionally scalable. The reason is simple: the more money that flows in, the larger the profits become. Interestingly, the cost of capital remains relatively stable, primarily because the bank is financed through the capital contributed by its founders. This setup isn't just about steady growth; it's about accelerating profits while maintaining consistent foundational costs, a winning formula in the banking sector. And you are still monopolists, so you can scale the banking business almost indefinitely.

The invention of the Siena Bank gave rise to a new form of economic activity: an efficient commercial banking sector. Economics laws proved to stay firmly against societal and governmental manipulation. An institution like a bank, thanks to easy access to credit and systematic accounting, freed entrepreneurs from political and religious dependencies. It mattered whether

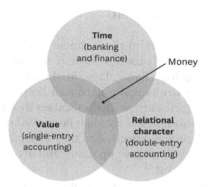

Figure 1.2 The relationship of money to time, value, and relationality.

the borrower had a plan for his business and whether lending him money was associated with a high (appropriately expensive) risk. Such a model spread first in Europe, and then, thanks to colonial activity, all over the world. That's how the financial sector was created—equipped with modern accounting methods, organized banking institutions, and human creativity, stimulated by the desire for profit.

We see how the emergence of banking brought a new aspect to financial analysis: the element of time (Figure 1.2). Our discussion so far has centered around transactions between two key players: the lender and the borrower. The borrower agrees to return the loan within a set timeframe, a commitment reflected in accounting records that date back to the era of Pacioli, marked by the classic two-column format. But, what happens when a borrower delays their repayment? In these cases, they face the consequence of higher interest rates.

Flipping the perspective, as a lender, my goal is to motivate the debtor to repay the loan swiftly. Repayment is crucial for me because it liberates my capital, allowing me to channel it into new investment ventures. To encourage the debtor to repay faster, I employ a strategy of offering them more attractive terms. I'm not just encouraging prompt returns—I'm also optimizing the financial health and fluidity of my own resources. In financial theory, this basic relationship is expressed by the time value of money.[19]

From a "mountain of mercy" to a well-oiled banking machine, the evolution of banking sure does have its twists and turns. Sure, the way we do accounting or use financial services has changed big time, thanks to computers and new technologies. But our world still runs on nearly the same principles laid down by those Italian accountants and bankers back in the day. It's like what Isaac Newton said, "If I have seen further, it is by standing on the shoulders of giants."[20] We're basically playing the same game, just with some upgraded gear.

1.4 3,500 YEARS OF HUSTLING

In today's language, especially in the business world, the term *hustler* has become incredibly popular. It used to have a negative meaning, linked to shady deals or prostitution. These days, in the business world, "hustler" refers to someone who works really hard and keeps pushing to do better. "Hustlers" often start their entrepreneurial career at a young age and work hard to develop their business, not through borrowed or given capital. What motivates them are their aspirations, and they're ready to do everything to achieve their goals. They don't give up easily and are eager to take on challenges to get what they want.[21]

Could we call Venetian merchants, Pacioli, or Sienese bankers "hustlers?" I believe so. The history of financial development is, in many ways, a history of hustling. However, this story started much earlier, with the Phoenicians and their invention of money. Despite geographical, cultural, and technical limitations, all these people devoted their time, effort, talent, and creativity to accumulate wealth, satisfy their needs, and at the same time do something for their society or—as history has shown—all of humanity.

As we consider the future of finance, we must ask: does Blockchain technology have the potential to revolutionize this field as previous innovations have? Could it be as significant as the financial solutions I've described? Only time will tell. Importantly, behind every great human achievement, there are always brave individuals. Sometimes these are anonymous Phoenician money inventors—brilliant merchants whose identities we will probably never know. Other times—Luca Pacioli, well known to history. What connects all these people with Satoshi Nakamoto, the alleged creator of Blockchain and the originator of its first application in the form of Bitcoin? Does the world of crypto millionaires differ from the world of wealthy individuals who initiated similar revolutions in global finance centuries ago?

The economic systems I described in this chapter have evolved over 3,500 years—from the invention of money to the creation of advanced financial institutions. I describe this history in such detail for two reasons. First, writing this book, I saw how little material on this topic is available in popular science books. I learned some of these stories in fragments during finance classes at New York University. I reached others on my own. Second, I have been observing the development of Blockchain technology since 2015 when I started leading a group of programmers. With my team's involvement in this space, we're developing cool and innovative products using Blockchain technology. To me, Blockchain's evolution is more than a tech trend—it's a key part of significant social transformations. It's essential in understanding the future of a decentralized economy. Who will build it? Let's find out in the following chapters.

NOTES

1 https://biztekmojo.com/robert-kiyosaki-quotes/
2 N. Arvidsson (2019), Money: The Greatest Innovation in the History of Humanity, in: *Building a Cashless Society*, SpringerBriefs in Economics, Cham: Springer, https://doi.org/10.1007/978-3-030-10689-8_1
3 A. Smith (1954), Badania nad naturą i przyczynami bogactwa narodów, tom I, Państwowe Wydawnictwo Naukowe, Warsaw, pp. 21–22.
4 Lev 25, 35–37.
5 UNESCO World Heritage Centre, World Heritage List Statistics, unesco.org, arc. 14.05.2011.
6 D. Puga, D. Trefler (2021), International Trade and Institutional Change: Medieval Venice's Response to Globalization, National Bureau of Economic Research, Cambridge [online, PDF].
7 T. Morgan (2018), This 14th-Century African Emperor Remains the Richest Person in History, History.com, 19.05.2018, access: 21.12.2021.
8 Ibid.
9 In comparison, even during the greatest contemporary crises, the Forex market didn't suffer from such drastic changes. For instance, the fluctuations in the exchange rate of the British pound against the German mark were "merely" 15% when George Soros speculated on this rate in 1992. Federal Reserve Bank of St. Louis, The Vulnerability of Pegged Exchange Rates: The British Pound in the ERM, pp. 43–44, access: 26.05.2021.
10 https://www.saltworkconsultants.com/salt-taxation/
11 J.-C. Hocquet (1999), Venice, in: Bonney, Richard (ed.), *The Rise of the Fiscal State in Europe* c. 1200–1815, Clarendon Press, p. 393.
12 Fodor's Italy (2011), Random House Digital, Inc., p. 190.
13 https://ritholtz.com/2013/12/birds-boats-and-bonds-in-venice-the-first-aaa-government-issue/
14 Pacioli biography, www-groups.dcs.st-and.ac.uk, access: 24.03.2016.
15 R. Sosnowski (2006), Origini della lingua dell'economia in Italia. Dal XIII al XVI secolo, FrancoAngeli, p. 87.
16 Boland V. (2009), Modern Dilemma for World's Oldest Bank, "Financial Times," 12.06.2009, access: 23.02.2010.
17 Voce del Monte dei Paschi di Siena, bankpedia.org
18 The florin was a coin used in Tuscany from the 13th to the 16th century. It contained 3.53 grams of gold. However, such a conversion would not reflect its purchasing power. Historians estimate that, converted to today's money value, one florin was worth between 140 and 1,000 US dollars—M. Bernocchi (1976), Le monete della repubblica fiorentina, III, Leo S. Olschki, Editore, p. 66.
19 S.V. Crosson, Needles B.E. (2008), *Managerial Accounting* (8th Ed), Boston: Houghton Mifflin Company.
20 Newton I., Letter from Sir Isaac Newton to Robert Hooke, Historical Society of Pennsylvania, access: 7.06. 2018.
21 https://www.indeed.com/career-advice/career-development/types-of-entrepreneurship

Chapter 2

Let Blockchain be Blockchain

2.1 OCCUPY WALL STREET

In 2008, the titan of investment banking called Lehman Brothers crashed, triggering the financial crisis. It exposed a plethora of problems—or even huge fuck-ups—in the banking world. Back then, I was just an 11-year-old kid, completely clueless about economics. As I began studying Economics, it all started to make sense. I understood the mechanics of the crisis and what led to it. What sparked my interest, you ask? Hip-hop. Yes, you heard that right.

As the biggest fan of street culture, I remember when Jay-Z released T-shirts printed with "Occupy All Streets."[1] This was a shout-out to Occupy Wall Street, a massive protest that sprung up in 2012 right outside the iconic New York Stock Exchange. The protestors voiced their harsh criticism of the actions of the American financial sector. This movement, with its raw expression of dissent, resonated with the core ethos of the hip-hop community. The slogan "We are the 99 percent" highlighted the unfair privileges enjoyed by bankers and financiers, while the rest of the society, the "99 percent," struggled to make ends meet. Many rappers, themselves products of tough neighborhoods, added their voices to the chorus, rapping about the unequal distribution of opportunities. But what sparked these powerful slogans? Why did Jay-Z decide to sell shirts that carried economic messages?

To answer that, we need to rewind to the late 1990s and early 2000s. Back then, Wall Street was heavily regulated. Each institution had a distinct role to play. Consumer banks handled customer service and simple financial operations, making money from loan interests or account management fees. Unexciting yet safe job. On the other hand, separate entities like funds and investment banks had the leeway to "play hard." They could choose investments that were less safe and aim for higher returns by taking on more risk. This division of roles and responsibilities was closely overseen by the stringent Securities and Exchange Commission.[2]

That system was established in 1933 with the Glass-Steagall Act, passed in response to the Great Depression.[3] It separated commercial and investment banking, protecting the financial system from risky business. It's scary

DOI: 10.1201/9781032621456-3

to think that the bad economy back then made 23,000 Americans take their own lives.[4] Messing with such an important system seems really dangerous, kind of like playing with live electric wires and hoping not to get electrocuted.

Despite the firm line drawn in the sand by the Glass-Steagall Act, the Congress of 1999 had a different plan in mind. They passed the Financial Securities Modernization Act, turning the financial world upside down. Until then, there was a clear demarcation: commercial banks operated with caution, earning less but with a high level of certainty. Investment banks, in contrast, embraced risk, making them more susceptible to the fickle winds of market fluctuations. They either hit the jackpot or lost big during a crisis. The repeal of the previous law, which had served well for nearly 70 years, resulted in the integration of investment and commercial banks. However, the new act failed to outline an optimal strategy. How much risk could the combined banking entities bear? Lured by the prospect of increased profits, these merged banks chose to follow a risky path.[5] That strategy worked wonders during an economic boom. However, the potential fallout during an economic downturn, or worse, a crisis, was not given due consideration.

But that wasn't the only change. Investment banks also started creating innovative securities based on mortgage loans. Their strategy was to cover many risky borrowers under mortgage action. These individuals were granted subprime loans, sometimes also referred to as "NINJA loans" (No Income, No Job, No Financial Assets)—loans for people without a steady income, jobs, or financial security.[6] Less affluent Americans were lured into buying homes with such risky mortgage loans. Stories even circulated about individuals buying several houses as "investments" or "savings." The concept of homeownership was sold with a heavy dose of ideology—investment brochures touted the idea of "realizing dreams" and achieving the "American dream."

In reality, the way banks were making money from those deals was quite clever and diverse. First, they offered loans with higher interest rates to people who weren't very rich. This was a way to balance the risk of these people not being able to pay back their loans. The banks thought, "If these people can't pay us back, we'll charge them more from the start." Second, the real estate market in America was doing well at that time. House prices kept going up, year after year. So, the banks had the following idea: if someone could not repay their loan, the bank could have just taken their house and sold it. They'd still make considerable profit because house prices were so high. Third, banks found another way to make money. They started selling other financial products, adding even more ways to profit from these deals.

However, the banks got too focused on making more money and missed some important risks that should have been put into the equation right from the beginning. They started offering a new type of bond that grouped many home loans into one big financial product. The market thought these bonds were safe. It was either not seeing the risk of people going bankrupt and not being able to pay their loans, or it was too confident that selling the houses would cover any losses. What went wrong? Well, supply and demand. Banks ended up with a bunch of houses that no one wanted to buy. They had to pretend these houses were worth more than in reality.

This led to two big issues. First, banks had to sell these houses quickly, but they lost money because they had set the prices too high. They operated on the plans based on the assumption that house prices would continue to climb by 6.5% every year, based on data from 1996 to 2006.[7] As their predictive models failed, they had to pay for their mistakes big time. Second, a kind of panic started among the banks. They realized they had guessed wrong about how many people wanted these houses. Hence, they tried to quickly get rid of them, selling them to other companies or investors. This rush to sell the houses caused the housing market bubble to burst. It was a big problem that couldn't be ignored anymore. And that's when the financial crisis hit (Figure 2.1).

Banks had been creating more and more securities related to the housing market.[8] The bursting of the housing bubble suddenly changed the direction of these instruments. It was like watching a domino effect in the American financial sector—one piece falling after another. This chain reaction was brought to light by some determined bank employees. Everyone then realized the extent of risk taken by financial institutions, which led to both the creation and bursting of the housing bubble. This crash in the housing market quickly spread to the traditional financial sector, heavily reliant on mortgage-linked products. This sparked a wave of massive sell-offs and short selling, which is essentially betting against the market. This entire process was vividly described by Michael Lewis in his book, *The Big Short*.[9] And yes, it's the same scenario

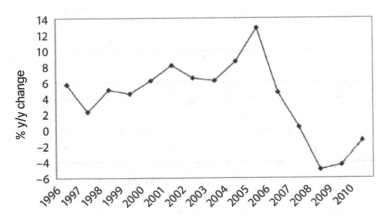

Figure 2.1 The annual housing price dynamics in the United States from 1996 to 2010.

(*Source*: **Data from Office of Federal Housing Enterprise Oversight report.**)

discussed by Margot Robbie in the movie, where she's in a bathtub with a glass of champagne.

What were the direct consequences of the subprime crisis? First and foremost, it spread beyond the traditional financial sector. The crisis of 2008–2009 was the biggest since the Great Depression. It's estimated that during the financial crisis, the net worth of American households fell by about $17 trillion, taking inflation into account (that's 17 with 12 zeros). This meant that as much as 26% of household wealth simply "evaporated."[10] Those weren't just abstract numbers and Excel functions. They represented the hard work and savings of ordinary people. From 2007 to 2009, approximately 7.5 million Americans lost their jobs.[11] So, it wasn't just about speculation on financial products but a real problem of playing with people's assets, their homes, and sometimes even their lives. Finally, the crisis "leaked" into other countries. Countries like Greece or Spain haven't recovered from the crisis to this day.[12]

What's important for us right now is how the events of 2008–2009 led to a lack of trust in the financial sector. In this atmosphere of distrust and a sense of betrayal, Bitcoin was born. It represented the first use of a radically new data recording technology: Blockchain. Bitcoin wasn't just a cryptocurrency—it was a symbol of a shift in trust and the search for a more transparent and decentralized financial system.

2.2 THE NEW DEAL

The story of Bitcoin's creation is shrouded in mystery, half-told stories, and plenty of conspiracy theories. Unlike earlier significant achievements in the world of finance, Bitcoin doesn't have an identified author. How can a creation without a clear creator be so valuable? In today's world, popularity, marketing, and reputation matter. This is true for cryptocurrencies as well. The world has been quick to embrace them with enthusiasm. In fact, it's amazing how quickly they've been valued so highly. This is especially impressive when you think about how long it took for past financial inventions to be adopted. For instance, the first application of Blockchain technology in the form of Bitcoin was worth over $730 billion in 2023[13] (Figure 2.2).

In the previous chapter, I shared the story of how accounting was born. The invention of double-entry bookkeeping was a revolution similar to what Blockchain turned out to be. The problem with the accounting rules created by Pacioli was that they could be easily manipulated. Simply recording a transaction between two parties is just the beginning of success, while another challenge is proving its authenticity. Who ensures that the bookkeeping records are accurate? Regardless of the system, whether the bookkeeping records match reality depends on the legal status in a given country. But what if the law fails to perform its function? What if the government creates regulations that allow for manipulation and artificial boosting? Put

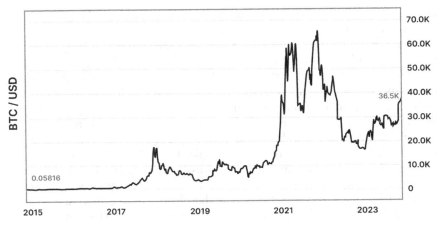

Figure 2.2 BTC/USD exchange rate from 2013 to 2023.

(*Source*: Data from CoinMarketCap.)

simply: what if legislators begin to prioritize the interests of banks over the good of society?

As a Blockchain-related entrepreneur, I regularly follow the discussion about the advantages of Bitcoin and other cryptocurrencies. This allows me to assess both the pros of Blockchain technology applications and the explanations of problems in "traditional" finance. The most frequently mentioned advantage of cryptocurrencies is decentralization. It doesn't involve storing transaction data in one place but creating a network where all users, or at least a big chunk of them, have equal and public access to the data registry.

Although Blockchain only recently put this concept into practice, the idea of decentralization has been known for over 200 years. It dates back to the early days of the European political order we know today. The chaos following the French Revolution began to subside in 1794. Soon after, the French dictionary introduced *centralisation* as a term for a new way of governing, focused on concentrating power within one group or place. The term *Décentralisation* was created in opposition. It was like the yin to centralization's yang.

The libertarian philosopher Alexis de Tocqueville visibly promoted that concept. He praised the possibilities of getting people involved in public affairs, exercising their freedom, and creating a counterbalance to the government's powers. Incredibly, such words were written down nearly 200 years ago. Yet I find the same arguments in Blockchain project pitches from my clients. Let's leave the political analysis aside for a moment. Just look at how people's aspirations haven't changed. Blockchain isn't just a technological revolution. It's an expression of age-old, contradicting desires: the dream to live in an equal, free society and the ambition to make a quick fortune, thanks to the emerging digital economy.

2.2.1 Cryptographic experiments and the digital counterculture

Since 2009, when the Bitcoin mechanism was described for the first time, the world has gone crazy for cryptocurrencies. However, digital cash experiments were in progress long before the implementation of Blockchain. In total, about 550 patent applications appeared. The rise of creativity wasn't just a coincidence—it signified a race of minds. Each author tried to figure out the details of distributed ledger technology with different levels of complexity and technological readiness.[14]

Before cryptocurrencies appeared, no one even thought about using the word *crypto*. Cryptographers—mathematicians and programmers dealing with data encryption—were focusing on a key question: how to create a document authenticating mechanism? The idea was to start with encrypting confidential and sensitive data securely, so it couldn't be misused. Encryption began with the sender, wrapping the data in a secure digital envelope. Yet, on the receiver's side, there was a missing piece—a reliable way to "release" the data, ensuring it was used exactly as intended. The challenge of safe decryption isn't a modern puzzle.

Data encryption is a very old invention. For example, 2,600 years ago, ancient Spartans used a device called a scytale to send secret messages during a battle. The device consisted of a leather strap wrapped around a wooden rod. Letters imprinted on the strap would make no sense unless the receiver had a rod of the exact size to make the message readable.[15] Fast forward to more recent times, cryptography played a key role in the history of World War II. Especially due to Enigma, a German encryption machine, whose code was supposed to be unbreakable, and which was finally decoded by Polish and British cryptographers. Thanks to Enigma, Alan Turing gained his first fame.[16] He is considered the creator of modern computer science and the father of such pioneering fields as artificial intelligence. There's even the Turing Award, sort of the "Nobel Prize of Computing."[17] As one of many examples, the case of Enigma shows that the issues of encryption and cryptography are the foundations of the digital technologies we know today, including Blockchain.

The application of encryption and cryptographic techniques was crucial in transmitting information. During war, it's all about tactics, human life, and victory. In times of peace—protecting assets. Cryptography therefore allowed security to be provided in those areas that have always been of the greatest value to people. Therefore, governments often research cryptographic techniques. Take the United States, for instance. Main institutions related to security, the CIA, NSA, or NRO (National Reconnaissance Office), concentrate heavily on cryptography and encryption. According to the Washington Post, those three institutions account for 68% of the so-called black budget—top-secret money spent on defense and public safety.[18] I think that for this reason, all the crypto and encryption stuff wasn't quite right for the business world, just like the tales of projects before Bitcoin showed. The issues of cryptography and encryption until 2009 were ill-suited to business realities or even suppressed by the government administration. Bitcoin was likely so successful because it simply escaped from under the shadow of state control.

Encryption became front and center in the discussion about digital cash technology. The thread was born long before everyone had computers and the Internet was a thing. In the community of theoretical computer scientists, a challenge appeared, originally only a cryptographic experiment: how to build a perfect and unbreakable system that keeps all transaction records, including the history of any data changes?[19] How to make every change in the data as well as the mark of modification visible? Ralph Merkle set for himself such a brain teaser. He was a pioneer of public key encryption and one of the precursors of distributed ledger technology (DLT). Now you know where Blockchain technology originated—from the field of DLT.

Even during his undergraduate studies at the University of California, Berkeley, Merkle stood out as an outstanding computer scientist. As work for credit, he developed a cryptographic solution known today as Merkle's puzzles. Think of that concept as a way to communicate through an unsecured channel—kinda like using the public key. Merkle's solution allows two parties to agree on a common secret by exchanging messages, even if they previously had no common secrets.[20] The challenge of puzzles is to solve a computer "riddle," which, over 30 years later, inspired the mechanism behind Bitcoin. However, we will get to that soon.

Merkle developed his work from undergraduate studies, working on his doctorate at Stanford University. In 1979, he defended his PhD thesis on how information can be linearly combined into a tree structure, known today as Merkle's hash tree.[21] The structure of connected "packs" of information brings us very close to the concept of Blockchain. Merkle came up with hashes—mathematical algorithms that map any amount of data into fixed-size packages).[22] To put it simply: the invention of the hash tree made it possible to save data in a constant format of neatly packed, single data block.

Merkle's solution was created in 1974. In my opinion, the most brilliant element of this story is the time aspect. I can't imagine designing cryptographic systems at such an early stage of development of the computer science. Remember that in the 1970s, there was no Internet for the public and computers did not have a graphical interface. Apple introduced the first computer with that feature in 1984 by launching Macintosh. So, things were way tougher than we could even imagine.

While Ralph Merkle may have had the potential to claim the title of the first crypto millionaire, he instead chose a more theoretical career path, primarily in academia. Despite brief episodes in business, like at Xerox PARC in the R&D department, he returned to the scientific community in 2003. Merkle accepted the title of Distinguished Professor at Georgia Tech, where he led the Tech Information Security Center.[23] Simultaneously, he shifted his focus toward nanotechnology. His research work won him nine industry awards, including the prestigious Richard W. Hamming Medal, sponsored by Qualcomm, a major microchip manufacturer.[24] However, the broader community remembers Merkle as one of the characters in Neal Stephenson's sci-fi novel *The Diamond Age*. Stephenson features him along with other notable scientists like Richard Feynman. In the storyline, Merkle holds a prophetic voice foreseeing that nanotech will enable cheap diamond production soon.[25] The character hints at a world where technology could fundamentally shift the economic landscape.

Cryptology may have been a niche hobby for computer geeks in the 1970s, yet by the 1980s and 1990s, a real-world business challenge emerged. How to implement the solutions developed by researchers? Encryption and cryptography had a clear use: the nascent world of the Internet needed a secure data transfer. The flow carried valuable information, including confidential data, monetary transfers, and access passwords to fundamental IT systems, which had to be protected. The most intuitive idea, therefore, was to build a digital cash system. Enter David Chaum.

Alongside Ralph Merkle, but entirely independently, Chaum conducted even more advanced research on the precursor of today's Blockchain. Like Merkle, he studied at the University of California, Berkeley. In 1982, he defended his PhD thesis, the first-ever proposal of a Blockchain protocol. Chaum investigated how computer systems could be used to build and maintain trust among groups that didn't necessarily trust each other.[26] In such a system, data were packed into "vaults" and connected to a distributed ledger system, with public access to the database.[27] Along with code samples, Chaum's work pretty much described all the elements of Blockchain, detailed almost 30 years later by the anonymous author of Bitcoin. The only missing piece of the puzzle was a mechanism verifying the value represented by the data packed into blocks.

Sadly, Chaum's work went largely unnoticed in the academic world. He never really pushed to publish it at a conference or in a scientific journal.[28] Maybe, he didn't have the same determination for an academic career as Ralph Merkle. However, unlike Ralph, Chaum was keen on applying his ideas in the business world. That's why he is recognized as the inventor of the first secure digital cash solution. Shortly after defending his PhD, in 1983, Chaum developed a relatively primitive solution for a blind signature—a digital certification confirming you've got the funds in your account. The blind signature allowed transactions to be validated and enabled multiple purchases with the same digital coin unit.[29] In 1988, Chaum recruited two programmers and cryptographers from Tel Aviv, Amos Fiat and Moni Naor. Together, they developed a system that provided the same functionality but also worked offline.[30]

Chaum's solution was, of course, very revolutionary back in the early days of the Internet and widespread computer use. The users could get digital currency from a bank and spend it, while the transaction remained invisible to the bank and anyone else.[31] The bank only knew if someone had funds but not where or on what they were spent—just like cash once you pull it out of an ATM.

The concept of digital cash became a technical groundwork for the vision promoted by the Cypherpunk movement.[32] That was a group of activists operating in the late 1980s, who were faithful to cryptography and privacy-enhancing technologies. The goal of the Cypherpunks was to pave the way for major social and political changes through technology. Their manifesto stated:

> Privacy is necessary for an open society in the electronic age... We cannot expect governments, corporations, or other large, faceless organizations to grant us privacy... We must defend our privacy if we expect to have any... We know that someone has to write software to defend privacy, and ... we're going to write it.[33]

I see the beginnings of what later became Bitcoin's first Blockchain implementation in the Cypherpunk ethos. The vision, which aimed to highlight crucial values, was pushed too far by theorists and blinded activists. Instead of trying to change the data exchange and money circulation systems, the original Bitcoin crowd was too proud, or perhaps simply obtuse. Of those who remained in this environment, Julian Assange, the Australian journalist and creator of WikiLeaks, is mainly known in public opinion. His work exposes cases of power abuse by state intelligence and corporations resulting in privacy breaches online. But this fight had a heavy cost. Assange was under an international arrest warrant for nine years, then ended up in Belmarsh in London—one of the world's most restrictive prisons, where terrorists pursued by British intelligence serve their long sentences.[34] Julian's case highlights the unpredictable paths of those involved in the digital revolution.

Since the late 1980s, the Cypherpunk movement has been a very diverse environment. Stories like Assange's are rare exceptions that broke into mainstream news. But what about the rest of the activists, hidden on niche Internet forums or, at best, working as university researchers? Many of the Cypherpunks found themselves in a vicious cycle: the more someone believed in the ideals of the movement, the more likely he shared his ideas as open source—free code with no moneymaking potential for the creator. It's worth noting that most of the initiatives of the first Cypherpunks either weren't registered or operated as non-profit foundations. After all, the goal was to create solutions for the community, not for business.

The only people who managed to escape were those who, at some point, put business thinking above political activism. Take Marc Andreessen and Bram Cohen as examples.[35] Cohen is a clear-cut crypto millionaire and the co-founder of the world's most famous startup investment fund, Andreessen

Horowitz. Meanwhile, it's worth remembering Andreessen as a business success developed from pure activism. He gave public access to his secure browser project (Netscape) and, afterward, sold it to tech giant AOL for a cool $4.3 billion. So, those Cypherpunks from the 1990s became millionaires 20 years later. Some of them even turned into crypto millionaires.

2.2.2 Business implementation

The ideals of social movements are one thing, but business? That's a whole other story. David Chaum, not quite in line with the profit-averse Cypherpunks, began working on turning his cryptographic ideas into a business. In 1990, he created his own electronic money company called DigiCash to make money from the solution he had come up with eight years earlier. DigiCash used a unique blind signature system to create secure keys for verifying digital transactions between users. It seemed like the perfect answer to the market's prayers. Was that a unicorn in the making?

Unfortunately, no. Even though Chaum had the right technology, was a pioneer in the market, and had enough money, he couldn't make it happen. He even received a $10 million funding round from a business angel and investor—David Marquardt, who had sat on the boards of companies like Microsoft and Sun Microsystems.[36] Despite the allocation of funds and strong contacts, Chaum was unable to scale his business. He struggled to partner with new banks. In the United States, DigiCash only worked with Mark Twain Bank. Not exactly a major player in the Midwest, far from the business centers, fintech (financial technology) hubs, and big banks. The second and last bank to operate DigiCash systems was Deutsche Bank.[37] Having such a small group of partners wasn't enough for Chaum's project to succeed.

In 1998, eight years after its debut, DigiCash declared bankruptcy. The company was dissolved, and its assets were taken over by another fintech startup, eCash Technologies.[38] There was no talk of any earnings, just legal shuffles and company takeovers. Chaum's technology, even though it was really interesting and groundbreaking, became a confusing math thing in the paperwork of companies that were bought and sold. DigiCash's final act played out as part of the Internet bubble tragedy, on the grand stage of Wall Street, watched by an audience fascinated by businesses with "-dotcom" in their name.

DigiCash failed not only because of the low number of business partners but mainly because of customers. They couldn't grow their user base. In three years of testing, only about 5,000 people signed up.[39] In an interview in 1999, Chaum stated that the DigiCash project and its technological system hit the market before e-commerce fully integrated with the Internet.[40] That explanation makes sense. DigiCash was founded in 1990 when only 0.8% of the American population had access to the Internet—that translates into 2 million people.[41] It wasn't until 1995 that the United States saw a massive jump in the number of Internet users. Unfortunately, too late for Chaum's project. Now, there are around 289 million Web users in the United States. So, it seems Chaum's timing was off, he was just too early to the party.

While Chaum's point about the Internet's limited reach at DigiCash's start is valid, his later reasoning isn't acceptable. Sure, DigiCash started before the times of widespread internetization, but by the time the company declared bankruptcy, 30% of Americans were already connected to the network. We can calculate that during the eight years of DigiCash's existence, the population of Internet users in the United States grew 40 times. So, what theory had Chaum begun to pose? A year after the project's shutdown, he said: "As the Web grew, the average level of sophistication of users dropped. It was hard to explain the importance of privacy to them."[42]

Blaming business failure on privacy ideals showed that Chaum was still mentally stuck in the 1980s—the era of the Cypherpunks. Despite the passage of time, he sounded just like one of the activists. After all, Cypherpunk groups prioritized political ideals of online anonymity over practical business applications of cryptographic solutions. When the Internet was just finding its feet, the world was actually waiting for a digital payment solution that would make life easier. Simpler payments would have lowered operational costs for banks, and improved sales results for producers and distributors in literally every sector of the economy. The goal was to give consumers the easiest, fastest, and most effective system for transferring money in exchange for goods or services. No one cared about the anonymity issues that were so dear to Chaum. So, while one foot of his was stepping into the business world, the other was still firmly planted in the Cypherpunk mindset.

Back in the day, still young e-commerce and fintech opted for debit and credit cards. Although early websites were encrypted with appropriate protocols, they simply required the cardholder's data. It was simple to use for people. Unlike DigiCash's complicated blind signature system that users just didn't understand. Credit and debit cards were familiar to everyone because people carried them in their wallets every day. So, all they had to do was enter the card numbers on the Internet. Budding fintech, therefore, showed that customer needs and business practices are more important than lofty ideas of dreamy inventors and inflexible entrepreneurs. The market wants easy and cheap solutions, not ones that seem interesting to programmers detached from reality.

Since the late 1990s, there have been attempts to revive digital cash ideas. Like in 1996, the e-gold project tried to create a digital currency based on real gold. At its peak, over 5 million users were on e-gold, and the platform's annual turnover was over $2 billion.[43] But with great scale came great responsibility, and, eventually, big troubles.

Right from the start, e-gold was plagued by technical problems and phishing attacks by Russian and Ukrainian hackers. The system was a security nightmare. Scammers found ways to get into people's e-gold accounts by finding weaknesses in Microsoft Windows and Internet Explorer.[44] Hackers could easily piece things together, like tracking money transfers and collecting data. According to the FBI, they stole data from more than a million accounts and credit cards from 40 different websites.[45]

Now, let's look at things from a different perspective. Using fake names online made it easier for people to do illegal things. The criminal investigation revealed 3,000 instances where e-gold was used to pay for child pornography.[46] Also, some scams started using e-gold, and people with ordinary usernames like user 1234 sold fake items or things that didn't even exist on eBay. International criminal groups preferred their victims to pay in e-gold, as it was the most accessible, fastest, and hardest-to-track method for transferring funds abroad.[47]

However, we must remember that the platform had both technical issues and faced serious legal problems. E-gold introduced something called the "e-gold Special Purpose Trust," which was like a special bank account for gold. The trust held gold on behalf of users, and users had full control without any legal obligations. All the legal responsibility was on the company, and they couldn't safely deal with users who had access to their digital tool without verifying who they were or what they were doing. Such a legal setup spread out the money transfers among users and put all the responsibility (and legal liability) on the company. Disastrous framework: money transfers were decentralized, but responsibility was centralized. It was a bad idea and caused a lot of problems.

Next, there were some tough legal problems to deal with. Five years after e-gold started, they had to follow strict rules set by the government and face the risk of getting in trouble with the law. This became even more serious after the 9/11 terrorist attacks. The government wanted to make sure that money transfers didn't support terrorism. So, they passed a law called the Patriot Act in 2001.[48] This law made it very strict to check and control money transfer services, especially when they operated internationally, like e-gold.

The Patriot Act had a rule stating that transferring money without a state money transfer license in any state that requires such a license is a federal offense.[49] This meant that e-gold had to get 49 different licenses to avoid breaking the law. Big players like Western Union or MoneyGram could afford good lawyers and obtain the necessary permits. For a small fintech startup, however, the legal costs were simply too overwhelming.

The company faced a lot of legal problems and had to close down in 2009.[50] High-ranking administration, like the US State Department, was involved in the proceedings. In support of the person who started e-gold, Douglas Jackson, even the prosecution admitted,

> Digital currencies are at the forefront of international money transfers. E-gold is the most well-known digital currency and captures the attention of the whole world. This world is now a bit like the Wild West. People are trying to find the right legal path, understand the rules and their consequences.[51]

Douglas Jackson eventually pleaded guilty to running an illegal, unlicensed cash transfer service and money laundering. He faced up to 20 years in prison and a $500,000 fine. Ultimately, the court limited it to 300 hours of community service, a $200 fine, and three years of probation, including six months of house arrest with electronic monitoring.[52] The court recognized Douglas Jackson did not have bad intentions and had troubles due to non-compliance with restrictive financial regulations. E-gold didn't intend to act against the law. It was simply an underdeveloped business—both legally and technically. Plain and simple: it was a business failure. However, the issue of digital cash was not settled. As it turned out, it came back in just a few years. And it returned in grand style.

2.3 BLOCKCHAIN: THE REAL DEAL

Before the release of Bitcoin's code, all attempts to create digital money using public key cryptography failed. There was always at least one factor, technological imperfections, impractical solutions, bad timing, inappropriate market research, or legal issues. Ralph Merkle, a pioneer in distributed ledger technology, had great ideas but didn't have the business skills to make them big. David Chaum, with DigiCash, began implementing academic and theoretical cryptographic solutions, but he was too early. Way before the essential elements for digital cash popularity (like widespread Internet access) were in place. Plus, he thought about digital money in a way that was too idealistic and impractical. And don't forget Douglas Jackson and his e-gold project. His solution had too many technical and legal flaws. None of them succeeded in this industry. None of them became the first crypto millionaire.

Around the start of the 2000s, there was a major shift in fintech and e-commerce. Digital financial services started to be in high demand, not just from everyday people but also from many emerging online businesses. They all recognized—fair enough—the huge potential for making money through the growing trend of online shopping. Bill Gates, one of the authors of this great digital revolution, wrote his thoughts on this in his 1996 book, *The Road Ahead*: "I can't say exactly when we reached the point of no return, but by the end of 1995, we had crossed a threshold. More users meant more content, and more content meant more users."[53]

This exponential growth wasn't just in users but also in what was offered to them. While there were about 2 million WWW sites in mid-1998, in less than two years, this number had increased five times. Just check out these statistics: from 1994 to 2002, the value of the global e-commerce market doubled every single year[54] (Figure 2.3).

Back then, consumers without Internet access (57% of the US population in 2000) relied on TV shopping and mail-order products. Placing orders at a distance wasn't a problem. But what about making payments?

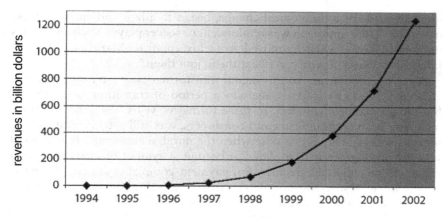

Figure 2.3 The worldwide revenues of e-commerce industry from 1994 to 2002.

(*Source:* **Data from NUA Internet Studies.**)

PayPal was a pioneer in digital money transfers, launching its first electronic payment system in 1999. Initially dealing with security software for mobile devices, PayPal didn't do well in that business model. So, they shifted their focus to a digital wallet. After merging with Elon Musk's x.com, PayPal zoomed in on Internet payments and achieved spectacular success. By 2002, they had gone public and raised $61 million.[55] Soon, eBay, the e-commerce monopoly of the time, came calling. For $1.5 billion—25 times its IPO value—eBay took over PayPal, turning it into its main payment channel. Over 70% of all eBay auctions accepted PayPal, and 40% of eBay's revenue was flowing in from transactions processed by Musk's company.[56] That American fintech firm also created strong partnerships with financial giants like MasterCard.

So, what sets stories like PayPal apart? The financial sector always jumped at new tech opportunities. Take NASDAQ, for instance, the world's first electronic stock trading system, launched in 1971.[57] However, until the early 2000s, the financial sector didn't care about bringing services closer to consumers using new technologies. Credit cards have been in the picture since 1958, but they don't quite fit in here. They're even familiar to the American baby boomer generation. The real game-changer was about to be the birth of the Internet.

With the widespread use of the Internet, the whole game of finance changed. Services that were traditionally confined to physical locations, like banks and stores, suddenly became available from anywhere with an Internet connection. Imagine transforming any room in your house into a personal shopping center or bank branch just by going online. This massive shift was unstoppable, and it marked the beginning of a new era in Finance. Fintech startups, blending finance and technology, began to emerge and collaborate with traditional banking institutions. These older banks, recognizing the inevitable tide of technological change, began to adapt and embrace these new tools. Their approach was reminiscent of soccer player Michael Owen's pragmatic stance when he moved from Liverpool to Manchester United, famously stating, "If you can't beat them, join them."

However, the journey to this digital transformation wasn't immediate or complete. The early Internet age was a period of transition rather than a full-blown digital revolution. In these formative years, the general public, including both entrepreneurs and consumers, was still getting used to how fintech worked. This was a time when the durable and iconic Nokia 3310 was just hitting the market, later to become a symbol of nostalgia and a testament to robust electronics. So, payment companies focused on what people knew best: credit and debit cards. It wasn't about creating brand-new financial services but improving what we already had. It was like updating an old car model to make it better, not making a whole new car.

One big issue with using this kind of payment method was that it was really expensive, and all the costs were passed on to the consumers. On the one hand, they paid a commission to the payment gateway from the transaction. On the other hand, they had to pay interest to their bank for the credit card they had. Both payment operators and banks found this arrangement quite lucrative.

Just look at the statistics of credit card use at the time of the technological boom of the early 2000s. First, at that time, the value of payments transferred by debit and credit cards was growing almost twice as fast as in cash transactions. This was most likely due to the widespread use of cards in Internet transactions[58] (Figure 2.4). American families were able to spend on credit partly because the economy was doing pretty well at that time. From 2000 to 2005, the average growth in America's GDP was 2.8%. But it's important to remember that using a credit card for transactions can be very pricey. In contrast, using cash is almost cost-free, even if you think about inflation. And it was these card fees and interest payments that were making the banks a lot of money.

Second, and even more importantly, the early 2000s marked a time of unprecedented credit consumption. In the previous chapter, I mentioned NINJA loans, given to people without jobs, income, or savings. Starting from the 1980s, Americans' credit card debt began to skyrocket. This gap between wealth and debt grew even faster at the turn of the millennium with the rise of electronic payment gateways. Consequently, credit card debt was growing four, then five times faster than consumer incomes (Figure 2.5).

This excessive debt was very profitable for banks. Between 2000 and 2005, the bank interest rate on credit cards in the United States fluctuated between 12% and 15%.[59] This means that on consumer loans alone, banks could have earned up to $190 billion.[60] And that's not even counting the extra fees charged to those who didn't pay off their credit cards on time. Sometimes, late fees could be as high as 30% of the owed amount. And there must have been plenty of late payers, especially since banks had been

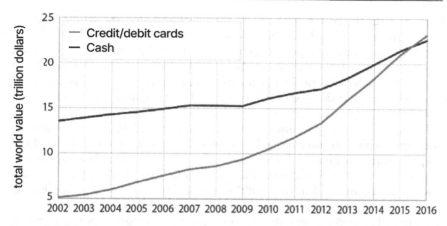

Figure 2.4 The dynamics of credit/debit cards and cash payments 2002–2016.

(*Source:* Data from Euromonitor International.)

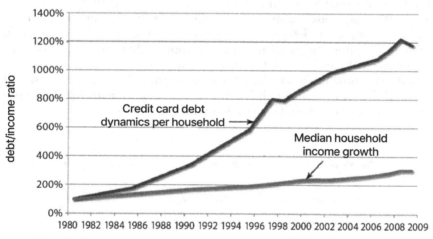

Figure 2.5 The debt-to-income dynamics of US households.

(*Source:* Data from Federal Reserve & Census Bureau 1980–2009.)

handing out those NINJA loans and not really educating people on financial management.

When the big financial crisis hit in 2007–2008, it was like a wake-up call. The laws of Economics could no longer be bent: the extended credit action had to have some limits. Banks had been taking big risks with people's money, and it backfired. Governments had to step in to prevent a total economic disaster. They decided to save the banks that were about to collapse. Interestingly, the bankers who took these risks often didn't face serious consequences. Governments started doing what's called bailouts. These were plans to help the banks get back on their feet and stop the whole banking system from crashing down. No one wanted another situation like Lehman Brothers, the fourth-biggest investment bank in the United States, which went down and showed everyone how fragile the financial system is. If one part of the system has problems, it can affect everything else. This crisis was a big moment that showed how complicated and fragile our global financial system is.

In the economic and political climate of the early 2000s, a game-changing anonymous publication emerged. This wasn't just a big deal for the world of cryptography—it posed a huge challenge to the traditional banking sector. On October 31, 2008, someone using the name Satoshi Nakamoto released a white paper, an article laying out the technical blueprint of a groundbreaking technological concept. Nakamoto chose to share this innovation through a mailing list popular among cryptographers, metzdowd.com. The paper was titled *Bitcoin: A Peer-to-Peer Electronic Cash System*.[61]

Nakamoto's white paper detailed a brand-new system for recording and exchanging information as a distributed ledger (Figure 2.6). This was a big shift from the usual accounting and IT methods used in digital money transfers. Unlike previous accounting and digital financial transfer solutions, Bitcoin's transaction ledger wasn't stored on a central server. Instead, Bitcoin's algorithm "packed" information about individual digital currency units into blocks and then linked them in a network.

And that's how the term *Blockchain* was born. This concept represented a radical departure from traditional financial systems, marking the beginning of a new era in digital transactions and currency.

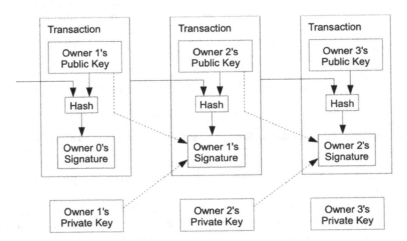

Figure 2.6 Simplified diagram of the Bitcoin network presented in an article by Satoshi Nakamoto.

(*Source*: Modified from Nakamoto, S. (2008) Bitcoin: A Peer-to-Peer Electronic Cash System. https://bitcoin.org/bitcoin.pdf)

This approach to the idea of money is diametrically different from the paper cash we use daily. For example, in the United States, the only issuer of money is the Federal Reserve System. The FED institution guarantees the value of money, which all people and companies "agree on." Such money is called fiat money—from another Latin word, *fiat*, meaning "let it be, let it happen."

With cryptocurrencies, it's different. They are not tied to any country or specific institution. Instead, the crypto community itself manages and issues new units. New bitcoins are created in the mining process, which involves solving a "cryptographic puzzle" by the author of a new block. Such a solution ensures the independence of the Bitcoin network from the power of specific people and their intentions. But does it work like that in practice? You'll find out later.

The Bitcoin community highly values the system for its strong resistance to hacking. Once a block is added, it's easy for existing users of the Bitcoin network to verify. Creating or "producing" it is a challenging and time-consuming task. That's because adding a block to the Bitcoin network requires solving a complex "cryptographic puzzle" using the computer power of a network user. This makes the Bitcoin network incredibly secure against hacks. To break it, you'd need to replace the code of over half of all bitcoins ever created. In simpler terms, hacking into the Bitcoin system would mean using enough electricity to power my home country, Poland, for nine months, and directing all that energy toward machines attempting to crack Bitcoin's code. But why bother hacking when all that effort could be used to mine your bitcoins? Why destroy a system when you can use it to make money?

But what the early Bitcoin community saw as a big security benefit turned out to be a major downside, especially for the environment. Confirming new Bitcoin transactions uses a lot of energy, wastes resources, and hurts the environment. As the Bitcoin network adds more units, it needs more and more electricity. The bigger it gets, the more costly and environmentally damaging it is to produce the next Bitcoin. In short: Bitcoin's model isn't scalable in the long run without hurting the planet. As of 2023, the Bitcoin network consumed around 120 terawatt-hours of electricity. That's the annual output of 37.5 medium-sized coal-fired power plants.[62] If wind turbines were to generate that much energy, you'd need over 225 million of them.

Even if one day all energy comes from eco-friendly, renewable sources, there's still the opportunity cost to consider. The electricity used for the energy-hungry Bitcoin could be put to better, more efficient use—like powering better-designed Blockchain networks. Even when the last Bitcoin is mined, and no new units are introduced, the network will still need to be maintained. Bitcoin's energy consumption is undeniable.

But let's put the tech talk aside and dive back into the story. Shortly after publishing his paper, Nakamoto also released the Bitcoin code on SourceForge. That included the first block (block number 0) of the decentralized network managing Bitcoin transactions. By making the software public and allowing users to add new blocks and their encoded cryptocurrency units, Nakamoto fired up the Bitcoin network and put it into circulation. Downloading and running the Bitcoin program and solving the first puzzle came with a reward of 50 bitcoins.[63] With the value of BTC in mid-March 2024, this amount would translate into $3,300 million.

But it's not just about the value. It's about the strong message hidden in its very first block. Nakamoto released the Bitcoin code right after a big news story hit the headlines: British banks were about to get a huge £37 billion bailout. In Bitcoin's first block, he left a note about this: "The Times 03/Jan/2009 Chancellor on brink of second bailout for banks."[64] This was like a clever hint at his views on politics and society. Bailout programs, funded by taxpayer money, provoked extreme emotions. Many people, regardless of political views, felt that the traditional financial sector had cheated society. Bitcoin quickly turned from a cool tech idea into a big change in the finance world. It wasn't just about making a new kind of money—it was about making a point against the old financial system. By including that headline from *The Times* in the first Bitcoin block, Nakamoto was saying something powerful about the state of finance, and this message connected with people who were tired of how things were. Bitcoin was the start of a whole new financial era.

NOTES

1 https://www.rollingstone.com/culture/culture-news/jay-z-announces-occupy-all-streets-t-shirt-69337/

2 United States Securities and Exchange Commission, Office of Legislative Affairs (24.07.1994), Timeline of Bank Securities Activities [PDF], s. 1–35, zarch. w Wayback Machine (web.archive.org) 4.08.2012, access: 11.02.2012.

3 G.J. Bentson (1990), *The Separation of Commercial and Investment Banking*, London: McMillan, pp. 47–89; H.B. Cleveland, T.F. Huertas (1985), *Citibank, 1812–1970*, Harvard University Press, pp. 172–187.

4 https://economictimes.indiatimes.com/industry/miscellaneous/market-crash-of-1929-some-facts-of-the-economic-downturn/articleshow/61166918.cms?from=mdr

5 J.E. Stiglitz (2008), Capitalist fools, "Vanity Fair", access: 9.11.2016.

6 D. Reed (2004), Loan Fraud: Just Don't Do It, "Realty Times", access: 21.01.2014.

7 B. Aziz (2012), Financial Crisis 2007 – 2009: How Real Estate Bubble and Transparency and Accountability Issues Generated and Worsen the Crisis, "Estudios fronterizos", 13(26), pp. 201–221.

8 Swaps can be an example here, for example, credit default swaps. They operated on the principle of "insurance" for lenders in case debtors failed to repay their obligations.

9 Lewis, M. (2011). The Big Short. New York: W.W. Norton & Company.

10 J. Bricker, B. Bucks, A. Kennickell, T. Mach, K. Moore (2011), Surveying the Aftermath of the Storm: Changes in Family Finances from 2007 to 2009, Federal Reserve Board Finance and Economics Discussion Series Working Paper 2011–17, March 2011.

11 Ibid.
12 M. Serapioni, P. Hespanha, Crisis and Austerity in Southern Europe: Impact on Economies and Societies, e-cadernos CES, 31 | 2019 [online], http://journals. openedition.org/eces/4068
13 CoinMarketCap.
14 A. Sherman, F. Javani, H. Zhang, E. Golaszewski (2018), On the origins and variations of blockchain technologies, "IEEE Security & Privacy" 17 (1), http:// arxiv.org/abs/1810.06130
15 https://www.thalesgroup.com/en/markets/digital-identity-and-security/ magazine/brief-history-encryption
16 P. Hilton, NOVA | Transcripts | Decoding Nazi Secrets | PBS, arc. 29.08.2019.
17 A.M. Turing Award, amturing.acm.org, dostęp 12.06.2015.
18 https://www.washingtonpost.com/gdpr-consent/?next_url=https%3a%2f %2fwww.washingtonpost.com%2fwp-srv%2fspecial%2fnational%2fblack-budget%2f
19 A. Sherman, F. Javani, H. Zhang, E. Golaszewski, On the origins..., op. cit.
20 S. Garfinkel (1994), Pretty Good Privacy, O'Reilly and Associates.
21 A. Sherman, F. Javani, H. Zhang, E. Golaszewski, On the origins..., op. cit.
22 S. Halevi, H. Krawczyk, Randomized Hashing and Digital Signatures. https:// webee.technion.ac.il/~hugo/rhash/
23 Cybersecurity Pioneer Selected to Lead Information Security Center at Georgia Tech (inf. prasowa), Georgia Institute of Technology, 15.07.2003, arc. 5.09.2006, access: 17.03.2007.
24 IEEE Richard W. Hamming Medal, IEEE, dostęp: 29.05.2011.
25 R. Merkle (1997), It's a Small, Small, Small, Small World, "MIT Technology Review" 25.
26 A.T. Sherman, F. Javani, H. Zhang, E. Golaszewski (2019), On the Origins..., op. cit., s. 72–77. https://arxiv.org/abs/1810.06130
27 Ibid.
28 Ibid.
29 Ibid., p. 403.
30 Ibid.
31 D. Chaum (1983), Blind Signatures for Untraceable Payments. Advances in Cryptology [PDF], in: Advances in Cryptology: Proceedings of Crypto 82, Springer, pp. 199–203.
32 A. Narayanan, What Happened to the Crypto Dream? Part 1, "IEEE Security & Privacy", Volume 11, Issue 2, March – April 2013, pp. 75–76.
33 E. Hughes (1993), A Cypherpunk's Manifesto.
34 T. Kirk, Wikileaks Founder Julian Assange Is Planning to Get Married Inside Top-Security Belmarsh Prison, "Evening Standard", access: 31.08.2021.
35 M. Casey, P. Vigna, The Truth Machine: The Blockchain and the Future of Everything, St. Martin's Press, p. 52.
36 J. Pitta (1999), Requiem for a Bright Idea, "Forbes", access: 16.10.2014.
37 https://www.chaum.com/ecash/articles/1996/05-07-96%20-%20DigiCash_s %20Ecash%E2%84%A2%20to%20be%20Issued%20by%20Deutsche%20 Bank.pdf
38 J. Pitta, Requiem..., op. cit.
39 T. Clark (1998), DigiCash loses U.S. toehold, CNET, 2.09.1998.
40 J.-I. Brodesser (1999), First Monday Interviews: David Chaum, "First Monday" [online], 4(7), access: 8.06.2016.

41 M. Roser, H. Ritchie, E. Ortiz-Ospina (2015), Internet [online], OurWorldInData. org, https://ourworldindata.org/internet

42 J. Pitta, Requiem…, op. cit.

43 e-gold Statistics. E-gold.com., zarch. w Wayback Machine (we.archive.org) 9.11.2006, https://web.archive.org/web/20061109161419/http://www.e-gold.com/ stats.html

44 [e-gold-list] Large Criminal Hacker Attack on Windows NT E-Banking and E-Commerce Sites, Mail-archive.com. 8.03.2021, access: 20.9.2013.

45 e-gold Blog: Buy Online Privately (but not Anonymously) with e-gold, Blog.e-gold.com, 12.9.2007, access: 20.9.2013.

46 J. Meek (2007), Feds out to Bust up 24-Karat Web worry, "NY Daily News", 3.06.2007, access: 20.9.2013.

47 e-gold Security Alerts. E-gold.com, access: 20.9.2013.

48 Pełna nazwa: Uniting and Strengthening America by Providing Appropriate Tools Required to Intercept and Obstruct Terrorism Act of 2001.

49 e-gold Statistics. E-gold.com., zarch. w Wayback Machine (we.archive.org) 9.11.2006, https://web.archive.org/web/20061109161419/http://www.e-gold. com/stats.html

50 archive.org. 2006-11-09. Archived from the original on November 9, 2006. Retrieved 2014-12-19.

51 Minutes of the Judgement Annoucement, p. 95, PACER, 20.11.2008, access: 13.01.2015.

52 S. Condon (2008), Judge Spares e-Gold Directors Jail Time, CNET.

53 B. Gates (1996), The Road Ahead (Revised Edition), New York/London: Penguin Books, p. xi.

54 http://www.digitalsuperhighway.com/Future/InfoSuperhighway.html

55 K. Regan (2002), PayPal IPO Off to Spectacular Start, "ECommerce Times", access: 11.11.2014.

56 D. Kidder, R. Hoffman, H. Hindi (2012), The Startup Playbook: Secrets of the Fastest Growing Start-Ups from the Founding Entrepreneurs, San Francisco, CA: Chronicle Books, pp. 214–216.

57 R. Buckley, D. Arner, J. Barberis (2016), The Evolution of Fintech: A New Post-Crisis Paradigm?, "Georgetown Journal of International Law", 47, pp. 1271–1319.

58 https://avpsolutions.com/blog/payment-cards-now-set-to-surpass-cash/

59 https://www.valuepenguin.com/average-credit-card-interest-rates

60 Calculations based on FED data.

61 S. Nakamoto (2009), Bitcoin: A Peer-to-Peer Electronic Cash System [PDF], arc. 20.03.2014, access: 5.03.2014.

62 https://digiconomist.net/bitcoin-energy-consumption/

63 J. Davis (2011), The Crypto-Currency: Bitcoin and Its Mysterious Inventor, "The New Yorker", 10.10.2011.

64 Ibid.

Chapter 3

Who is Satoshi?

3.1 THE MYSTERIOUS AUTHOR

At any point, Satoshi Nakamoto revealed neither his true identity nor personal data. We don't know if it was one person or a team of programmers. Satoshi always either discussed technical issues or published comments on traditional paper money banking. On his P2P Foundation profile, Nakamoto claimed to be a 37-year-old Japanese man. But some doubted his nationality and Japanese name due to his fluency in English.

More revealing than his identity, however, were Nakamoto's views. Satoshi never openly stated his ideological approach, but he gave some signs. The Bitcoin Whitepaper contains at least one indirect political reference. Nakamoto refers to Wei Dai, with whom he had a brief email conversation.[1] Wei Dai is a Chinese computer scientist and University of Washington alumnus. Since the 1990s, he was one of the Cypherpunks who published articles about encryption systems and cryptography at the peak of its popularity. His 1998 article B-money begins as follows:

> I am fascinated by Tim May's crypto-anarchy. Unlike the communities traditionally associated with the word "anarchy," in a crypto-anarchy the government is not temporarily destroyed but permanently forbidden and permanently unnecessary. It's a community where the threat of violence is impotent because violence is impossible, and violence is impossible because its participants cannot be linked to their true names or physical locations.[2]

Nakamoto's views are also reflected in the choices he made while programming Bitcoin. In the summary of the Bitcoin Whitepaper, he outlines his reasoning for selecting specific technical solutions in the Bitcoin algorithm. He wrote,

> We have proposed a system for electronic transactions without relying on trust. (...) To solve [verification problem] we proposed a peer-to-peer network using proof-of-work to record a public history of transactions

DOI: 10.1201/9781032621456-4

that quickly becomes computationally impractical for an attacker to change if honest nodes control a majority of CPU power. The network is robust in its unstructured simplicity.[3]

This approach aligns closely with the philosophy of Adam Smith, known as the father of free-market economics. He said that when people look out for their interests, they end up helping society more than if they tried to help society on purpose.[4] Nakamoto made a system where everyone looks after their transactions, and by doing that, they make the whole Bitcoin network safer and stronger. It's like everyone is working for themselves, but that ends up making the whole system work better for everyone.

The design of Bitcoin's mechanism seems to appeal to libertarians or even anarcho-capitalists—those who strongly believe in extreme individualism and freedom. Wendy McElroy, a Canadian feminist and anarcho-capitalism writer, talks about this in her book *Satoshi's Revolution: A Revolution of Rising Expectations*.[5] She points out some features of Bitcoin that would attract libertarians, using quotes from Nakamoto's article:

- *Radical Decentralization*: The first line of the abstract of the White Paper states, "A purely peer-to-peer version of electronic cash would allow online payments to be sent directly from one party to another without going through a financial institution." No leaders, no bureaucracy, no position of power beyond what the individual wields over himself.
- *Privacy*: Section 10 of the *White Paper* is entitled "Privacy." While not perfect, the anonymity sought and offered by Bitcoin is far superior to that of other forms of online payment. Section 10 ends with a warning and, perhaps, an indication of an improvement Satoshi was planning to make to the Blockchain.

  As an additional firewall, a new key pair should be used for each transaction to keep them from being linked to a common owner. Some linking is still unavoidable with multi-input transactions, which necessarily reveal that their inputs were owned by the same owner. The risk is that if the owner of a key is revealed, linking could reveal other transactions that belonged to the same owner.

- *Pro-capitalism*: The *White Paper* stresses Bitcoin's advantages to commerce and merchants as a free-enterprise payment system. It states, "With the possibility of reversal [which Bitcoin does not accommodate], the need for trust spreads. Merchants must be wary of their customers, hassling them for more information than they would otherwise need." It's difficult to imagine a socialist having this insight or caring about merchants at all.

- *Anti-government*: Although the government is not mentioned in the *White Paper*, Bitcoin is a direct attack on an allegedly vital state function—banking. The message in the Genesis block was a slap at the Chancellor as much as at the bank bailout.
- *Anti-baking*: The entire purpose of Bitcoin is "online payments ... without going through a financial institution." Satoshi explained,

> The root problem with conventional currency is all the trust that's required to make it work. The central bank must be trusted not to debase the currency, but the history of fiat currencies is full of breaches of that trust. Banks must be trusted to hold our money and transfer it electronically, but they lend it out in waves of credit bubbles with barely a fraction in reserve. We have to trust them with our privacy, trust them not to let identity thieves drain our accounts.

- *Anti-inflation*: Section 6 of the *White Paper* entitled "Incentive," claims that "once a predetermined number of coins have entered circulation, the incentive can transition entirely to transaction fees and be completely inflation-free." The predetermined number is 21 million coins that are each divisible down to a tiny fraction of a whole coin.[6]

As Bitcoin emerged as a popular option for making stratospheric profits, the mood in its community shifted to a more playful one. Members started creating funny memes that made light of traditional investments. This was coupled with dreams of wealth, often expressed through hashtags like #Lambo and #ToTheMoon. "#Lambo" symbolized the luxury goals of long-term crypto investors, while "#ToTheMoon" reflected their high hopes for Bitcoin's soaring value. This shift brought a lighthearted and hopeful vibe to the Bitcoin community, blending humor with big dreams in the world of cryptocurrency.

A side note: look at how the "hodlers" and Bitcoin enthusiasts communicate. I found it interesting that Wendy McElroy's work wasn't released as a typical e-book. It was shared piece by piece on niche cryptocurrency forums. This method, more common in the past, really shows the almost secretive nature of the early Bitcoin community. They used encrypted emails, peer-to-mail and peer-to-peer systems, special chat platforms, and anonymous forums like Reddit to talk with each other. This setup created a feeling of being in an exclusive club among the most committed "hodlers." It was like they were part of a digital elite that had figured out the secrets of decentralized finance. It reminds me of one of my favorite books from elementary school, *The Paul Street Boys*. Just like those brave boys defending their playground, the Bitcoin devotees seemed ready to stand guard over their digital domain.

Now, let's get back to the essence of Wendy McElroy's arguments. Essentially, each of the arguments she cites can be turned against her, criticizing the extremely liberal elements of Bitcoin. BTC, unlike some other cryptocurrencies, faces significant technological constraints. It doesn't support transactions based on complex smart contracts, a topic I delve deeper into Chapter 6 about Vitalik Buterin. Its primary function and advantage lie in the functional nature of digital money, and that's pretty much it. This brings us to question whether its features of decentralization, anonymity, anti-government stance, and anti-banking nature are truly beneficial.

Contrary to Nakamoto's assertions, we can't ignore the possibility of malicious actors in the Bitcoin system. The human nature also has dark sides. In some cases, the anonymity offered by the Bitcoin network isn't an advantage but a significant drawback. It puts a powerful economic tool in the hands of people whose intentions we neither know sufficiently nor can fully trust as a consequence. This becomes particularly problematic in the absence of government oversight or regulatory frameworks. The risks aren't just theoretical. According to data from the US Federal Trade Commission, from October 2020 to May 2021, the number of reported cryptocurrency scams increased sharply. Nearly 7,000 people reported losses totaling over $80 million, with a median loss of $1,900 per person.[7] Imagine what would happen if monitoring institutions didn't exist since fraud occurs even with their hard work and supervision.

As we look back at the chaos of the financial crisis and the rampant excess of money supply, Bitcoin's stance against traditional banking seems partially beneficial. The meteoric rise of BTC and other cryptocurrencies sent a clear message to banks: people are ready to challenge the unfair financial system and devise new ways to regain control over it. On the other hand, practice shows that removing institutions from the oversight or involvement in the circulation of money would eventually lead us downhill. The perception of Bitcoin as a fully decentralized, intermediary-free system is somewhat misleading.

True decentralization would mean a digital economy where bitcoins could be used for everyday purchases, from groceries to electronics. But in reality, despite some marketing efforts to accept Bitcoin, most businesses still operate with traditional currencies. Accepting Bitcoin or another cryptocurrency is just a problem for them, even due to strong price fluctuations. In this situation, there is, in fact, an intermediary. It's the exchange that accepts traditional money from investors and earns on the exchange of cryptocurrencies for a commission or using the spread mechanism. Moreover, even simple transactions like transferring bitcoins from one wallet to another involve fees. For instance, the average fee for a Bitcoin transaction is around $5, but it can increase during network congestion. During the last price boom, the fees were almost $60—a rate that even the most expensive banks wouldn't charge (Figure 3.1). This brings us to question just how much these wallet operators and cryptocurrency exchanges are earning from these transactions. I'm going to talk more about that later.

Now, look at the role of exchanges and wallet operators in the Bitcoin ecosystem. They're the middlemen in the Bitcoin world. It kind of goes against the idea of Bitcoin being totally decentralized. While the Bitcoin network itself doesn't have central control, getting into the network isn't

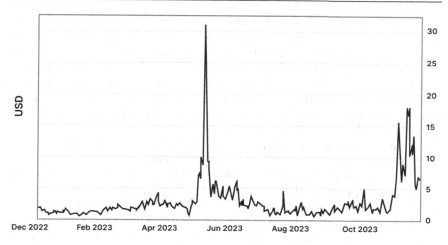

Figure 3.1 Average transaction fees for a bitcoin transfer.

(*Source*: Data from Blockchain.com.)

direct. As someone who runs a software business, I see it as the difference between the back end and front end of a program. The back-end is like the engine (Bitcoin, in this case), but you need a front-end—a user-friendly way for people to use the system. In the Bitcoin world, cryptocurrency exchanges and wallet operators are this front-end, acting as the real intermediaries. Because these intermediaries exist in the Bitcoin community, they can be targets for hackers, just like any digital system. That's why we sometimes hear about big thefts from cryptocurrency exchanges. The biggest of these was the 2014 hack of the Japanese platform Mt. Gox. At its best 70% of all bitcoin traffic went through Gox. During the hacker attack, 850,000 BTC with a total value of $460 million vanished into thin air in seconds.[8]

Let's finally tackle the argument about anti-inflation. For sure, free-market economists are criticizing inflation as a hidden tax—inflation means you can buy less stuff, and the only "winner" is the government, which sees its tax revenue grow on paper. Inflation often results from so-called quantitative easing policies, where the central bank can "print" more money. In my opinion, the issue of inflation makes the most sense out of all the arguments Bitcoin believers use. The cryptocurrency's algorithm is programmed so that the maximum supply of BTC is 21 million units. Wendy's argument, when detached from a broader economic context, is logically sound and hard to fault.

But the real problem isn't the potential inflation of paper money. The issue lies in Bitcoin's extreme deflation. What does that mean? Well, any economic exchange can be described using ratios. This applies to both currencies and goods. For example, one euro unit can be exchanged for roughly $1.10, and one BTC for $73,135 (which is a new all-time high price set by Bitcoin on March 13th 2024). But these economic units are currencies. This means they can be exchanged for goods or services. After all, that's what cash is ultimately for. In a normal situation, the goal is to avoid extreme fluctuations in these exchange rates. If I have $1,000 in my account, I need to make sure that today, tomorrow, and a year from now, I should be able to buy 30 lunchboxes with it. In other words, good money must be stable. It must be predictable.

But what happens when we get deflation (an increase in the purchasing power of money) or inflation (a decrease in purchasing power)? In case of deflation, suddenly I can buy more products with the same amount of cash. When inflation occurs, it's the other way around—my money allows me to buy less and less over time. For example, inflation would mean that with $1,000, in a month I would no longer be able to buy 30 lunchboxes but maybe just 25. Conversely, deflationary pressure would mean that all of a sudden, I could buy more, maybe even 35 or even 40. So, would you think that deflation is okay and inflation isn't, right? Well, hold your horses.

Let's get back to Bitcoin. Imagine we wake up in the dream world of Wendy McElroy and Satoshi Nakamoto, where Bitcoin with its limited supply is the global currency. Everyone knows that the number of bitcoins won't increase, so everyone tries to buy their own and keep it as long as possible. What does this lead to? Such extreme deflationary pressure makes trading unprofitable for people. And if no one wants to trade, people hoard the assets they accumulated, and the exchange stops. Ultimately, when the deflationary spiral continues, production stops, too. Everything stops. That's how a deflationary spiral works.

History has taught us that neither extreme inflation nor deflation is beneficial. For effective and long-term economic planning, a stable and predictable financial environment is essential. Particularly when it comes to currency stability. Accepting this argument, we can tame our fears about what Bitcoin is. It's neither a magic fix for all problems the world is facing, nor is it just a way for criminals to hide money. Instead, Bitcoin is the first implementation of Blockchain technology, which has enormous potential to streamline many key processes in the digital economy. A technology that can still make a lot of money—not only because of its hype and noise but also its actual value.

3.2 LOOKING FOR NAKAMOTO

Nakamoto kept working with other programmers on Bitcoin's software until mid-2010, modifying the source code himself. He then handed over control of the source code repository and the network alert key to Gavin Andresen and transferred several related domains to various prominent members of the Bitcoin community and stepped away from the project. In April 2011, he sent a note to a developer involved in Bitcoin development, saying he had "moved on to other things."[9] Since then, his trail has gone cold. And that's when the real search began.

Some believed that Nakamoto could be a team of people, not just one programmer. The perspective of Dan Kaminsky, a cybersecurity specialist, is especially interesting here. According to his mother's stories, Dan got his first primitive computer at the age of four, and a year later taught himself how to program.[10] Dan Kaminsky is known for discovering a terrifying flaw in the WWW protocol that would allow a skilled programmer to take over any website, or even shut down the Internet.[11] That was back in 2008. Kaminsky alerted both the US authorities and the management of Microsoft and Cisco about the issue. He worked with these corporations to fix the flaw. He's one of the most skilled practitioners of "penetration testing," or breaking into computer systems at the request of owners who want to know the weaknesses of their software. At first, he thought Bitcoin was an easy target—after all, it was created by an anonymous author, and it's open source. However, he was quite surprised when he read BTC's code.

In an interview with the New Yorker, Kaminsky said,

> When I first looked at the [Bitcoin] code, I was sure I was going to be able to break it. The way the whole thing was formatted was insane. Only the most paranoid, painstaking coder in the world could avoid making mistakes.[12]

But for every doubt Kaminsky had, there suddenly was a line of BTC code that answered the imagined problem. When analyzing Bitcoin and trying to find its weak point, there was a sort of chess game going on: Satoshi Nakamoto versus Dan Kaminsky. Despite Kaminsky's good preparation, Nakamoto not only complicated his moves but was able to anticipate each move at least two moves ahead. That's why Kaminsky immediately concluded that Nakamoto must be either a "team of people" or a "genius"— because such programming was "just crazy."[13]

The crypto community turned into a band of digital detectives, poring over every byte and bit for clues. First up, the language clues. Using British English both in the source code comments and in forum posts—using expressions like *bloody hard*, terms like *maths*, and spelling *grey* or *colour* (instead of the more popular American forms *math*, *gray*, and *color*). It sparked speculation that Nakamoto, or at least one person in such a consortium, comes from the United Kingdom. Additionally, a reference to the London newspaper *The Times* in the first BTC block mined by Nakamoto suggested a special interest in the British government. For sure, it's making everyone wonder if Nakamoto is sipping tea by the Thames.[14]

The more people looked into Satoshi Nakamoto, the more mysterious he became. The forum posts—over 500 of them—were sifted through like a digital detective novel. And guess what? Almost no posts between 5 AM and 11 AM British Time GMT. That's afternoon (from 2 PM to 8 PM) in Japan.[15] Now, why would a supposed Japanese Nakamoto be offline when everyone is working, going to a restaurant, or spending time with their family? Each clue, each guess just deepens the mystery. Is Nakamoto a lone genius typing away in a dimly lit room in London? Or a collective of brains scattered around the globe? The more people tried to understand, the more confusing it all got.

3.2.1 Hal Finney, the first BTC transfer recipient

By September 2021, those bitcoins would have been worth more than $400,000. Finney was so involved early on that some people even thought he might be Nakamoto. If he were still around, we would consider him the first crypto millionaire.

Finney was an active player in the cryptographic community. He was really influential, especially after he created the first reusable Proof-of-Work system (RPoW) in 2004. Nakamoto used later a similar solution to build the Bitcoin transaction verification mechanism. As early as the 1990s, Hal Finney was setting up newsletters and peer-to-mail networks in the cryptographic community.[16] What's interesting is that he wasn't a big theory guy; he only had a basic engineering degree from CalTech. But he was great at doing things in practice. For a long time, Finney designed computer games. He worked at Mattel, where he helped develop games for Atari computers and early gaming consoles. However, his real love was cryptography, so he eventually switched to that field. He worked at PGP Corporation until he retired in 2011. The PGP company produced software called Pretty Good Privacy, which was really important in the cryptography world.[17]

Like the other members of this community, Finney saw cryptography as a tool for building a free society. When David Chaum began his pioneering work with digital cash projects, Finney commented:

> Here we are faced with the problems of loss of privacy, creeping computerization, massive databases, more centralization—and Chaum offers a completely different direction to go in, one which puts power into the hands of individuals rather than governments and corporations. The computer can be used as a tool to liberate and protect people, rather than to control them.[18]

Andy Greenberg, a journalist from *Forbes* and *Wired*, shared the moving story of Finney. In March 2014, when Finney was in the last stages of ALS, a disease without a cure, Greenberg wrote *Nakamoto's Neighbor: My Hunt for Bitcoin's Creator Led to a Paralyzed Crypto Genius*.[19] Finney, who battled ALS for five years, was known for his healthy and active life, especially as a runner.[20] Even as the disease progressed, he and his wife Fran participated in a Santa Barbara marathon to raise money for ALS research foundations. Finney was a well-known member of the Cypherpunks community and later in the Blockchain world.

Finney shared his experiences on his blog, Less Wrong, starting in 2009.[21] From 2013, he was almost completely paralyzed and bedridden. Despite his deteriorating health, he kept programming and stayed active in the Bitcoin community until his last days. However, this did not prevent some anonymous bastards from taking advantage of his situation. In his final year, the Finneys received anonymous calls where frauds demanded a payment of 1,000 BTC. They threatened to use "swatting" if not paid. Swatting is a dangerous trick where someone falsely reports a serious crime, like a bomb threat, at someone's house to make the police, especially SWAT teams, respond aggressively. The worst part of this story is that the blackmailers demanded more bitcoins than what Finney had left after paying for his medical care.[22] A cruel, heartless act, targeting someone at their most vulnerable, adds a deeply distressing and unfair layer to the challenges Finney and his family were already bravely facing.

3.2.2 Gavin Andresen

Most Bitcoin activists suspected of being Satoshi Nakamoto, the pseudonymous creator of Bitcoin, had one thing in common: they were very mysterious. They didn't reveal themselves publicly or did so very cautiously. They didn't give interviews and didn't appear at conferences. But Gavin Andresen was different.

Gavin Andresen, with his "nerdy" glasses and hair combed down, resembled his peers in the industry. For the most important tech conference in the world, the Web Summit in Lisbon, he wore a dark gray crumpled jacket. Yet, his appearance wasn't a priority. What mattered more was his programming talent. Andresen studied computer science at the prestigious Princeton University and then worked in a 3D graphics studio in Silicon Valley.[23] Like his IT colleagues, he had initially followed a standard, safe career path. But by the late 1990s, he started his own business. He was a serial entrepreneur, engaging in many diverse business ventures. Among these was an early Voice over IP project, the precursor to today's Internet voice calls. He also founded a startup that developed multiplayer gaming software for mixed teams of visually impaired and fully abled individuals.

The story of Andresen strikes a personal note with me. Despite the importance of such projects in Corporate Social Responsibility, he probably would have remained unknown to the larger business community if not for Blockchain technology. This resonates with my own journey. I implemented my first serious project in high school: a sign language communicator for deaf people called FiveApp. However, I saw the opportunities emerging with the rise of Blockchain. In 2015, I decided to enter the industry, more specifically: exploring Ethereum. This makes me appreciate what a challenge it must have been for Andresen. He decided to change his previous development path 180 degrees and bet on such a fledgling technology. And doing this as early as 2010.

Andresen discovered Bitcoin independently and joined the project because he was impressed by its technical sophistication. He started by sending patches and improvements to the BTC code to Nakamoto. The founder of Bitcoin liked his work, and soon Andresen's email address became the only one on the project's main page. It is said that Satoshi Nakamoto first chose him to lead the developers and then to be his successor. Gavin's resume included relevant experience. He had led projects as a technical leader and CTO, Chief Technology Officer, in Silicon Valley. He became the "custodian"—the chief programmer (core maintainer). He supervised five other, younger programmers.[24] On the *Bitcointalk* forum, he opened a thread called Development Process straw-man. His post read:

> With Satoshi's blessing, and with great reluctance, I'm going to start doing more active project management for Bitcoin. Everybody please be patient with me; I've had a lot of project management experience at startups, but this is the first open source project of any size I've been involved with.
>
> I've created an integration/staging tree at GitHub [code sharing site for developers]... Discussion, feedback, etc, especially from people with experience leading or working on other open-source projects, is very welcome.[25]

Andresen's understanding of HR processes and project development, especially in its original non-profit format, is the best proof of his business skills. An entrepreneur is someone who can efficiently utilize available resources to build value. In managing the early Bitcoin project, Andresen was able to maximize the effort of programmers working for free. He mentions this in his official post on the Bitcoin forum, where he describes the organization of work. Volunteers from around the world would send their code and paste it onto the GitHub platform. Statistics show that at peak times, there were over 40,000 added lines of code per week, which were then tested. Initially, this was done by a handful of programmers, but soon dozens of regular contributors joined in.[26] With these resources, the group of programmers around Andresen refined and organized the delivered solutions, integrating them into the existing code. This efficient way of working is something many IT entrepreneurs would dream of, despite the high hourly rates they pay programmers in profit-driven organizations. However, this work model makes sense, especially considering that Bitcoin has always been an open-source initiative. Andresen could count on the commitment of volunteer programmers because everyone felt that they were contributing to the creation of a new, exciting project—Bitcoin.

The Bitcoin project mirrors many aspects of typical startups, except it wasn't set up as a profit-driven company. In Bitcoin's early days, the management style was much like that of a young startup, focusing more on technical development than on business and marketing. Early-stage projects often have a flat management structure. This means fewer or no middle managers between the core team and the top leaders.[27] Employees in such setups have broad responsibilities and a big say in the project's direction. This contrasts sharply with corporate environments, where there are many layers of hierarchy. In corporations, you find departments with managers, partners, consultants, and various other roles, all adding to a complex structure. Despite the initial belief that remote work during the pandemic would boost efficiency, people ended up working longer, with an average increase of 49 minutes per day.[28]

After sorting out key programming and business matters, in 2012, Andresen made a game-changing move in the organization of the Bitcoin community. Up until that point, Bitcoin's development had a kind of "wild west" feel—anyone could jump in, write code, and throw it up on GitHub for others to check out. But as time went on, this freewheeling approach either lost its utility or started causing headaches. With the Bitcoin code now more structured and security beefed up, the era of anonymous volunteer coders was fading.

But then, a new hurdle appeared. Bitcoin, by then valued at tens of millions of dollars, lacked legal representation. Contrary to the original vision in Nakamoto's article, this situation was far from ideal. The community was growing and generating value, but it lacked formal management. To address this, Andresen established The Bitcoin Foundation in Washington, D.C. Its mission? The primary goal of the foundation was to promote this new form of digital cash and educate the public about its functionality and legitimacy, dispelling any myths about it being a financial pyramid.[29]

Using foundations to manage projects is common in the IT sector. Look at Mozilla's web browser, courtesy of the Mozilla Foundation, or the Linux operating system from the Linux Foundation. Bitcoin was headed down a similar path. The foundation Andresen established was designed to mirror the management style of programming whiz Linus Torvalds. By setting up the foundation, Andresen formalized his influence on the project while smartly avoiding the top leadership position. He joined the Foundation as the "chief researcher," with a BTC salary of about $209,000, which was relatively modest for someone of his programming and business skills. Was there a hidden agenda behind all this?

Whether working independently or within the Foundation, Andresen acted as the person responsible for the final product (product owner). Gavin often spoke about this period not in terms of his own work but in relation to Satoshi Nakamoto's contributions. In 2010, as cybersecurity expert Dan Kaminsky put it, the Bitcoin code was messy, chaotic, and not quite fit for purpose. Andresen was always concerned about potential security flaws. He recounted to *The Technology Review* how in 2010, someone pointed out a bug to Nakamoto that could let someone spend bitcoins they didn't own. Nakamoto's response? "Satoshi just changed the code and told everyone: »Run this new code, I won't tell you why," Andresen recalls.[30]

Having learned from programming errors, as early as 2014, Andresen warned: "It's why I say Bitcoin is an experiment and you shouldn't invest your life's savings."[31] He linked those issues to the organizational structure of the Bitcoin project, noting, "Unfortunately, the best defense against security flaws—having people review other people's code—is hard to deploy for Bitcoin. Unpaid volunteers prefer to write their own code rather than laboriously read other people's."[32]

Those insights into the organizational dynamics of the Bitcoin project are crucial. I mention these details for a reason. In my own journey as an entrepreneur and investor, I've seen many promising ideas fail, sometimes due to lack of founder commitment, other times because of a flawed organizational structure leading to avoidable conflicts. The stats are pretty startling. For example, in the United States, managers spend a third of their time sorting out conflicts, leading to an average loss of $12,000 per year for every difficult employee.[33] Yet, despite these hurdles, the underlying drive in all companies is to generate profit and make money. This profit motive often brings out more rational behavior in people, steering them toward collaborative solutions rather than fighting over ideals or egos.

Initially, the Bitcoin project was more about activism and volunteering, with no real profit motive. In such environments, personal conflicts can become more common without a clear, shared objective and the promise of financial rewards for the participants. This is where Andresen's management skills really shone. He not only transformed the organizational culture and set new objectives but also successfully motivated the team and expanded it.

Andresen faced the classic startup dilemma: needing more programmers while also having to focus on scaling and promoting the project. Balancing product development with promotion is a tough act. It requires multitasking, creativity, and smart marketing strategies. Eager to have more people using Bitcoin, Andresen launched a website in 2010 called Bitcoin Faucet (Figure 3.2). This site offered a novel approach: it gave away 5 free BTC to every visitor, just for completing a captcha code.[34] Andresen's goal was to spread cryptocurrency to a broader audience and generate excitement around Bitcoin. Instead of slowly building a community, he opted for a more aggressive tactic, using sheer force to quickly elevate Bitcoin from a niche computer project to a global sensation.[35] That approach wasn't just about incremental growth—it was a strategic move to catapult Bitcoin into mainstream awareness and use.

The *Bitcoin Faucet* website operated for two years, until 2012. During this time, Andresen gave away a total of 19,700 BTC. This was during a time when the cost of mining (or "producing" a unit of Bitcoin) was almost nothing. The Bitcoin network was in such early stages of development that a basic computer was sufficient to process the calculations needed to confirm new BTC blocks on the network. Between 2010 and 2012, when the Internet really started paying attention to Bitcoin, the average cost to produce a Bitcoin fluctuated from 16 cents to $29.[36] That's when the ongoing hype around Bitcoin started, which was precisely what Andresen was aiming for.

Figure 3.2 Archived screenshot from the *Bitcoin Faucet* website.

(Source: Freebitcoin website. Available at: https://freebitco.in/site/faucet/. Used with courtesy.)

Discussing how Gavin Andresen promoted Bitcoin is so interesting that it's worth looking at the marketing costs during the project's early stages. It irritates me that the Blockchain community often treats this subject like a religion or ideology, rather than a business. However, the efforts to promote Bitcoin we're talking about here are real examples of business development.

In startup theory, there's a lot of focus on customer acquisition cost (CAC). This helps measure how much you spend on marketing. The costs for promoting Bitcoin through *Bitcoin Faucet* are detailed in Table 3.1.

Table 3.1 Estimated calculation of user acquisition costs via the Bitcoin Faucet website

BTC business model variable	Value
Period of Bitcoin Faucet operation	2010–2012
The cost of mining 1 BTC in 2010–2012	$0.16–$29.33
The average cost of mining and transferring 1 BTC (2010–2012)	$5.20
The number of bitcoins spent on the Bitcoin Faucet website	19,700 BTC
Number of users acquired (5 bitcoins per person)	3,940
Total cost of The Bitcoin Faucet campaign	$102,507
User Acquisition Cost	$26

Imagine being a judge at a startup competition. How would we view spending about $100,000 to give away bitcoins for promotion? The Bitcoin Faucet ran for two years, so if this wasn't working, Andresen had plenty of time to change it. This strategy of giving away bitcoins wasn't just a quick marketing trick, like the ones I've seen from inexperienced entrepreneurs.

Consider scenarios like hiring high-priced influencers for a budding project, leasing fancy cars, or committing to long-term office leases in upscale areas without a solid plan to attract upscale clients. From my perspective, these are examples of unwise marketing expenditures that don't necessarily lead to generating revenue. They seem more like lavish spending without a clear return on investment. Andresen opted to invest his own funds into powering his computers and sharing enigmatic pieces of code, which, at first, were nothing more than an Internet meme.

In 2010, someone looking at Andresen's decision might have thought he had been either too naive or a complete idiot. But 10 years later, we understand why Gavin made that choice. He took a big gamble on a certain kind of marketing because he really understood the project he was working on. His job was to make something known worldwide that was either unknown or not trusted by people. Both the finance world and online users remember digital money projects that failed due to technical issues or fraud. So, Andresen couldn't promote Bitcoin the usual way, like how most financial tech projects grow. First demonstrating its advantages, then launching a trial with a bank or fund, and finally spreading it to broader markets. This approach wasn't possible, partly due to the ideology and political manifesto of the Cypherpunks. Even if Andresen managed to convince traditional financial institutions of the advantages of Blockchain, negotiations would immediately fail when a bank employee asked:

"Well, who invented it? Can we talk to the Bitcoin creator?"—Andresen would have no choice but to respond.

"Ladies and Gentlemen, this is Satoshi Nakamoto. He's said to be a Japanese math genius, but you can't meet him. He hides his identity."

That's a dealbreaker. Banks hate anonymity. They crave transparency, clarity, and mutual trust. And just after this initial hiccup concerning the creator of BTC, another would pop up. Bank employees negotiating the first implementation of the technology sold by Andresen would certainly take issue with what Nakamoto and the entire Bitcoin community had to say about their business. Remember, distributed ledger technologies (DLT) were designed to bypass banks, accounting and auditing institutions, or simply the entire financial sector. So even when comparing the current CAC in the "normal" fintech world, an expenditure of about $26 as CAC doesn't seem that large. It's the lowest such value among "competitive" solutions—if you can compare Blockchain and the world of "regular" finances at all.

For instance, digital banks (like Revolut, N26) have CACs of around $38.[37] Of course, today the rates for successful marketing campaigns have gone down, as traffic and user interest primarily come from social media, which have mastered the use of data and targeted campaigns. It's much easier to reach a customer today. But Bitcoin started when there were 197 million people on Facebook (today it's 3 billion).[38]

Andresen also knew the huge innovation he was dealing with. Even for specialists in cryptography and computer science, Bitcoin was a significant challenge in terms of both usage and understanding the code in depth. Therefore, Andresen couldn't adopt another common marketing strategy of educating his target group about the promoted product. He had to create the simplest possible mechanism for people to suddenly get their hands on a bunch of bitcoins and start exchanging them, thereby building their value. It couldn't have been simpler. On a basic website, all you had to do was transcribe a code from an image to receive five units of this new, interesting currency. Although it sounds brutally honest, it's the truth—just like in 2010, the majority of the Bitcoin community consists now of people who just don't fully comprehend this subject. The challenge with understanding Blockchain technology lies either in the general level of knowledge in society or the complexity of the technology itself. The barriers to entering Blockchain technology are significant. People need to be equipped not only with cryptocurrencies but also with knowledge about what they really are and the value they bring to society. The problems of this ignorance—regardless of their origins—are well evidenced by statistics.

Research conducted in 2021 shows that only 16.9% of investors who purchased cryptocurrencies "fully understand" their value and potential. Meanwhile, 33.5% of buyers have either zero knowledge about cryptocurrencies or would describe their level of understanding as "beginner."[39] This means that a third of people who own cryptocurrencies know nothing about them. So why did they buy them? The reason is simple: human need, or even primitive instinct—the desire to get rich. The study was conducted by Cardify, which monitored the behavior of cryptocurrency investors from February 5 to 12, 2021, when the BTC price rose from $37,000 to $47,000.[40] Hence, I think Gavin Andresen chose the strategy of interaction with the emerging crypto community because he anticipated people's line of thought. Instead of getting into unnecessary technical details, he launched a mechanism that triggered people's subconscious desire to make money with zero or minimal effort—whether physical or intellectual.

Finally, it's crucial to ask whether Andresen's marketing efforts brought the planned effect. It was all about getting bitcoins into circulation and then allowing for their organic growth. Not only of awareness of Bitcoin's existence but also of the opinion that it's a new, interesting idea for the cash of the future. This action started a chain reaction, where in the end, the community itself was supposed to build a critical mass of users to give Bitcoin actual value. Through Bitcoin Faucet, Andresen introduced almost

20,000 units of the new cryptocurrency into circulation—enough to form a market. If Andresen had released too few bitcoins into circulation, transactions would have slowed down or even stopped, leading to a potential market collapse. This would have undermined Bitcoin's primary purpose: facilitating exchanges between users. By introducing Bitcoin into circulation in such a quantity, Andresen allowed it to achieve any actual value. To a casual observer, it might seem like Andresen lost a fortune by giving away bitcoins—about $1.3 billion at the rates of early 2024. However, this perspective misses the bigger picture. This move was far from a financial loss. It was a crucial step in building the foundation and credibility of Bitcoin, which proved to be so crucial in the long run.

Gavin Andresen's approach showed his exceptional skills not just in programming and business but also in microeconomics. He understood the technical details of Bitcoin and used this knowledge to establish a market and speculative environment around it. So, what was the genius of his approach? Through the Bitcoin Faucet, Andresen released a large number of Bitcoin units into circulation when they were valued at just a few cents each. In contrast, other early Bitcoin platforms, which we'd now recognize as exchanges, sold Bitcoins for a small fee in dollars. This set a low initial price for each cryptocurrency unit. It was thus either a cheap novelty for tech geeks or an object of minor speculation. For example, 1 BTC bought at the end of August 2010 for 7 cents was worth around 30 cents three months later—nearly four times more. The prospect of quick earnings thus attracted new people to this "game" (Figure 3.3).

In the early days, people didn't think about splitting Bitcoin into smaller parts. A famous story from those times is when someone bought two pizzas for 10,000 Bitcoins each.[41] Now, that seems crazy because Bitcoin is worth so much. The cryptocurrency community even celebrates this transaction's

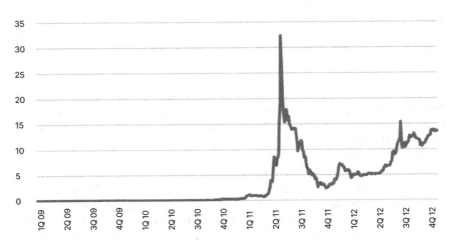

Figure 3.3 BTC to USD exchange rate in the first years of the project.

anniversary on May 22—*Bitcoin Pizza Day*. Back then, Bitcoin was a novelty, and large quantities were exchanged for just a few cents. Gavin Andresen, recognizing Bitcoin's potential, started to distribute the cryptocurrency generously through the Bitcoin Faucet site. He gave five Bitcoins to everyone who visited. At first, these Bitcoins were only worth a few cents, but their value quickly grew. By the end of 2010, one Bitcoin was worth 30 cents, and a year later, it was over $13. Andresen knew that the prospect of quick earnings with low risk would attract people who would still want to invest small amounts. At first, you could get a lot of Bitcoins for just a dollar. But as the value went up, people didn't want to buy whole units anymore.

Gavin Andresen showed a big benefit of Bitcoin without making a big announcement about the economic principle behind it. Unlike traditional currencies, where you divide a dollar into 100 cents, Bitcoin allows for much finer divisibility. You could buy 0.5 Bitcoin with just $2, and someone else could do the same with $20 a few months later. This made Bitcoin accessible to everyone, rich or poor, unlike other investments. There weren't really any barriers to getting involved, aside from perhaps some insider knowledge. Whether someone bought 10 BTC or one-tenth BTC—everyone, investing in Bitcoin, only proved that there was a demand for it. This demand, largely speculative, started a trend that increased Bitcoin's value and continues to drive its growth today.

Gavin Andresen was a psychological genius. He recognized that the Bitcoin community was its own ecosystem: the issuer, the theoretical creator, and the source of its value. This required a careful balance. Andresen knew how to foster a sense of belonging in the digital community while also maintaining his physical presence in offline meetings. He navigated the delicate line between valuing the anonymity of ordinary users and the transparency of project leaders. In his communication, he was presenting just enough technical knowledge to make the community feel exclusive but not so much that it would have overwhelmed non-tech users.

Andresen was a pioneer in the crypto world, starting to speak at meet-ups and even banking conferences. His appearances at events like the Milken Global Conference, where tickets cost thousands of dollars, demonstrated his ability to monetize community engagement effectively.[42] Andresen was also a trailblazer in using social media for communication, moving away from niche forums to Twitter. This strategic shift broadened his reach, making Bitcoin more accessible to a wider audience. Through all these efforts, Andresen crafted the ideal atmosphere within the Bitcoin community, paving the way for others like Vitalik Buterin to follow in his footsteps. His blend of community engagement, strategic communication, and psychological understanding was key in shaping the early narrative and growth of Bitcoin.

The increasing value of Bitcoin was a clear sign that Gavin Andresen's strategies in management, marketing, and communication were effective.

Due to the anonymity of the Bitcoin network, it is impossible to estimate how much money Andresen actually has. In interviews, he mentioned that his contract with the Bitcoin Foundation stipulated payments in BTC, converted to dollars every three months.[43] Officially, most of his wealth, estimated at "only" $3 million, comes from this source.[44] Although for an ordinary person, it is still a lot of money, doesn't this amount seem strange to you?

How has Andresen been making a living since 2014, after withdrawing from the role of Bitcoin's main manager? If he were not to have his own benefits from the rapidly growing Bitcoin, why would he spend $100,000 to promote the project four years earlier? Also, Andresen's decision to step back from Bitcoin coincided with its first major crash, when its value dropped by $1,100 to just over $400, adds to the intrigue. The early days of Bitcoin are filled with unanswered questions and mysteries. From the true identity of Satoshi Nakamoto to the decisions and motivations of key figures like Gavin Andresen.

Gavin Andresen's influence on Bitcoin's code and its operation is significant, arguably more than anyone else's. His contributions have been crucial in shaping how Bitcoin functions. This significant role has fueled speculation, leading some to suggest that Andresen might actually be Satoshi Nakamoto, the mysterious creator of Bitcoin. However, Andresen has consistently denied these claims. "I am not Satoshi Nakamoto. I have never met him. I had many conversations with him via emails; it was only correspondence," Andresen stated in April 2014. Two years after Andresen's denial, the topic came up again. This time, the spotlight turned to Craig Wright, who claimed to be Bitcoin's founder.

3.2.3 Craig Wright

Gavin Andresen was the person who led a new cryptocurrency to great heights. Under his leadership, Bitcoin's value soared from almost zero to more than $1,000. In just four years, Bitcoin, which was once just a piece of computer code, became worth over $6 billion. Andresen became a highly respected name in the field because of their great success. However, he also gained a reputation for causing divisions. He often set members of the cryptocurrency world against each other, as seen in his conflict with Craig Wright.

Andresen began as a leader, guiding a group of independent, anonymous volunteers. However, he quickly managed to turn their efforts into a solid business plan. New startups started popping up, all using Bitcoin's protocol. The amount of fresh concepts turned into competing ideas about the direction Bitcoin should take. Groups of programmers, originally under Andresen's guidance, started creating their own versions of Bitcoin. This caused two big problems. First, there wasn't a single clear goal for the project anymore. People's personal goals began to interfere. Second, there were technical issues like changes to data block sizes, but the bigger issue was the disagreement over what Bitcoin should become. New groups like Bitcoin Core and Bitcoin Unlimited formed. Some of those groups still followed Andresen, but others created their own start-ups, using Bitcoin's technology but aiming to find new uses for it. As a result, the Bitcoin community broke apart, which weakened Andresen's influence and position.

At the start, technical challenges were a big deal in the world of crypto-currency. People mainly talked about how to make Bitcoin better and faster. For instance, when Andresen tried to improve Bitcoin, it could only do seven transactions per second. That's a really small amount, especially for a tech-nology with global aspirations. And as more people used Bitcoin, this num-ber was going down even more. Back then, most people bought Bitcoin for speculation rather than actual payment. To put things into perspective, Visa processes nearly 480 transactions per second all over the world. They can even go up to 47,000 if needed.[45] So, Bitcoin had to figure out how to keep up with the established players.

Big plans were on the horizon for speeding up Bitcoin, and the man behind them, Gavin Andresen, was determined to implement them. More and more people, other members of the Bitcoin community, conceded that he had become despotic. Gavin decided to focus more on business matters, so he let some programmers he trusted handle the coding part. By April 2014, Wladimir van der Laan was leading the programming crew. But there was a problem. The original Bitcoin volunteers and Gavin were not seeing eye to eye. He was no longer doing what he used to, like checking the code others wrote on GitHub and helping new programmers learn. Instead, he was deep into business stuff, talking with big Blockchain companies like Coinbase and BitPay. Andresen promised them that he would increase the efficiency of the Bitcoin network to further boost its market value.[46] This shift in focus caused some early supporters to feel let down, as they saw Gavin moving away from his earlier, more hands-on role in the community.

In 2015, Andresen and his team demonstrated their big dreams at the Coinscrum conference in New York.[47] Gavin Andresen, the leader of their project, had a panel discussion with top volunteer, Mike Hearn. They both belonged to the same Bitcoin team and shared a vision for its future. They wanted to make some technological changes to Bitcoin. A few years earlier, Mike Hearn left a well-paying job at Google in Switzerland to work on the Bitcoin project. He agreed with Andresen's ideas about growing the business side of Bitcoin. Mike was very interested in scaling the project and getting the most out of Bitcoin's increasing success.

"Why do we still argue about the block size limits after so many years? Why is scalability such a big topic?" Mike asked provocatively.

An awkward silence followed. Gavin took the mic and turned to the audience:

"Many people are pressuring me to be more of a dictator," he said as Hearn took a sip of his beer and pointed to himself. Everyone understood the implication. Mike, who works closely with Andresen, was pushing him to make a clear declaration about the upcoming changes in the BTC code.

Initially, Andresen explained the attempt to take over such an open project as Bitcoin with a change in programming vision and "nerdy" techniques:

"Ummmm ... ummmm... Maybe such a change is inevitable"—he began to ramble.

This was followed by a suggestion from the audience:

"Maybe [Gavin] shouldn't be a dictator, but more of a traffic cop. You probably mean decision-making."

Andresen just smiled and explained that managing such a project was just an "icebreaker." And after a while he added openly:

"Frankly, that may be what has to happen to the block size. I may just have to throw my weight around and say: 'this is the way it's going to be and if you don't like it find another project'"

The authoritarian approach, where one person or group has all the power, first peeved the Cypherpunks who built decentralized technology, and then they started to disagree with the direction of its development. The world of Blockchain is known for being tough and not controlled by just one subject. This is a big deal for people who work on those projects, and that's why strong such actions upset them a lot.

"It wasn't really about block size. It was about the fact that people thought [Gavin] was trying to bypass code review, it made everyone nervous."[48]—Eric Lombrozo, who's been working on Bitcoin programming since 2011 as a volunteer, said that.

Bryan Bishop, another volunteer from the anti-Andresen team, was even stronger:

"The issue here is that Andresen claimed to be a guru shot in Bitcoin's development, but in reality, anyone on the team can suggest ideas."[49]—he said, criticizing Andersen for moving away from community ideals and not checking code made by volunteers.

He accused Andersen of focusing on business, which led to the problem of using unsecured solutions. Ultimately, it was a matter of communication:

> "We think Core [Andresen's group] isn't listening because a lot of people were having secret conversations with Andresen. And he didn't really bridge the gap and talk to the creators who actually developed the project." [50]

Bitcoin's original goals got mixed up with personal issues, which overshadowed some genuinely good ideas. After all, the solution for BTC was meant to be improved. In the world of Blockchain, updates that make things work better or enhance security are called forks. Andresen, with his right-hand Mike Hearn, pushed for a fork called Bitcoin XT. Their goal was to make the network faster, jumping from seven transactions per second to about 24.[51] It was a massive revolution—both technological and organizational. *The Guardian* wrote that Bitcoin was facing a "civil war." [52] Bitcoin XT would only happen if at least 75% of the network's users agreed to it. So, the struggle started.

Leaders of both the original and new groups within the Bitcoin community faced threats, including death threats. It was a battle where both sides applied the "all moves allowed" tactic. In an interview with *The New York Times*, Hearn talked about receiving the threats, but he never showed any messages to prove it.[53] The mutual destruction game tactic affected both sides: those who supported changes, led by Hearn, and their strong opponents who faced computer attacks using Denial-of-Service methods.

At its worst, hackers started spreading harmful software named Bitkiller. The program targeted computers downloading Bitcoin XT by flooding them with so much Internet traffic that they couldn't cope. In Long Island, New York, an Internet service provider reported that Bitkiller attacks caused a big network outage in a significant part of the district for several hours.[54] The biggest crypto company in the United States, Coinbase, even had to shut down for a while after they showed support for XT. No wonder that scared off many Bitcoin users from getting the new software or declaring support for it. Later on, the hacker behind those attacks, who seemed to be from Russia, told Hearn online that someone paid him to kill XT. However, the Russian hacker didn't reveal the identity of his employer.[55]

Despite the initial success of the fork proposed by Hearn and Andresen, users quickly lost interest in the improved Bitcoin. Later, in January 2016, Mike Hearn became frustrated by the mass rejection of his proposal. He told the whole world through the news that "Bitcoin has failed, … maybe we've miscalculated (its) future value." [56]

The creators of Bitcoin XT tried to convince the community of their solution. They tried their best, even at the largest Blockchain conference in New York, called the Consensus. In 2016, it attracted over 1,300 participants—quite a lot for the still-developing technology community. No one expected that the topic of Bitcoin XT would take a back seat in conference discussions. All because of a suspicious character who suddenly appeared in the cryptocurrency mainstream: Craig Wright.

In December 2015, during a major discussion about the fork happening in the Bitcoin world, some exciting news started spreading throughout the media. People began to claim they had figured out the true identity of Satoshi Nakamoto. Two independent websites, "Wired" and "Gizmodo," even published articles about it. Journalists and Blockchain researchers started connecting the dots that led to a man named Craig Steven Wright. He was an Australian IT specialist, statistician, and philosopher, and he had been part of the Bitcoin community from its early days.

Among the journalists unraveling the Nakamoto mystery was Andy Greenberg. The author of a touching story about the paralyzed Hal Finney. He initially relied on an anonymous source close to Wright, who under the pseudonym Gwern Branwen provided the Wired editorial office with important documents. That information was supposed to prove to the Bitcoin community the connection between Nakamoto and Wright.[57] It was a surprising twist. Additionally, the fact that leading technology media like "Wired" got involved in the mystery.

In 2008, there was a suspicion that someone named Wright might be using a Japanese name to hide their identity. That suggestion was supposed to start a whole chain of events a few months before the Bitcoin White Paper became available. Craig ran a cryptography blog where he was to mention working on Bitcoin even before Nakamoto published the article. He called the new system "triple-entry bookkeeping."[58] Obviously, the name referred to the Pacioli accounting method developed in Italy 500 years earlier. Instead of just keeping track of money going back and forth between two people, triple-entry bookkeeping linked ledger entries, showing the flow of money. That made it clear where the money came from and who was the current owner. However, that idea didn't originally belong to Craig. It was a reference to a scientific article from 2005, which already presented several ideas similar to Bitcoin.[59]

Apart from the fact that the supposed post was meant to discuss Bitcoin even before Nakamoto published the official White Paper, there are some interesting technical similarities in how they communicated. In another blog post, Wright asked people to use a special code known as a PGP (Pretty Good Privacy) key if they wanted to contact him. This key acts like a secret code to ensure messages stay safe. The key shared in 2008 on Craig's blog was linked to the MIT server and the email address satoshin@vistomail.com. It was almost identical to the satoshi@vistomail.com address that Nakamoto used to send out the Bitcoin White Paper to a cryptography mailing list.[60]

There's no solid proof, no copies of the posts I talked about before, but things became clearer when someone found screenshots from Wright's blog. The archived copy of the now-deleted post dates back to January 10, 2009.

That's right, it was the day after the official launch of Bitcoin. In Craig's short post, he wrote:

> Well, e-gold is down the toilet. Good idea, but again centralized authority. The beta of Bitcoin is live tomorrow. This is decentralized... We try until it works.[61]

Later on, Wright changed the post that I referred to. He replaced it with a mysterious message that said, "Bitcoin—AKA bloody nosey you be... It does always surprise me how at times the best place to hide [is] right in the open..."[62] A few months later, the post was taken down. What's really interesting is not what was in the post, but when it happened. But do you know what was really intriguing? It was not the content, but the time.

Wright was based in Sydney's time zone. If he had posted on his blog just after midnight on Saturday, January 10th, then in New York, it would have been a few minutes past 9:00 am on Friday, January 9th. However, Satoshi Nakamoto's archived message with Bitcoin software No. 0.1 was released on Thursday, January 8th, at 10:27 am New York time.[63] Why did Wright claim in his blog post that "the beta version of Bitcoin is coming out tomorrow" (Figure 3.4)? There were many things in his story that didn't make sense.

Soon, news outlets from around the world started paying attention to Wright. Bitcoin was worth more than $400 back then, with a total value of

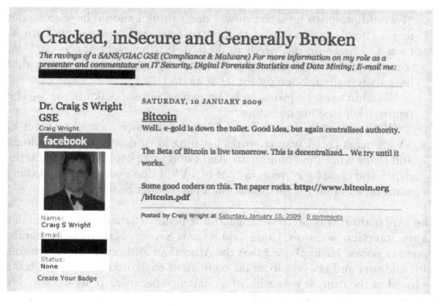

Figure 3.4 Archived screenshot from Craig Wright's website.

about $7 billion. Wright's story was featured in magazines like *The Economist* and *GQ*, and it even made it to the BBC website. At the beginning of May 2016, the BBC interviewed him. Sitting in front of his computer, a guy with an Australian accent explained everything to the BBC journalist. So, let's dive into this, shall we?

> "My name is Craig Wright and I'm about to demonstrate a singing of a message with the public key that is associated with the first transaction ever done on Bitcoin."
>
> "And who does the world think did that first transaction? What's the name associated with that first transaction?"—The journalist asked. He immediately found out from Craig that the person in charge was himself, under the nickname—Satoshi Nakamoto.
>
> "So you can say with hand on heart to me that Satoshi Nakamoto is you?"
>
> "Yes. Some people will believe, some people won't. And to tell you the truth I don't really care. I was the main part of it, other people helped me."

Craig didn't tell the world who it really was until three years later.

"Why did you feel you had to keep secret for so long?"

Craig replied without any hesitation:

> "I would prefer to be secret now. I don't think I should have to be out there. There's nothing owed to the world where I have to say 'I am X. I am Y.' I mean no one needs to do that. It is my right not to say I did something. If I released a paper that actually benefits people. Why do I have to actually take credit for it? Why do I?"
>
> "Wouldn't you be proud to be known as Satoshi Nakamoto?"—The reporter kept asking questions.
>
> "Yeah, but that doesn't mean I have to bounce around in front of TV cameras [...] I wanna work. I wanna keep doing, what I'm doing and that's what I'm going to do. And I don't work and invent and write paper and code by coming in font of TV's. I don't want money. I don't want fame. I don't want adoration. I just wanna be left alone."

The explanation was pretty strange and it definitely made people wonder. As the interview went on, Craig said he was Satoshi Nakamoto to handle some tax issues. He explained that the Australian authorities were working with auditors and lawyers from his companies to figure out how much tax he owed at the time. It was a bit of a challenge because, in his words, "No one understand Bitcoin very well."[64]

But then, the journalist went back to the most interesting part: who actually created Bitcoin?

"People assume that the inventor of Bitcoin must be fabulously rich. The inventor of Bitcoin must have wast stores of Bitcoin in there to be incredibly rich."

"What matters isn't how much I have, it's when I use it. Because I've got an asset class that has gone up in value, doesn't mean I pay tax on it now. I pay tax when it's deployed—only on the bits that are deployed, no more."

"Are you planning to deploy any of that Bitcoin?"

"I've deployed enough and I'm happy where I am. I'm not looking for money and this is one comment I wanna make to people: 'I don't want money. I don't want help.' And I'm categorically going to say this and I'm making sure that things are being put in place with lawyers and whatever else. If anyone puts me up for awards or anything like that I will never, ever accept a cent. Ever. If you put me in for a Noble prize, if you put me for an ACM Turing medal, if you put me up for some honor, I will never accept a cent from any of you, for anything."[65]

Let's pause for a moment and appreciate how bold and daring Wright was. Here's a man who revealed himself in front of a community that had been focused on a mysterious crypto project for more than seven years. He said he would have "preferred to stay secret" and started dropping hints about awards he'd never have accepted. Eventually, Satoshi Nakamoto was nominated for a Nobel Prize in Economics in 2016.[66] To top it off, the Bitcoin community must have been buzzing.

The fact that Wright was not exactly a no-name added some spice to the whole situation. At a cryptocurrency conference, he proudly claimed to have lots of degrees: "a master's degree in law, statistics, and several doctorates." But strangely, he never really said what he did for a living. He called himself an "entrepreneur" without explaining what kind of business he was into. People knew for a fact that he came from Australia. He said he had a Ph.D. in theology and comparative religious studies, which he supposedly earned in 2003, but he never told which university gave him that degree.[67] Wright also said he had a Ph.D. in computer science from Charles Sturt University.[68] But during the identity scandal, the university said they never gave him such a degree—he had only studied there for a master's degree.[69] Wright's LinkedIn profile stated that he was the author of books and dozens of articles on cryptography. Then in 2020, his former universities started checking whether his works were plagiarized.[70]

Craig Wright made people suspicious not just because he lied about his background but also because of his past. He talked about having IT experience, like working for banks in Australia and a company called BDO Kendalls.[71] He even said that the first online casino in 1999 was his creation.[72] He also had something to do with the Australian Church of Reconciliation.[73] That's a strange mix for a cryptocurrency activist.

Wright's case gained the attention of Dan Kaminsky, one of the first Bitcoin code explorers. Kaminsky wrote on his blog that Wright's claim was a clear fake. Other influential figures in the industry felt the same way. They accused Wright of copying an old signature from a 2009 transaction made by Satoshi.[74] So, here's what happened: The Bitcoin community suddenly split into different groups. Apart from the ongoing debate about a tech update and the Bitcoin XT fork in the crypto world, there was a new argument: whether to trust Craig Wright's words.

Now, let's talk about Gavin Andresen, who's kind of a guru in the Bitcoin project. Besides supporting the Bitcoin XT upgrade, he got involved in the debate about Wright's real identity. Along with other community leaders, like Jon Matonis from the Bitcoin Foundation, Andresen confirmed that Craig Wright is indeed the actual creator of Bitcoin. On the same day Wright's interview aired on BBC, Andresen wrote a blog post titled simply "Satoshi":

> I believe Craig Steven Wright is the person who invented Bitcoin.
>
> I was flown to London to meet Dr. Wright a couple of weeks ago, after an initial email conversation convinced me that there was a very good chance he was the same person I'd communicated with in 2010 and early 2011. After spending time with him I am convinced beyond a reasonable doubt: Craig Wright is Satoshi…
>
> During our meeting, I saw the brilliant, opinionated, focused, generous—and privacy-seeking—person who matches the Satoshi I worked with six years ago. And he cleared up a lot of mysteries, including why he disappeared when he did and what he's been busy with since 2011. But I'm going to respect Dr. Wright's privacy and let him decide how much of that story he shares with the world.
>
> We love to create heroes—but also seem to love hating them if they don't live up to some unattainable ideal. It would be better if Satoshi Nakamoto was the codename for an NSA project, or an artificial intelligence sent from the future to advance our primitive money. He is not, he is an imperfect human being just like the rest of us. I hope he manages to mostly ignore the storm that his announcement will create, and keep doing what he loves—learning and research and innovating.
>
> I am very happy to be able to say I shook his hand and thanked him for giving Bitcoin to the world.[75]

The cryptocurrency community was abuzz. The backing from high-standing individuals like Andresen and Matonis showed immense trust in Wright. It was a kind of public acknowledgment that he was telling the truth. This was a hot topic throughout the community during the Consensus conference in 2016. Even though another much more crucial debate was happening simultaneously, one that was vital for the strategic development of the project. Why did Andresen get involved in a scandal with Craig? Simultaneously, he was trying to convince the community to accept the Bitcoin XT. He cared about the proposed strategy; nothing made sense. In my opinion, Andresen supported Craig as a strategic move to draw attention away from the controversial fork. I won't go into whether Craig being revealed as Satoshi Nakamoto was planned or accidental. But what makes me suspicious is what happened afterward. First, there was a leak to major tech news outlets, followed by exclusive interviews in international media. Then, came the support of the busy and neglected project leader.

You might expect that when such a big crisis hits Bitcoin, its value would drop a lot, if not go to zero. All because someone claiming to be Satoshi Nakamoto had come forward, which challenged the idea that Bitcoin was created by a community, rather than by one individual. If it turns out that one person is behind Bitcoin, it changes the balance of power and influence. So, was Bitcoin like Satoshi said, decentralized, anonymous, and truly independent? To put it simply, did it live up to the values Satoshi wrote about?

Nakamoto's supposed real identity came out alongside the most crucial emails in the whole issue. Before he wrote an article about Bitcoin, Wright talked to his buddy David Kleiman, who's a computer expert. Before publishing an article about Bitcoin, Wright had discussed his idea with a close friend and a computer forensic specialist, David Kleiman.[76] In those emails, Wright talked about purchasing his work and investing in hundreds of computer processors to "develop the idea." There's also a PDF by Kleiman where he says he'll take care of a trust fund called Tulip Trust. The fund's strategy was to gather lots of bitcoins from one institution and keep them safe for their owners. They registered the fund in Seychelles and intended to collect between 820,000 to 1.1 million BTC and then sell everything in January 2020. At the monthly rate back then, it would be worth more than $8 billion.

That story might seem like just another unproven rumor in the cryptocurrency world. But there's something worth noting here. The PDF file seems to have been officially verified by Kleiman using his PGP signature. It's a cryptographic technique ensuring that no one can change the document after he signed it. Now, when it comes to the so-called conspiracy involving Kleiman and Wright, it's a mystery that will forever remain unsolved. Tragically, David Kleiman left this world in 2013, taken by natural causes right in the comfort of his own home.[77] He was just 46 years old. The cause of his death were the complications arising from MRSA.

BTC transactions were anonymous. Thus, it was impossible to determine how many bitcoins the newly revealed creator had. If one person had had so many, they could have influenced their value. If people knew that, they might have wanted to sell their bitcoins quickly and get their money back. But that didn't happen. Even when there was a lot of talk about Craig Wright being the creator of Bitcoin, the price of Bitcoin stayed at about $400. Then, it suddenly went up to over $650 (Figure 3.5).

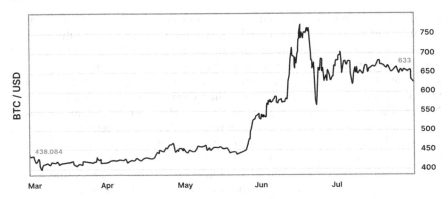

Figure 3.5 BTC to USD rate in the period March to July 2016.

(*Source:* Data from CoinMarketCap.)

Craig got everyone curious by saying he'd prove his identity as Satoshi Nakamoto, but he never delivered on that promise. Instead, things took an unexpected turn when Andresen withdrew his support for Craig's claim. All twists and turns took place either in blog posts or controversial articles. The ending of this saga left behind lots of Internet chatter and many wondering about the true identity of Satoshi Nakamoto.

The first to question Wright's story—Dan Kaminsky, recalled his email exchange with Gavin Andresen in a post from May 3, 2016:

> "What is going on here? There's clear unambiguous cryptographic evidence of fraud and you're lending credibility to the idea that a public key operation could, should or must remain private?"—Kaminsky sent an email and got a reply from Andresen, who said it was okay to share the message.

> "Yeah, what the heck? I was as surprised by the 'proof' as anyone, and don't yet know exactly what is going on. It was a mistake to agree to publish my post before I saw his—I assumed his post would simply be a signed message anybody could easily verify. And it was probably a mistake to even start to play the Find Satoshi game, but I DO feel grateful to Satoshi."[78]

In the whole Wright case, something that stood out as strange was the dynamic of the events. Less than a day after the BBC interview with Wright, things got even more confusing. Andresen had just confirmed some surprising claims, and then Kaminsky posted an email where Wright basically took back what he had said earlier. Remember, Andresen had even claimed he met Satoshi Nakamoto and saw his key. So, how come he changed his mind about Craig Wright so quickly?

We will probably never know why Andresen kept changing his version of events. Despite being a former leader, he was completely excluded from the community after the scandal with the identity of Wright/Nakamoto. He lost the ability to share his work on GitHub, a platform where many developers collaborate on Bitcoin.[79] Since then, his activity has been mostly limited to blog posts, where he was active until May 27, 2020. He still comments on cryptocurrency stuff on social media—more than 170,000 people follow him on Twitter. In one email, Andresen said: "I've been avoiding getting myself into any press lately, and that's been going well so I'm going to keep doing that."[80] What has he been doing for almost five years? How does he pay the bills? Those questions still haven't been answered.

The Wright/Nakamoto case is more complicated than it seems. It all happened a few months after Gavin Andresen and Mike Hearn tried to convince the Bitcoin community of their idea to increase Bitcoin's bandwidth. But their plan didn't work out. The Bitcoin XT project didn't succeed and Mike Hearn gave up. So, the former leader of Bitcoin was left alone. In such situations, people often do things that don't make much sense. A good example of this is how they got deeply involved in talking about rumors about Wright and Nakamoto. It's just like in Murphy's laws: people start doing the right thing only after everything else they've tried failed.[81]

Why did Andresen take such a big risk when he was the top person in charge of the Bitcoin project and a highly respected member of the Bitcoin community? He trusted a guy he knew either through email exchange only or, if we believe Andresen's first blog post, from a brief one-time meeting. I'm not a Bitcoin expert, and I'm not into conspiracy theories. I'm an entrepreneur, and I always make sure to double-check my information from reliable sources. However, there are several unclear things here that I want to point out.

What really makes me curious about this story are Andresen's next steps. Maybe he thought a lot about the risks and feared the consequences of his actions. Was there some kind of secret agreement between Wright and Andresen? Did Wright use the supposed Nakamoto reveal to boost his reputation in the Bitcoin community? Did he get something in return? I don't know and I don't want to be the detective. But here's something important to keep in mind: if we believe the reports about Wright, he set up the Tulip Trust fund before the Bitcoin project even started.[82] The goal was to sell a bunch of bitcoins all at once. This kind of transaction would show up on the network, but we wouldn't know who actually did it. The way the market behaves doesn't suggest that this planned sale ever happened. Now, there's a talk that Dave Kleiman was supposed to sell those bitcoins from the Tulip Trust, but he passed away three years before this whole scandal erupted. So, it would be logical for Wright to look for a new partner. Could that partner have been Andresen?

We might never find the absolute truth. The version of the facts I consider has one significant flaw: it assumes that everyone involved, from Andresen to individuals investing in cryptocurrency, acted rationally. But how can you explain that during the whole scandal around Wright, there was no massive Bitcoin crash? If the project leader confirmed that Satoshi Nakamoto had a huge influence on Bitcoin's value, it should have turned the cryptocurrency world upside down. Even though Bitcoin was supposed to be all about privacy and fairness, people should have lost faith in it. But that didn't happen. It's weird, right? Why did the Bitcoin community accept those strange reports without any resistance? Maybe it's because rumors about Nakamoto's identity are as old as Bitcoin itself. Over time, it seems that Wright was the first to convince the masses of cryptocurrency investors until the main initiators withdrew.

After many years, we can think about why Gavin Andresen supported Craig Wright's claims. Forget about the Tulip Trust fund, it's quite puzzling. Did Andresen use the Wright situation to benefit himself in some way? What was his goal? Maybe it was about money or maybe it had to do with psychology. Or perhaps he had some secret strategy we'll never know about. Was it a bad move to calm down all the talk about "Nakamoto Speculations?" You should make your judgment.

Think about history for a moment. During the Napoleonic wars, the Russians actually burned Moscow themselves to escape from the French army. Surprisingly, that helped them win because the fire destroyed what Napoleon needed to survive the Russian winter.[83] So, sometimes self-destruction can be a powerful move in tough situations. Andresen's role in the Bitcoin world was fading after his attempts to make changes didn't work out. Instead of causing chaos in Bitcoin, he sort of caused chaos in his own career. He completely stepped away from the cryptocurrency scene. Some say he was advising the zCash project, but he wasn't as influential and powerful as before.[84]

Two years after the Satoshi scandal, his case finally went to court. Ira Kleiman, on behalf of his brother, filed a lawsuit against Wright in the United States, asking for the rights to bitcoins worth more than $5 billion.[85] As the estate administrator, she claimed that Wright had deceived Dave Kleiman regarding both bitcoins and intellectual property rights. The lawsuit alleged that Wright and Kleiman had collaborated in mining bitcoins during the early days of cryptocurrency. According to Ira, after his brother's death, Wright was executing a plan to take over his former collaborator's bitcoins. When Ira raised concerns about the authenticity of the documents provided by Wright, he attempted to resolve the matter outside of court by offering to settle the debt owed to Dave. However, those payments never reached the Kleiman family. And that's how a never-ending legal battle has begun.[86]

In the court of first instance, Wright lost. The court's decision had two important parts. First, it required Wright to reveal how many bitcoins he originally owned. Second, it said that the fund in charge of Kleiman's estate should get half of the bitcoins that Craig and Dave mined together from

2009 to 2013. Nevertheless, the story gets yet another twist here because the court told them to stick to their agreement without specifying how. In plain English, the court said what should happen but not exactly how. In the explanation, it said the court didn't need to decide if Wright was Satoshi Nakamoto or how many bitcoins he had.[87] So, basically, the verdict didn't really solve anything.

In August 2021, Wright's lawyers said he couldn't join the hearings because of COVID-19 and the tough situation in Afghanistan.[88] The court proceedings continued in December 2021. As I write those words Wright still hasn't succeeded in proving that he was Satoshi Nakamoto. However, all of the judgments concerned company property distribution or the legality of defamation—not the identity. In *Wright v. McCormack*, Wright sued for defamation. He won the case, but only got a symbolic $1 in damages because he couldn't prove that he suffered from it financially.

The case of *Magnus v. Wright* in Norway had a different outcome. The Norwegian court decided that Magnus' statements about Wright didn't count as defamation according to their law. Again, that didn't really touch on whether Wright was Satoshi Nakamoto. Perhaps the most anticipated case is *COPA v. Wright*, scheduled for trial in 2024. This case directly tackles Wright's claim of being Satoshi Nakamoto. It's a big deal because it could finally shed light on who really created Bitcoin.

Craig Wright's journey didn't stop when Andresen left the first-ever successful cryptocurrency project. Despite all the confusion, Wright stayed active in the Blockchain world. Shortly after the scandal quieted down, Craig sat down for an interview with Reuters and declared:

> I will sell [my BTC] when I do this for goods on a daily basis, or I will go down with it. Past the basics of my family's well-being, all I have is dedicated to building the systems and institutions needed to make Bitcoin successful globally. I will never dump Bitcoin.

Craig Wright is still active in the world of Blockchain. He leads nChain, which works on developing DLT. His company has about 100 employees, according to its Crunchbase profile. Over three years, Wright and his team developed over 800 patented solutions for various Blockchain projects, significantly enhancing the company's value. That achievement is particularly beneficial for Wright since he helped to start the company and most likely holds a major stake in it. The company's growing portfolio of patents has likely contributed to its increasing worth. In 2017, nChain received an investment from the Maltese High Tech Private Equity Fund. Reports from Reuters suggest it could be as much as $300 million.

Wright keeps changing his stories about Satoshi Nakamoto. In a 2019 interview with *Finder*, he said that Bitcoin had been created by a group he had led, along with Dave Kleiman and Hal Finney, who both died a few years before. Wright also connects his past work to his current projects. At nChain, he made a new version of Bitcoin called Bitcoin SV, which stands for Satoshi Vision. That version changes how Bitcoin works. Instead of having a fixed-size block, it depends on what the market needs. It's a solution for the big problem with the original Bitcoin: it couldn't grow enough. One of the biggest issues with scaling up Bitcoin was that it used a lot of energy and transactions took longer. Bitcoin SV can handle 9,000 transactions every second. That's a big step up from the original Bitcoin, which can only do about 4 transactions per second.

In 2019, Bitcoin SV became its own type of digital money. By 2021, it was worth $2.3 billion, which is really impressive for merely a fork of the original coin—especially, for a project led by a man who is widely considered a liar and sued for an amount many times larger. The people who invest in cryptocurrencies like Bitcoin SV don't seem to be worried about those issues. In the past, even big scandals haven't stopped the hodlers from doing their thing. Craig's story is like a rollercoaster ride with lots of surprises. Even experts who study Blockchain and lawyers agree that we may never find out for sure if he's the real Satoshi Nakamoto. But one thing is certain—Craig Wright joined the list of people suspected of creating Bitcoin.

3.2.4 Nick Szabo

Elon Musk, known for his work at Tesla and SpaceX, is a big name in tech. In a podcast chat with AI researcher Lex Fridman, Musk said what he thinks about the true identity of Satoshi Nakamoto. He mentioned a well-known person in the cryptocurrency field, Nick Szabo.

Nick Szabo's life is full of secrets. He was born in the United States, and not much is known about his early life. However, there's one important detail that Szabo shared about his background. It's a glimpse into the events that shaped his worldview. Szabo's father was a participant in the Hungarian uprising against the Soviet Union in the 1950s.

> My path goes a long way back, my father fought in the 1956 Hungarian revolution against the Soviet Union, and he along with many other people from communist societies that I've encountered have plenty of horror stories to tell about the oppression, the killing of people, the stealing of their property and so forth. So, if you had just been born and raised the US, you might not have known as much about the potential for the government to be abused.
>
> So, to my mind if you can substitute—there's many important functions government does—if you can substitute less violent and less abusable ways to perform those functions, that's a big win.[89]

The family history of Nick Szabo had a big impact on his life. His dad went through tough times with governments. Clearly, that must have had an effect on how Nick saw power and control. He grew up hearing about fighting against unfair rules, and that made him think differently about authority and centralization.

In 1989, Szabo graduated with a computer science degree from the University of Washington. He didn't stop there though. He also studied law at George Washington University Law School. The combination of tech and law gave Szabo a unique perspective. It helped him to understand how technology, regulation, and economics intertwine. His studies also profited in his later work in cryptography and digital money.

In 1996, Nick Szabo came up with a digital innovation called "smart contracts." Those were meant to be digital, self-executing agreements or actions between two (or more) actors. A new concept at the time that later became key in Blockchain and cryptocurrency technologies. Back then, the Internet was still in its early stages. Szabo, with his unique blend of legal and computer science expertise, foresaw the future. Smart contracts, as envisioned by Szabo, were designed to automate deal execution with minimal reliance on trust. That concept would later prove integral to the cryptocurrency ecosystem.

Szabo also conceptualized a form of decentralized digital currency named "bit gold," in 1998.

Even though it was never implemented, it's often recognized as a precursor to the architecture of Bitcoin. The structure of bit gold was uncommon in its approach to generating digital currency. In Szabo's design, people would use their computer power to solve complex cryptographic puzzles. Once they cracked the code, they shared it with a fault-tolerant public register. Then, the solutions were linked to the solver's public key. Each solved puzzle not only contributed to the creation of new digital property but also became a part of the following exchange. This method created a growing chain of new properties and served as a mechanism for the network to verify and time-stamp new coins. It also made sure everyone agreed on what was legit. If most people didn't like a new solution, they'd say no and move on to the next puzzle.

In the digital world, replicating data is as simple as copying and pasting. Therefore, there is a risk that someone would use the same money more than once. Most digital currencies avoid the double-spending problem. How does it work? They give some control to a central authority that keeps an eye on the amount of money in each person's account. However, Szabo was determined to find a decentralized solution, one that didn't rely on a central authority. He aimed to create a digital system that could be as secure and trustworthy as gold.

Nick's deep understanding of economics, cryptography, and digital technology, coupled with his contributions to the field, has led many to speculate about his possible identity as Satoshi Nakamoto. His work on Bit Gold and smart contracts lines up with the rise of Bitcoin, making people wonder if he's Satoshi.

In 2014, the Aston University Centre for Forensic Linguistics conducted a linguistic analysis of the Bitcoin White Paper to identify Satoshi Nakamoto. Their investigation pointed to Nick Szabo as a likely candidate. One reason was that both the Bitcoin White Paper and Szabo's writings used a tool called Latex to make documents. They also found similar phrases and writing styles in both documents. While not definitive, that analysis suggested a strong linguistic link between Szabo and the Bitcoin document. Nick Szabo has denied that he was the creator of Bitcoin. In 2014, he responded to claims linking him to Nakamoto, by saying, "I'm afraid you got it wrong doxing me as Satoshi, but I'm used to it."[90]

But let's circle back to Elon Musk's perspective. Musk provided his view on the Satoshi Nakamoto mystery in a podcast with AI researcher Lex Fridman. "Obviously, I don't know who created Bitcoin ... it seems as though Nick Szabo is probably more than anyone else responsible for the evolution of those ideas." So, Musk doesn't crown Szabo as Nakamoto but rather highlights Szabo's influence in the developments that led to Bitcoin. I deeply agree with the thought Musk shared later in the podcast. One for the books: the true value lies not in the name "Satoshi Nakamoto" itself but in the ideas and changes that the name represents.

Whether Szabo is Satoshi Nakamoto or not, his influence on the crypto world cannot be denied. His ideas have had a huge impact on the Blockchain technology. When we think about Musk's words and Szabo's legacy, it reminds us that great innovations often come from the growth of ideas and the effort of many people working together. And that's the main point of that story.

3.2.5 Dorian Nakamoto

In a peaceful neighborhood in California, Dorian Nakamoto led a life much like anyone else's. His days were filled with ordinary routines and simple pleasures, with no hint that soon his name would echo across the globe. But Dorian's life was about to change in a way he never imagined, taking him from a life of routine to one of unexpected attention and mystery.

He was born in the serene city of Beppu, Japan, in 1949. Young Dorian's life took its first major turn when he, along with his family, migrated to the sun-kissed shores of California. This new world opened up avenues of possibilities and challenges for Nakamoto. Dorian's academic journey led him to California State Polytechnic University, where he studied physics. In 1973, he changed his name to "Dorian Prentice Satoshi Nakamoto." The significance of this name change would only become apparent decades later, tying him to a technological revolution he never claimed to be part of.

His professional path was marked by his work at Hughes Aircraft, a place where his talent in math and science came to the forefront. Dorian's colleagues remembered him as a man of remarkable intellect, often challenging conventional norms and thinking. His career in the defense and electronics sector hinted at his involvement in complex and secretive projects, adding layers to his already enigmatic persona. The turn of the century saw Dorian navigating through various phases of life, including being a father to six children. In 2014, as he waited around, his world suddenly flipped upside down in ways he could never have predicted.

In March 2014 *Newsweek* released an article "The Face Behind Bitcoin" by journalist Leah McGrath Goodman, which suggested a startling possibility: Dorian might actually be Satoshi Nakamoto. The publication drew specific parallels between Dorian and the elusive Satoshi. Both were noted to have libertarian views, a detail that aligns with the decentralized, government-independent ethos of Bitcoin. Additionally, they shared Japanese heritage (Satoshi Nakamoto was believed to be of Japanese origin). Also, Dorian lives in Los Angeles, which is a place where people suspected of being Satoshi also live or have connections.

Perhaps the most compelling parallel drawn in the article was their backgrounds in physics and involvement in classified defense projects. Dorian's work history and educational background in physics matched the profile of someone capable of creating Bitcoin. This task requires a deep understanding of cryptography and computer science. Moreover, the emergence of Bitcoin and the period when Dorian was active in relevant fields seemed to coincide, further fueling the theories linking him to the Satoshi identity.

The article's author also claimed Nakamoto said he was "no longer" involved with Bitcoin: "I am no longer involved in that and I cannot discuss it," he says, dismissing all further queries with a swat of his left hand. "It's been turned over to other people. They are in charge of it now. I no longer have any connection." Nakamoto refused to say any more […]."[91] So strange and suspicious, isn't it? Later Dorian obviously publicly denied any involvement with Bitcoin, claiming a misunderstanding. He clarified that his comments, which seemed to imply a connection to Bitcoin, were actually about a secret project he had worked on with Citibank, completely unrelated to the cryptocurrency.

To determine whether Dorian Nakamoto had any connection to Bitcoin, a significant clue can lay in a post published on the P2P Foundation Forum. P2P is where the Bitcoin code was first published.

This post surfaced shortly after the publication of the *Newsweek* article. In it, the individual using the Satoshi Nakamoto moniker explicitly stated that they were not Dorian Nakamoto.

This statement in the forum post adds an intriguing dimension to the puzzle. It suggests a direct denial from the purported Bitcoin creator, distancing themselves from Dorian. This and the explanation from the Japanese mathematician did a lot to quiet some of the rumors, but the situation had already escalated. The Bitcoin community was upset by the way Dorian was portrayed and the invasion of his privacy. Revealing his home's image and location in the *Newsweek* article was seen as crossing a line that should not have been crossed—especially given the speculative nature of the claims.

People responded with a wave of support, rallying around him. They turned a challenging situation into a show of solidarity. In a heartwarming display of community spirit, tech entrepreneur Andreas Antonopoulos organized a crowdfunding campaign. It served as an apology for Nakamoto. More than 2,100 supporters donated 102.23 bitcoin worth roughly $34,500 in 2014. In March 2024, it was worth about $6.65 million.

Post-*Newsweek* article, Dorian Nakamoto became a celebrated figure within the cryptocurrency community. His image began appearing on posters, T-shirts, and stickers. He was invited to speak at cryptocurrency conferences, where he shared his story of being unwittingly thrust into the limelight and how it turned his life upside down. Despite always maintaining that he had nothing to do with Bitcoin's creation, Dorian's story had a lasting impact. It highlighted the power of media and public perception, and how they can dramatically change a person's life. It also showed the positive side of the Bitcoin community—they support someone they believe was unfairly treated.

3.2.6 Conclusion

Despite the numerous theories and speculations, the true identity of Satoshi Nakamoto remains a mystery. Over the years, various individuals have been suspected of being the elusive creator of Bitcoin, but none have been conclusively proven to be Nakamoto. The search for Nakamoto has led to the exploration of various personalities.

Among these is Hal Finney, a pioneering cryptographer, who played a significant role in Bitcoin's early days, receiving the first transaction from Nakamoto. His work on the reusable Proof-of-Work system was crucial in shaping the cryptocurrency's infrastructure. Finney's legacy is marked by resilience and a profound impact on the crypto world.

Gavin Andresen, with his Princeton education and shift from entrepreneurship to cryptocurrency, was pivotal in Bitcoin's development. His public involvement and significant contributions to Bitcoin's code and organization, including founding The Bitcoin Foundation and creating the Bitcoin Faucet website, were instrumental in the early growth of Bitcoin.

Craig Wright, an Australian computer scientist, stirred controversy by claiming to be Nakamoto. However, his lack of conclusive evidence and legal disputes over Bitcoin holdings have led many to question his claims, making him a contentious figure in the crypto community.

Nick Szabo, known for his work on "bit gold" and "smart contracts," emerged as another strong candidate. His expertise in law and computer science, coupled with linguistic similarities in his writings and the Bitcoin Whitepaper, fueled speculations. Yet Szabo has consistently denied being Nakamoto.

Dorian Nakamoto, a Japanese-American physicist, was spotlighted in a *Newsweek* article. Despite speculations fueled by his background and name,

Dorian firmly denied any involvement with Bitcoin, further supported by a P2P Foundation forum post.

Regardless of Satoshi Nakamoto's real name or even their actual existence, there's no doubt about the enormity of their wealth. With Bitcoin reaching its peak, exceeding $72,000, Nakamoto could be counted among the world's top 20 richest individuals. It's estimated that if BTC's price hits $182,000, this mysterious cryptographer could become the wealthiest person on the planet. Such an immense fortune is reason enough to remain hidden. It would surely attract the attention of intelligence services and financial regulatory bodies in almost every country. But that's Nakamoto's dilemma.

Yes, Satoshi Nakamoto is the first crypto billionaire. But money is a secondary aspect. The real deal is the potential of Blockchain technology to revolutionize the financial world. Instead of getting hyped up about the wealth of the first crypto activists and entrepreneurs, it's more crucial to understand the mechanisms driving the people responsible for implementing this technology in our modern, digital, and globalized world. This quest to uncover Satoshi Nakamoto's identity takes us through a tapestry of personalities, each contributing to the field of Blockchain and cryptocurrency in their unique ways. As of 2024, the mystery of Nakamoto remains unsolved.

NOTES

1 W. McElroy (2017), The Satoshi Revolution: Revolution of Rising Expectations. Chapter 1: Politics versus Ideology, Bitcoin.com, https://news.bitcoin.com/the-satoshi-revolution-a-revolution-of-rising-expectations-part-3/
2 http://www.weidai.com/bmoney.txt
3 S. Nakamoto (2009), Bitcoin: A Peer-to-Peer Electronic Cash System, (p 8)
4 A. Smith (1954), Badania nad naturą i przyczynami bogactwa narodów, PWN (pp. 21–22)
5 W. McElroy, The Satoshi Revolution…, op. cit.
6 Ibid.
7 Cryptocurrency Buzz Drives Record Investment Scam Losses, Consumer Protection: Data Spotlight, Federal Trade Commision, https://www.ftc.gov/system/files/attachments/blog_posts/Cryptocurrency%20buzz%20drives%20record%20investment%20scam%20losses/cryptocurrency_spotlight.pdf
8 https://www.makeuseof.com/worst-cryptocurrency-hacks-how-much-they-stole/
9 https://www.newyorker.com/magazine/2011/10/10/the-crypto-currency
10 N. Perlroth (2021), Daniel Kaminsky, Internet Security Savior, Dies at 42, "The New York Times", 27.04.2021, access: 27.04.2021.
11 https://www.newyorker.com/magazine/2011/10/10/the-crypto-currency
12 Ibid.
13 Ibid.
14 J. Davis (2011), The Crypto-Currency, The New Yorker.
15 B. Wallace (2011), The Rise and Fall of Bitcoin, "Wired", 23.11.2011, access: 31.05.2016.
16 Ibid.

17 Ibid.
18 A. Greenberg (2014), The Little Black Book of Billionaire Secrets Nakamoto's Neighbor: My Hunt for Bitcoin's Creator Led to a Paralyzed Crypto Genius, "Forbes", 25.03.2014, access: 17.04.2017.
19 Ibid.
20 B. Punzal (2013), In Finney Home, Fran Gives Care, Quality of Life to Husband Hal, Presidio Sports.
21 A. Greenberg, The Little Black Book…, op. cit.
22 Ibid.
23 T. Simonite (2014), The Man Who Really Built Bitcoin, "MIT Technology Review", 15.08.2014, Massachusetts Institute of Technology, access: 28.09.2021.
24 https://www.technologyreview.com/2014/08/15/12784/the-man-who-really-built-bitcoin/
25 https://bitcointalk.org/index.php?topic=2367.0
26 https://github.com/bitcoin/bitcoin/graphs/contributors?from=2009-08-30&to=2021-10-01&type=c
27 E.E. Ghiselli, J.P. Siegel (1972), Leadership and Managerial Success in Tall and Flat Organization Structures, "Personnel Psychology" 25 (4): 617.
28 Results of a Harvard Business School study of over 3 million corporate employees from 16 cities around the world—https://hbr.org/2020/12/the-pandemic-is-widening-a-corporate-productivity-gap
29 https://www.theguardian.com/technology/2012/oct/03/bitcoin-foundation-online-currency
30 https://www.technologyreview.com/2014/08/15/12784/the-man-who-really-built-bitcoin/
31 Ibid.
32 Ibid.
33 https://mediatorselect.com/blog/articles/how-to-resolve-your-workplace-conflict-peacefully/
34 https://www.technologyreview.com/2014/08/15/12784/the-man-who-really-built-bitcoin/
35 https://freebitco.in/site/faucet/
36 https://www.blockchain.com/charts/cost-per-transaction
37 https://irp-cdn.multiscreensite.com/91156662/files/uploaded/NeoBanks%20Performance%20and%20New%20Ideas%20Finnovate_v7_10_11_2018.pdf
38 https://www.statista.com/statistics/264810/number-of-monthly-active-facebook-users-worldwide/
39 https://www.cnbc.com/2021/03/04/survey-finds-one-third-of-crypto-buyers-dont-know-what-theyre-doing.html
40 Ibid.
41 https://www.marketwatch.com/story/bitcoin-pizza-day-laszlo-hanyecz-spent-3-8-billion-on-pizzas-in-the-summer-of-2010-using-the-novel-crypto-11621714395
42 https://www.technologyreview.com/2014/08/15/12784/the-man-who-really-built-bitcoin/
43 Ibid.
44 https://www.wealthypersons.com/gavin-andresen-net-worth-2020-2021/
45 https://www.technologyreview.com/2014/08/15/12784/the-man-who-really-built-bitcoin/

46 https://www.coindesk.com/markets/2017/05/19/where-is-gavin-andresen-the-quiet-exile-of-bitcoins-former-face/

47 https://www.youtube.com/watch?v=RIafZXRDH7w&t=1674s

48 https://www.coindesk.com/markets/2017/05/19/where-is-gavin-andresen-the-quiet-exile-of-bitcoins-former-face/

49 Ibid.

50 Ibid.

51 https://bitcoinchain.com/nodes

52 A. Hern (2015), Bitcoin's Forked: Chief Scientist Launches Alternative Proposal for the Currency, "The Guardian", 17.08.2015, https://www.theguardian.com/technology/2015/aug/17/bitcoin-xt-alternative-cryptocurrency-chief-scientist, access: 20.08.2015.

53 https://www.nytimes.com/2016/01/17/business/dealbook/the-bitcoin-believer-who-gave-up.html?_r=0

54 Ibid.

55 Ibid.

56 https://www.reuters.com/article/us-global-technology-bitcoin-idUSKCN0UT2II

57 https://www.wired.com/2015/12/bitcoins-creator-satoshi-nakamoto-is-probably-this-unknown-australian-genius/

58 Ibid.

59 Ibid.

60 Ibid.

61 https://www.the-blockchain.com/2015/12/09/has-bitcoin-and-blockchain-creator-satoshi-nakamoto-been-unmasked/

62 https://gizmodo.com/heres-all-the-evidence-that-craig-wright-invented-bitco-1747059371

63 https://www.metzdowd.com/pipermail/cryptography/2009-January/014994.html

64 https://www.bbc.com/news/technology-36168863

65 Ibid.

66 Satoshi was nominated for the Nobel Prize in Economics by an American professor of economics from the University of California. However, the application was rejected because the Nobel regulations require disclosure of the identity of the person nominated—https://www.newsbtc.com/news/bitcoin/bitcoin-creator-satoshi-nakamoto-nominated-nobel-prize/

67 I. Kaminska (2016), Craig Wright's upcoming big reveal, "Financial Times", 31.03.2016, access: 10.04.2016.

68 https://archive.is/Q66Gl#selection-1991.0-2009.106

69 https://www.forbes.com/sites/thomasbrewster/2015/12/11/bitcoin-creator-satoshi-craig-wright-lies-hoax/?sh=7c82ee6e6794

70 https://cointelegraph.com/news/craig-wright-accused-of-plagiarism-again

71 C. Wright, D. Kleiman, R.S. Sundhar (2008), Overwriting Hard Drive Data: The Great Wiping Controversy, in: R. Sekar (ed.), *Information Systems Security: 4th International Conference*, ICISS 2008, Hyderabad, India, December 16–20, 2008, Proceedings. Springer Science & Business Media, p. 243.

72 J. Wilkinson (1999), Gaming Commissions, Internet Gambling and Responsible Gambling [PDF], Parliament of New South Wales, pp. 28–29.

73 S. Thomsen (2015), The incredible career of the Australian scientist suspected of creating Bitcoin, "Business Insider", 9.12.2015.

74 J. Pearson, L. Franceschi-Bicchierai (2016), Craig Wright's New Evidence That He Is Satoshi Nakamoto Is Worthless, "Vice", 2.05.2016.

75 http://gavinandresen.ninja/satoshi

76 https://www.wired.com/2015/12/bitcoins-creator-satoshi-nakamoto-is-probably-this-unknown-australian-genius/

77 A. Greenberg (2015), New Clues Suggest Craig Wright, Suspected Bitcoin Creator, May Be a Hoaxer, "Wired", 11.12.2015, access: 4.09.2019.

78 https://dankaminsky.com/2016/05/03/the-cryptographically-provable-con-man/

79 HAL 90210 (2016), Bitcoin Project Blocks out Gavin Andresen over Satoshi Nakamoto Claims, "The Guardian", 6.05.2016, dostęp: 6.12.2019.

80 https://www.coindesk.com/markets/2017/05/19/where-is-gavin-andresen-the-quiet-exile-of-bitcoins-former-face/

81 http://czasopisma.isppan.waw.pl/index.php/kis/article/download/1419/1165/

82 https://www.prnewswire.com/news-releases/tulip-trust-files-lawsuit-against-ira-kleiman-over-billions-in-bitcoin-fortune-301268633.html

83 https://www.rp.pl/historia/art3547651-xix-wiek-kto-spalil-moskwe

84 https://www.coindesk.com/markets/2017/05/19/where-is-gavin-andresen-the-quiet-exile-of-bitcoins-former-face/

85 R. Browne (2018), Self-Proclaimed Bitcoin Creator Sued for Allegedly Stealing $5 Billion Worth of Crypto, Other Assets, CNBC, 27.2.2018, access: 27.2.2018.

86 J. Pearson (2018), The Man Who Claimed to Invent Bitcoin Is Being Sued for $10 Billion, "Vice", 26.02.2018.

87 https://www.forbes.com/sites/haileylennon/2021/01/22/the-battle-to-be-satoshi/?sh=7269b42856fe

88 https://coingeek.com/kleiman-v-wright-still-on-for-november-1-for-now/

89 https://medium.com/zulurepublic/towards-a-trust-minimized-world-an-interview-with-nick-szabo-90b900947683

90 https://www.nzherald.co.nz/business/elon-musks-cryptic-post-about-bitcoin-founder-goes-viral-over-the-internet/24PQOPDUK5SGYARGPQKEQO7XKA/

91 https://www.newsweek.com/2014/03/14/face-behind-bitcoin-247957.html

Chapter 4

Bitcoin fever
The digital El Dorado

4.1 FROM PROGRAMMING CURIOSITY TO MILLION-DOLLAR BUSINESS

The journey of the Bitcoin community traces its roots to the Cypherpunk movement, a collective committed to leveraging technology for enhanced freedom and privacy. This group, infused with libertarian ideals, championed the principles of independence, anonymity, and equitable access to digital resources. Their mission was to remain impartial, steering clear of both government and corporate influences. Yet, sustaining their vision required financial backing. As Bitcoin started capturing attention and gaining value, it unlocked new avenues for monetization and investment. This financial breakthrough allowed those driven by ideology—individuals and collectives alike—to fund their initiatives and maintain their operations. Here, a pivotal shift occurred: the pursuit of high-minded ideals started to merge with the realm of finance. As Bitcoin grew beyond a tech novelty, it was the business-minded people who first enjoyed the wealth it created through Blockchain.

In the early stages of Bitcoin, the community surrounding its development underwent a remarkable evolution. Picture the scene: a landscape initially dominated by a unique breed of individuals, often labeled as impractical nerds, completely absorbed in their own world. Among them was Wei Dai, rumored to have corresponded with Satoshi Nakamoto. These early pioneers exemplified this era, engaging in passionate discussions in the secluded corners of Internet forums and mailing lists. Their conversations were not just about technology. To them, this was more than just technological tinkering—it was about being part of a groundbreaking digital culture, a movement at the edge of the known and the possible.[1] As you might guess, most people just found them strange.

Then, individuals like Gavin Andresen came along. Andresen, with his experience in the IT sector, bridged the gap between introverted programmers and the business world. He had managed startups in the Silicon Valley and this experience helped him bring practical ideas to the Bitcoin community. Mike Hearn was another key person, handsome and well-built with impressive presentation skills and background at Google's Zurich office.

DOI: 10.1201/9781032621456-5

Despite leaving a prestigious career for a then-niche technology, Hearn's venture into Bitcoin was initially voluntary. He chose to work on Bitcoin, even though it was risky. He wanted to make Bitcoin better and more popular worldwide. The shift from idealistic tech lovers to business-smart people marks the Bitcoin community's growth. It's a move from just focusing on tech and ideals to learning how business and market forces work. This change is like Bitcoin's journey from being an interesting tech project to a major financial player.

In the midst of it all, Craig Wright made his entrance. Wright has demonstrated undeniable business skills, managing to carve out a technological and financial empire amid the chaos. His story, tangled in legal complexities, adds an extra layer of fascination to the Bitcoin narrative. Wright finds himself at the center of billion-dollar lawsuits (yes, another one), where he accuses key Bitcoin developers of pilfering his intellectual property. He pegged his losses at a staggering $5.7 billion in a 2021 lawsuit.[2] A twist in his tale came when a UK court recognized his copyright to the Bitcoin Whitepaper. Though this acknowledgment didn't come with a financial windfall, it's a noteworthy validation from a serious court. This recognition plays into the larger picture of the cryptocurrency sector, now an industry valued at $1.5 trillion, equivalent to almost a tenth of the Chinese economy, and a third of the German one. Today Wright's claim to be the elusive Satoshi Nakamoto still remains unconfirmed.[3] His legal battles haven't conclusively proven his financial losses nor solidified his identity as the creator of Bitcoin. The much-anticipated *COPA v. Wright trial*, set for 2024, might finally shed light on the true origins of Bitcoin.

But who really has the upper hand in this complex saga? It's a tough call. What's clear, though, is that the conflicts among the original Bitcoin community have persisted. Secrets dating back to Bitcoin's 2009 roots are still waiting to be unearthed after more than a dozen years. During all the early fights and problems in the cryptocurrency world, things started to change. Experienced business leaders and entrepreneurs began to get involved. These people knew a lot about theory, but they also had real business experience. Shifting away from the fraught community of Bitcoin activists, these entrepreneurs and tech-savvy users started creating their own ventures. Most of these were based on the Blockchain and facilitated the use of cryptocurrency wallets but did not directly participate in the Bitcoin project. They utilized its advantages, without getting involved in resolving the inherent (and probably incurable) flaws of the first cryptocurrency developers' environment.

4.1.1 Digital miners

In the age of epic voyages, when the Americas were the new frontier, I'm particularly captivated by the legend of El Dorado. Picture the 16th-century Spanish adventurers who, fueled by tales of the riches, braved unknown seas to reach the lands we now know as Colombia. The discovery of America wasn't just about unearthing unknown civilizations—it was also about the mystique of unverified legends. Among these was the tale of indigenous tribes crafting golden statues of their deities, known as El Hombre Dorado, or "the golden man," leading to the term *El Dorado*—the land of gold.[4]

The human desire for gold and riches is timeless. Across history, this quest for wealth has pushed people to seek their fortunes, no matter the era or circumstances. Post-El Dorado, the term *gold rush* came into play. In the mid-19th century, this was the drive to settle in previously uninhabited places, mainly on the West Coast of the United States. The empty plains and remote areas, devoid of infrastructure, lured fortune-seekers dreaming of striking gold and other precious metals. This was the essence of the California Dream—the belief that anyone could strike it rich overnight.[5]

One hundred and fifty years from the days of the gold rush, we find the pursuit of wealth transformed in the digital age with the emergence of Bitcoin. It introduces a novel concept of "mining," a far cry from the traditional pickaxe and shovel method. This contemporary form of mining is a high-tech endeavor, involving the solving of intricate cryptographic puzzles integral to the Proof-of-Work (PoW) algorithm. In this new digital gold rush, the "miners" are computers, engaged in a competitive race to decipher complex codes.[6] The reward here is not tangible gold but new units of Bitcoin, a digital currency. Each successful solution of a puzzle results in the award of a block of Bitcoins, symbolizing a virtual treasure trove. This modern mining echoes the spirit of the gold rush era, but instead of physically mining the earth, these 21st-century prospectors mine through layers of digital complexity, seeking wealth in the realm of cyberspace.

4.2 THE MAKING OF DIGITAL CURRENCY

Bitcoin mining changed how we think about money. Before Bitcoin, central banks like the Federal Reserve (Fed) were the only ones who could produce money. In economic terms, they had a monopoly on money issuance. To maintain the central authority's control over currency, police and courts pursue counterfeiters. Making fake money is a serious crime, governed by the Penal Code. It is sometimes seen as worse than theft or even more brutal crimes. In the United States, counterfeiting money can lead to up to 20 years in prison.[7]

In the United States, everyone uses dollars because the government says so, and everyone agrees to that. It's like a big promise that a piece of paper with "100 dollars" written on it is worth something. That works because everyone knows what a dollar is worth and what you can buy with it. To make sure people trust that money, the central bank, which is in charge of dollars, has a lot of rules to eliminate fakes. On one hand, the design of dollar bills hasn't changed much since 1963, so they're familiar. People can always recognize them. On the other hand, the Fed uses complex procedures to make sure the money we use is real, not fake. Dollar bills are made of a mix of flax and cotton, and they use unknown inks for that characteristic green color.[8] For security reasons, the composition of the blend is one of the most closely guarded secrets in the United States. Why does no one question the authority of the United States? Because they are a world power that hasn't been attacked by any army on its land for over 170 years.

Digital payments work with help from central authorities. Think about using a debit or credit card. Companies like Mastercard and Visa handle all the transactions, whether online or in a department store. They keep track of your purchases and make sure they're real. That's why your card might get blocked when you travel—to prevent fake transactions. That system is centralized and relies on trust. We trust central banks that issue money as well as global companies in tech and finance, like banks and card operators. They run everything centrally.

Seems like a world full of trust doesn't need anything else. Why would someone make a payment system where anyone can use it, no matter who they are, how old they are, or what's their (legal) background? It might sound weird, but that's what has happened. Satoshi Nakamoto created a system called Bitcoin. It doesn't need any central organization to control it. Instead, lots of computers around the world are supporting it. Those computers are called nodes. They do a job similar to what the Federal Reserve, Visa, and Mastercard do in the United States but with a few important differences.

In the world of Bitcoin, nodes keep track of all the Bitcoin transactions that have happened in the past. They're important because they check to make sure each transaction is authentic. What's cool about Bitcoin is that those nodes aren't controlled by just one company or government. Instead, they are spread all over the world, and anyone can see the list of transactions they keep.[9] In March 2024, a record number of over 56,000 nodes were active in the network.[10] Every one of them is a part of what's called "mining" centers. They're like the heartbeat of the Bitcoin network, helping it run smoothly.

Bitcoin works differently from regular money. Normally, we trust a bank or the government to make sure our money is safe. But with Bitcoin, you don't have to trust just one big organization. Instead, you rely on lots of different people who don't even know each other. But what connects those people is a reward in the form of Bitcoin. You might think that strangers wouldn't trust each other with money, especially when they're anonymous. In the case of Bitcoin, it works. Involved people keep the network running because they can earn big money from it. They use their own computers or even buy special computing machines. Such a designed network is virtually impossible to stop or turn off—or simply it's not profitable.

Satoshi Nakamoto, thought of something important when designing the model. To break into the Bitcoin network, someone would have to take control over at least 51% of the nodes. The attack would require a huge computing power. And guess what? Using that power to just mine Bitcoins would make you more money than trying to break into the network. There's another part of Bitcoin's security: private keys. They are passwords that let you access your Bitcoin wallet. Guessing someone's private key is almost impossible. Do you know how many different combinations of access keys there are? It's a number that's 2 to the power of 160 (2^{160}). That's a huge, almost unimaginable number:

1 461 501 637 330 902 918 203 684 832 716 283 019 655 932 542 976

We don't use such values on a daily basis, so it's not really important to keep a record of it. Let's put it in perspective: imagine all the grains of sand in the world—there are about 2^{63} of them. Now, think about Bitcoin keys.[11] The number of different keys you can generate is way bigger than the number of grains of sand. In fact, it's a hundred times more. That's a huge difference, right? Just compare the length of those two numbers:

9 223 372 036 854 775 808

Bitcoin and other cryptocurrencies are generally safe. Unless there's a security error, like someone hacking into the software of crypto exchange or a digital wallet. But usually, those systems are good at keeping an eye on the money flow.

People got really interested in Bitcoin for different reasons: they thought it was a smart idea, they saw a chance to make some cash, or they just got caught up in all the excitement. Bitcoin was the first of its kind, opening the door for other digital currencies. Those cryptocurrencies have started a whole new type of economy. They're changing the game in how we send and get money. The financial strategies and rules used in digital currencies are known as token economics. It's a big deal because it's not just about buying and selling but a whole new perspective on handling and thinking about money.

In the case of Bitcoin, the token distribution works in such a way that its maximum supply, encoded in the system, is 21 million units. Currently, there are just under 19 million Bitcoins in circulation. People are aware that time is running out, and at some point, the most popular cryptocurrency will become a luxury commodity that will no longer increase in quantity. Everyone, therefore, is trying to find their opportunity and own Bitcoin while its price is not too high. Approximately 900 new Bitcoins are added to the network each day, but one day this number will drop to zero.[12] As long as it's possible, everyone is trying to take advantage of the opportunity to earn from the "production" of Bitcoins, although the chances of doing so are decreasing rapidly. According to current estimates, the last Bitcoin, or BTC unit number 21,000,000, will be mined in 2140.[13]

The emergence of the Bitcoin network created a new opportunity to earn money through mining cryptocurrency. Many people felt the chance for a large profit. Unlike the first months of Bitcoin's operation, the interest in cryptocurrencies is now much greater than the actual ability to handle them by the computers of active users. The number of miners is limited, as the demand for computational power of cryptocurrency miners is continually increasing. Looking at data from around the world from 2020, just maintaining the Bitcoin mechanism and adding new transactions to the network brought miners an income of over $50 million per day.

To understand precisely the reward mechanism that miners receive for maintaining the network, we must go back to the roots of Bitcoin. When Satoshi Nakamoto published the first version of the BTC network software, every miner received 50 units of cryptocurrency in exchange for providing their computer to solve a programming puzzle and confirm a new transaction record. Such confirmation happens by packing transaction information into blocks (hence the name Blockchain).

To get a good grasp of how Bitcoin miners earn their rewards, we need to take a trip back to where it all began. Satoshi Nakamoto set a simple rule: miners got paid 50 Bitcoins for each puzzle they solved. Every new Bitcoin transaction was approved that way. Miners collected all the transaction details and packed them into what we call "blocks." That's how the term *Blockchain* came about—it's like a chain of blocks, each containing specific transaction information.

In simple terms, the amount of new Bitcoins created with each block mined is known as the "block reward." This reward is cut in half every 210,000 blocks, which happens about every four years. For example, it started at 50 Bitcoins in 2009, then went down to 25, 12.5, and was 6.25 in May 2020. The next time it will be halved is just around the corner, in mid-2024. Halvings reduce the pace of creating new coins and make them less common. Even though the number of Bitcoins miners receive is getting smaller, mining can still be very profitable. Why? As new coins are added slower and more people want them, their value goes up. The graph (Figure 4.1) shows that although the reward in Bitcoins goes down every four years, its value in dollars actually increases.

To confirm new transactions on the Blockchain, miners use special equipment—cryptocurrency miners. Their technological scheme resembles graphics cards (GPU), but the computational power of miners exceeds anything a user of even the best GPU unit could dream of. In the early days of Bitcoin, mining was something almost anyone could do with a regular computer. But as Bitcoin grew more popular around 2013, the complexity of these math problems increased. They became so challenging that only specialized equipment could handle them.[14] This is where cryptocurrency miners come in—machines designed specifically for mining Bitcoin. Now, how tough is the task? Imagine trying to solve a puzzle with a 1 in 16 trillion

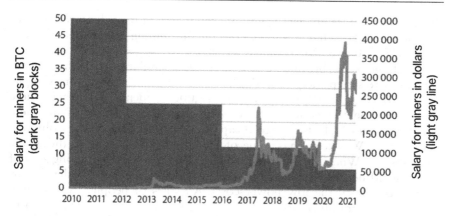

Figure 4.1 Rewards for miners for maintaining BTC networks.

chance of getting it right.[15] That's the kind of odds the mining machines face every time they work to verify a transaction in Bitcoin's PoW system.

Because of the immense difficulty and the special requirements of Bitcoin mining, companies started producing dedicated machines for this purpose. One of the biggest names in this industry is Bitmain, a Chinese manufacturer. Bitmain is a giant, responsible for producing up to 70% of all mining machines used worldwide.[16] Their equipment is essential in the process of validating transactions and maintaining the integrity of the Bitcoin network.

4.3 PROFESSIONAL MINERS IN DEFI

The mining realm draws many individuals because it looks like a cool passive income source. However, in practice, mining Bitcoin and other cryptocurrencies is a demanding task.

First off, the equipment, called mining rigs, is expensive. Plus, it's not just a set-and-forget situation. Those rigs demand constant care and attention. You've got to monitor them all the time, and sometimes parts break down and need replacing. If even a small component fails, your whole setup can stop working, leading to a drop in the profits. Thankfully, there are some mobile apps that make tracking everything a bit easier. Many miners delegate everyday tasks to a full-time employee. Some miners even construct specially adapted buildings and centers where thousands of mining rigs can operate at full capacity, generating much heat and noise in the process.

Bitcoin mining used to be something people did for fun in their own rooms. But now, it's changing. Continuously more people who are into cryptocurrencies are moving their mining setups out of their homes. From what I've heard from my clients and others in the crypto industry, they're now renting spaces in specialized science and technology parks. That shift allows them to mine more efficiently, without the worry of disturbing roommates or neighbors. The change shows how Bitcoin mining is moving toward a more dedicated and professional approach.

On a larger scale, big mining centers consider similar factors while choosing a place to set up. Take East Wenatchee in Washington state, for example. It used to be a quiet little town with 13,000 residents. The place where people from Seattle would go to get away from the city buzz. Living there was pretty affordable, thanks to cheap power from a dam on the Columbia River.[17] East Wenatchee has some of the cheapest electricity in the whole United States. When Bitcoin came around, this place started drawing a lot of attention. Miners of Bitcoin and other digital currencies saw a golden opportunity because of the low power costs. All sorts of people, from former Microsoft programmers to construction workers, started getting down to East Wenatchee.[18] For instance, in 2013, local entrepreneur Malachi Salcido started constructing special halls to install Bitcoin mining rigs. He was 41 at the time and had previously worked as the owner of a small construction company. Fast forward five years, and his company grew to have more than 50 employees. The company is responsible for maintaining infrastructure and providing services for local mining entrepreneurs.

Bitcoin mining is becoming a lot like other businesses. Just like in traditional industries, people in Bitcoin mining are doing things like making deals with power plants, finding land to build mining centers, and sometimes even getting money from investment funds that work with Blockchain technology. The world of cryptocurrency is really open to different kinds of businesspeople. Hence, there are a lot of ways to become a millionaire in the crypto world.

Starting out in mining doesn't mean you have to go big right away. You don't need a huge setup or even a physical location. You can actually get into mining Bitcoin in simpler, still profitable ways, all from the comfort of your home. It's really about being smart, diligent, putting in the effort, and having Internet access. Take Adam Gitzes, for example. He's been into Bitcoin since 2017. After spending four years in the industry, he decided to try mining Bitcoin himself. However, his wife did not agree to install the equipment in their home due to concerns about noise, heat emissions, and power consumption by the miners. So, Adam thought outside the box. He used his experience from working in marketing at Amazon and the money he'd saved from his day job.[19] He turned himself into a computing power broker. It was a clever way to get into mining without all the usual hassle.

Adam Gitzes decided to enter this business relatively recently, when the price of Bitcoin skyrocketed between September 2020 and January 2021. Gitzes understood the mechanism that drives the distribution of Bitcoin mining profits. In an interview with Business Insider, he said: "The price of bitcoin appreciated 500%. But the difficulty to mine bitcoin only appreciably only changed by 30%, which meant there was a really great opportunity to get into mining."[20] The gap between the price increase and the relatively smaller jump in mining difficulty created a golden opportunity for those looking to get into mining. Gitzes didn't just observe trends. He crafted his own business strategy based on the insights. Investing 1.1 Bitcoin, which was about $60,000 at the time, he purchased six mining machines. They were capable of generating up to 0.0048 Bitcoin daily. In October 2021, that amount translated to roughly $280 every single day.

Gitzes also pays mining fees to Compass Mining, to whom he "leases" miners. In exchange for allowing Compass Mining to use a portion of his miners' computing power, they take care of maintenance and upkeep. The average daily cost of energy for six machines is about $30, giving Gitzes a profit of $250.

Not long after Gitzes set up his new mining equipment and made it available for Compass Mining, some (favorable for Gitzes) big news shook the world of Bitcoin. The information came straight from China, which, before 2021, was a giant in the mining industry. In fact, experts think that China was responsible for producing nearly 65% of the world's Bitcoin[21] (Figure 4.2). Why the Land of the Dragon? They had really cheap energy costs and didn't worry much about pollution. In China, nobody seemed too bothered about the increasing use of electricity from sources that weren't good for the environment. Especially, since mining Bitcoin was so profitable. The official ban on mining was introduced due to concern for the environment, but analysts agree that it was actually about control. The Chinese government feared that Bitcoin could undermine its control over financial and monetary systems. They worried it might increase the risk of economic crisis, promote financial crime, and harm investors supported by the Communist Party of China.[22]

When China got stricter with its rules on cryptocurrency mining, it hit the Chinese miners hard. Many of them had to shut down. They turned off their

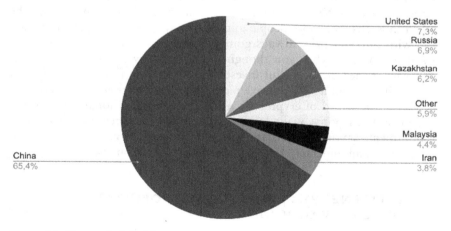

Figure 4.2 Share of global Bitcoin mined by country in April 2020.

(*Source:* **Data from Cambridge BTC Electricity Consumption Index.**)

equipment, which meant they couldn't contribute to the worldwide network of digital currency mining anymore. To maintain network continuity, computational power had to be increased. Now Gitzes comes in. He saw a chance and decided to buy more mining machines. He didn't say how many, but his plan was pretty smart: "It was very clear I'd be getting excess bitcoin from buying these miners than if I just bought bitcoin, and it was very good."[23] Gitzes explained his approach: "Now is a great time to be in mining... There's a reduced difficulty rate with the [Chinese] miners being offline. As the difficulty rate increases, the amount of bitcoin mined will decrease."[24] Gitzes estimated the investment would have paid off in about eight months.[25]

Renting mining machines at Compass Mining's main office is just the beginning of the story. Adam Gitzez bought the mining machines using Bitcoin in a very strategic way. He purchased the machines when the BTC rate was going up but before the price of the miner in dollars changed. It's a bit like a game: Gitzes tried to guess when the value of Bitcoin in dollars would have increased. When it did, more people wanted to buy mining machines because they wanted to profit from Bitcoin. But, Gitzes acts before miners would realize they could charge more for their work. He buys these machines while they're still priced lower before their manufacturers realize they could be charging more. That strategy significantly cut down his business costs. The only other major expense? Electricity. For remote miners, the day-to-day work is almost nothing. Compass' support team usually takes care of any repairs or times when the machines are not working.

Imagine trying to become rich by investing in Bitcoin and buying lots of mining devices. It sounds like a sure bet, right? But in reality, it's not that simple. Here's why: markets, whether it's in stocks or cryptocurrencies like Bitcoin, naturally find a balance. The idea in microeconomics called long-run equilibrium explains that well: over time, everyone has about the same chance to succeed. Now, what if lots of people try to do the same thing? The sad truth is, that the more people join in, the less profit each person makes. And with Bitcoin's price always going up and down, it's pretty risky. This risk can "eat up" what you thought you'd earn by investing in mining. However, stories of successful investments in crypto, like the example of Adam Gitzes, paint a very positive picture. It shows us there are still opportunities in the world of cryptocurrencies, even the traditional ways of getting in. But it's not a walk in the park. It just requires a high level of commitment, staying up-to-date with the industry news, learning about Blockchain, and understanding the basic rules of economics.

4.4 GREEN ENERGY, CLIMATE CATASTROPHE, AND THE FUTURE OF MINING

Cryptocurrency mining business generates high electricity costs. In my opinion, it only makes sense in two cases: in places where electricity is cheap or where it comes from renewable sources like wind and solar power. Using biological fuel sidesteps the environmental concerns associated with burning coal or gas. However, most of the leading countries don't follow that eco-friendly path.

After China decided to ban mining, a significant chunk of Bitcoin mining shifted to the United States. As of March 2024, more than a quarter (28.80%) of Bitcoin's Nodes was based in the United States. Then came Germany with 13.79% and China with 6.66%.[26] The policy toward mining in those countries raised many questions due to the considerable, negative impact on the environment.

The United States and Canada are big players in Bitcoin mining, sitting at the top spots (1st and 4th). They're doing great because they have advanced technology. But let's think about places like the former communist countries. They've got cheap gas and unregulated legal situation. Also, consider Venezuela. Despite being in a tough place with its economy and politics, they don't have strict rules on Bitcoin mining either. Siberia serves as another perfect example. After China changed the law, a lot of miners moved there with their businesses. In 2021, energy consumption in the Irkutsk region (central Siberia) increased by 159% compared to the previous year.[27] It's clear evidence of just how much Bitcoin mining was happening there.

The situation in Siberia and sudden spikes in electricity demand served as a warning sign for local authorities. Over time, cryptocurrency mining could become a burden for thousands of people living in the areas chosen by miners. For example, in Abkhazia—a region by the Black Sea in the Caucasus mountains—power shortages and voltage spikes caused malfunctions and sometimes even destroyed household electrical appliances, such as refrigerators and TVs. In some extreme cases, the unstable power supply even sparked fires. The root of those problems laid in the existence of over 150 large-scale cryptocurrency mining centers in the region.[28]

Abkhazia is a place stuck between Russia and Georgia, with both countries arguing over it. About 250,000 people call Abkhazia home. The ongoing conflict—initially military, now diplomatic—also affects other spheres of life. Since 2020, people there have had to deal with electricity blackouts for eight hours every day. The situation gets more complicated with Bitcoin businesses. The local political clans keep changing their minds about whether those businesses are okay or not.[29] The lack of decisiveness makes life hard for everyone, especially those trying to make a living with Bitcoin. Abkhazia is a self-proclaimed republic, but it leans heavily on Russia for money.[30] The sad part? It's got a reputation for being super corrupt, like one of those places where knowing the right people matters more than doing the right thing.

In this self-proclaimed republic, cryptocurrency mining isn't just a cool idea anymore, it's become a life necessity. It's gone from being a hobby for teenagers to something that matters on a global scale. Here's the story: a couple of years back, Abkhazia wouldn't let people bring in computers for mining. That's changed now. The new government has lifted any restrictions and even got a deal with Russia for the power needed. Speaking of Russia, they're big on pollution, ranking fourth in the world for CO_2 emissions. Few people seem to care about that. Why? Because Russia sits on the largest gas reserves and the second-largest coal resources on the planet.[31]

Countries like Russia are in a great situation; they can experiment with cryptocurrency mining because they have vast raw material resources. But Russia is not an isolated case. In 2018, Venezuela issued its own cryptocurrency, Pedro.[32] Overlooking the need to save the country from a massive economic crisis and hyperinflation, Pedro was meant to be an interesting experiment in developing the cryptocurrency mining industry in this country.[33] Plus, in Venezuela, the cost of mining is super cheap because the government helps out with fuel costs. It's actually the cheapest place in the world to mine Bitcoin. To put it in perspective, mining one Bitcoin in South Korea costs more than $26,000.[34] In Venezuela? Only about $530. That's like 50 times cheaper.

With rising electricity prices, the current mining business faces many challenges. Countries like Poland, which still rely on conventional resources for electricity production, are facing the so-called green transformation. For example, in Poland, only one-fourth of energy comes from renewable sources. Sixty-five percent comes from burning coal.[35] You can't walk away from such a non-ecological system in a few months, which means electricity prices will rise. The costs of CO_2 production permits and penalties imposed on electricity producers for exceeding emission standards are rising. And this negatively affects energy prices, which—as I showed you in this section— are one of the two main variables determining the economic sense of investing in cryptocurrency miners. How can this problem be solved?

The quickest answer: move the investment in miners to other places. Imagine you're a miner who works remotely. You could set up your mining setup in a country where electricity is cheaper because it's not as clean or eco-friendly. But, this isn't a good thing for our planet, and it won't work well in the long term. Nowadays, climate change is a big deal, and all the world's leaders know it. They're all trying to cut down on pollution and use of nonrenewable energy, moving toward green power sources instead. Take Russia, for example. It's known for not being very eco-friendly, but they've started a project that's getting attention in the crypto world. Gazprom Neft, a big government-owned gas company, created a mining center in Siberia. Normally, when they drill for gas, they release CO_2, which is usually just burned off and goes into the atmosphere. But now, they're using that CO_2 to generate electricity instead.[36]

What's innovative about that approach is the placement of cryptocurrency mining equipment right at the oil drilling sites. The gas that would have been wasted is now used to power the mining rigs. It's a creative solution that benefits the environment, the Blockchain community, and the oil industry. And it's not just in Russia, similar models are being adopted in the United States and Canada. It's a win–win situation, creating a synergy between the digital and traditional energy sectors, all while being mindful of environmental impacts.

The next proposed solution to the problem of expensive and unecological mining is the choice of the right cryptocurrency. Over the years, there have been no appropriate innovations in the token sector that could be mined ecologically. Blockchain specialists have experimented with various types of transaction confirmation protocols to reduce the environmental impact of the cryptocurrency network.

Notably, Vitalik Buterin has partially succeeded in making the field of cryptocurrency less harmful to the planet. He is the brain behind Ethereum, which ranks as the second-most popular cryptocurrency, right after Bitcoin. Ethereum works a bit differently. While Bitcoin uses special GPU circuits for its operations, Ethereum relies on regular computer processors, similar to the ones we use in our everyday computers. That's a big deal because it means Ethereum is not as tough on the environment as Bitcoin. However, it's important to note that Ethereum still uses a lot of power, so it hasn't completely solved the problem of high energy consumption. That's one of the reasons Ethereum stands out in the crowded world of cryptocurrencies. Bitcoin is still the largest cryptocurrency, holding approximately a 40% share in the cryptocurrency market.[37] Because of this, it has the largest share in the impact of cryptocurrencies on the environment. In nearly 12 years of operation in this sector, the Bitcoin network has grown so large that it turned into a power-hungry monster. In 2021, the amount of electricity Bitcoin used was crazy high. It was similar to what a medium-sized country, like Malaysia, where over 32 million people live, would use in a whole year.[38] That's a lot of power for just one type of digital money.

The excessive power consumption is largely attributed to the whole process. Bitcoin mining used to be tough on the environment because it needed powerful graphics cards, known as GPUs, which wasn't great for the environment. But then came a new kind of cryptocurrency called Chia, named after those healthy seeds you find in eco-friendly foods. The cool thing about Chia is that you can still mine it and make money, but it's way better for the planet. It's a big step forward in making crypto more eco-friendly.

The problem of unecological mining was, among others, that due to Bitcoin's technical limitations, miners had to use miners based on graphical units, that is, GPUs. However, an innovative cryptocurrency appeared, which can also be mined—and bring profits—but with a significantly lower impact on the environment, Chia.[39] It's named just like healthy seeds, very popular in ecological and healthy dishes. Brian Cohen, the guy who created BitTorrent, started the Chia project. Remember when I mentioned the Cypherpunk movement in Chapter 2? He was part of that too. Chia doesn't need a ton of computing power. It just uses memory space, which saves a lot of electricity. When Chia got really popular in 2021, the demand for hard drives and SSDs shot up, making their prices increase even by 50%.[40] Thus, many thought that in the modern, ecological world of Blockchain, your mining adventure could start by buying an ordinary SSD carrier.

The exchange rate of Chia token (XCH) is currently falling, but another value shows that you should be interested in the topic of mining this cryptocurrency, possibly by investing in computer memory.

To silence the right (or, unironically, righteous), critics concerned about crypto and its impact on the environment should consider that even the most rooted cryptocurrencies—like Ethereum—can change for the better, environment-wise. From the previous chapter you may already know how difficult it is to pass a change among any crypto community. Even the solid, value-adding forks are looked at by the community with a fair amount of skepticism. However, the second-largest crypto stands out here. In March 2023, Ethereum underwent the so-called Shanghai hard fork, named after the location of its announcement. That was a big deal for the crypto community and soon proved to be such for the environment as well.

When Vitalik Buterin first introduced Ethereum, it operated on a PoW principle—a very similar consensus mechanism for validation of transaction, compared to Bitcoin. Hence, it faced the same problems: power consumption and scalability. As ETH got more popular, so did the complexity of the consensus mechanism. So did the demand for power for network maintenance. So did the electricity consumption and environmental damage.

All of that changed, as the so-called ETH 2.0 was introduced. The old PoW mechanism was replaced by the Proof-of-Stake. Instead of needing computers to solve an ever-increasing cryptographic puzzle, the new Proof-of-Stake operated on the logic that validators stake their "contribution" to validate new transactions and allow for the flow of funds on the network. What were the consequences to the environment? Immediately the need for electricity for Ethereum maintenance dropped by 99%. And with other coins based on the Ethereum platform, other smaller altcoins followed suit. Quite rightly, some critics will (or even should) insist that the greatest impact on the environment still comes from the most important and the most sought-after crypto: Bitcoin. Since I simply don't believe in collective responsibility and instead prefer individual action, I have a straightforward message. If miners are aiming to profit in today's market, they should consider becoming self-sufficient in energy, moving away from expensive traditional electricity sources. Instead of expensive regular electricity, why not go for solar panels or wind turbines? That's not just about saving money. It's an investment. Plus, there's often government help available. Being a miner—like in any business activity—requires an open mind and creativity. Think big. Connect the dots. It's all about making the right moves.

On the other hand, cryptocurrency mining seems to be a good way to make money for many more years. Continuously more people and big companies are getting interested in digital money. Despite daily fluctuations, cryptocurrency rates are climbing. Even with the upcoming "halving" event, which will reduce the Bitcoin reward for miners, I believe mining will still remain profitable. Moreover, even in countries where ecological awareness is high, and electricity prices are rising, governments and central banks have already been convinced that cryptocurrencies cannot be fought. They must be properly implemented and legally regulated. It's becoming clear that technologies like Blockchain are no longer seen as threats by those in power but rather as valuable allies. This shift in perception suggests a promising future for cryptocurrencies.

In its latest strategy, the European Union lists two important topics for miners and the entire digital currency sector. First, they're setting their sights on creating their own hubs for researching and making high-tech gear like semiconductors and circuits.[41] I feel like it's a big step toward Europe being self-reliant and not having to depend on other parts of the world for those critical technologies. It's a significant shift, especially considering that right now 70% of cryptocurrency mining is happening in China. But that's not all. The EU is also considering the introduction of a digital Euro.[42] It proves that European institutions do not want to fight cryptocurrencies but to properly benefit from them. And this is a good sign for the entire sector. It turns out that even with the changing situation and rising electricity prices, such "typical" topics as cryptocurrency mining can inspire you to look for your chance in the Blockchain sector. You just need to have an open mind—just or as much as that.

NOTES

1 https://news.bitcoin.com/satoshi-revolution-chapter-2-satoshi-libertarian-anarchist-part-4/
2 https://www.reuters.com/article/us-britain-bitcoin-lawsuit-idCAKBN2CT1VZ
3 This case concerned proceedings before the High Court in London. The operator of the website Bitcoin.org, trading under the pseudonym Cobra, was forced to stop hosting the Bitcoin white paper—https://www.coindesk.com/markets/2021/06/29/uk-court-orders-bitcoinorg-to-remove-white-paper-following-craig-wright-lawsuit/
4 J. Ocampo López (2007), *Grandes culturas indígenas de América*, Plaza & Janes Editores Colombia S.A.
5 K. Starr (1985), *Inventing the Dream*, Oxford University Press.
6 https://www.investopedia.com/terms/b/bitcoin-mining.asp
7 https://www.law.cornell.edu/uscode/text/18/471
8 https://bestlifeonline.com/20-crazy-af-facts-dollar-bills/
9 https://cryptonews.com/news/this-is-how-satoshi-nakamoto-defended-bitcoin-mining-convert-9640.htm
10 https://cointelegraph.com/news/bitcoin-network-node-count-sets-new-all-time-high
11 https://privacypros.io/btc-faq/how-many-btc-addresses
12 https://www.buybitcoinworldwide.com/how-many-bitcoins-are-there/
13 https://finance.yahoo.com/news/90-bitcoin-total-supply-mined-112422242.html

14 https://spectrum.ieee.org/bitcoin-mining
15 Network Difficulty, Blockchain.com, access: 16 sierpnia 2020.
16 https://spectrum.ieee.org/bitcoin-mining
17 https://www.politico.com/magazine/story/2018/03/09/bitcoin-mining-energy-prices-smalltown-feature-217230/
18 https://www.politico.com/magazine/story/2018/03/09/bitcoin-mining-energy-prices-smalltown-feature-217230/
19 https://www.businessinsider.com/remote-bitcoin-mining-expert-compass-crypto-investing-strategy-adam-gitzes-2021-8?r=US&IR=T
20 Ibid.
21 https://medium.com/currency-waves/bitcoin-and-the-concept-of-economic-freedom-25284f0c121e
22 https://www.reuters.com/world/china/china-central-bank-vows-crackdown-cryptocurrency-trading-2021-09-24/
23 https://www.businessinsider.com/remote-bitcoin-mining-expert-compass-crypto-investing-strategy-adam-gitzes-2021-8?r=US&IR=T
24 Ibid.
25 Ibid.
26 https://bitnodes.io/nodes/all/
27 https://www.themoscowtimes.com/2021/10/13/siberia-sounds-electricity-alarm-over-chinas-crypto-crackdown-a75286
28 https://www.rferl.org/a/bitcoin-blackouts-russian-cryptocurrency-miners-minting-millions-sucking-abkhazia-electricity-grid-dry/30968307.html
29 https://en.cryptonomist.ch/2020/12/13/abkhazia-crypto-mining-farm-georgia/
30 https://www.emerald.com/insight/content/doi/10.1108/OXAN-DB207664/full/html
31 Country Analysis Brief. Russia, U.S. Energy Information Administration, April of 2007, access: 3.03.2008.
32 U.W. Chohan (2018), Cryptocurrencies as Asset-Backed Instruments: The Venezuelan Petro, available on SSRN, https://ssrn.com/abstract=3119606
33 https://jpt.spe.org/gazprom-neft-mines-bitcoin-as-an-alternative-to-flaring-unwanted-gas
34 https://www.cnbc.com/2018/02/15/the-cheapest-and-most-expensive-countries-to-mine-bitcoin.html
35 https://300gospodarka.pl/300klimat/transformacja-energetyczna-polska-2020-forum-energii-spadek-wegiel
36 https://www.ogv.energy/news-item/russian-oil-drilling-giant-opens-a-crypto-mining-farm-run-on-gas-energy
37 https://www.financialexpress.com/market/bitcoins-dominance-in-global-crypto-market-contracts-share-in-total-crypto-mcap-down-by-41-this-year/2339086/
38 https://hbr.org/2021/05/how-much-energy-does-bitcoin-actually-consume
39 https://www.zdnet.com/article/exbibyte-frenzy-how-mining-for-chia-crypto-turned-me-into-a-storage-junkie/
40 https://www.newscientist.com/article/2278696-bitcoin-rival-chia-destroyed-hard-disc-supply-chains-says-its-boss/
41 https://sciencebusiness.net/news/chips-act-way-help-eu-boost-semiconductor-rd-and-manufacturing
42 https://forsal.pl/finanse/waluty/artykuly/8210114,cyfrowe-euro-mozliwe-ze-pojawi-sie-juz-w-2026-roku.html

Chapter 5

The cryptospeculation

I'm part of a unique generation, the last one to grow up just as the analog world was giving way to the digital age. My childhood was a mix of old and new. Playing outside with friends from the neighborhood and living in an apartment with my family. But also getting my first computer and Internet connection as I was graduating elementary school. This blend of experiences gave me a special view on how important our surroundings and friendships are for growing up. I observed how being part of a community significantly influences our development and helps us achieve both shared and individual goals. This process, known as socialization, involves absorbing and adopting the values of our community and integrating them into society. We learn a lot from the people we hang out with and from the community around us. This learning from others and fitting into society is what people call socialization.

What really catches my attention is how the Internet has changed the way people of my age make friends and come together. It's amazing to think about how people who have never met in person can organize big movements against politicians or kickstart companies online. A prime example of this was the widespread protest against the Anti-Counterfeiting Trade Agreement (ACTA). Almost overnight, so many people on the Internet joined together to fight against something that could limit our freedom online. By the end of 2011, there was a surge of digital unity, a collective standing in opposition to a proposal that threatened the whole Internet. After nine years, history has come full circle.

At the start of 2021, countries around the world were slowly recovering from the big economic hit of the coronavirus pandemic. The stock market, in contrast, was riding a wave of unprecedented prosperity. The recovery from the pandemic losses was swift and dramatic, with major stock indices like the S&P500 experiencing their fastest growth since World War II.[1] Investors, banks, and big funds were all eager to make up for their pandemic losses and were looking for sure wins in the stock market. But nobody expected that a group of regular Internet users, especially those on a controversial forum like Reddit, could disrupt the well-oiled machinery of stock market speculation. This unexpected twist in the financial narrative came from a Reddit community known as WallStreetBets. Operating in a domain

DOI: 10.1201/9781032621456-6

far removed from the traditional financial world, this group became a unique blend of an investment chat, meme exchange, and candid advice. Its members, often outsiders to the financial sector, shared strategies, exchanged tips, and reveled in the absurdity of stock market gambles. WallStreetBets was a place, where tales of fortunes made and lost on penny stocks (stocks worth mere cents) were commonplace. The language was raw and unfiltered, with members often referring to each other as "idiots," "monkeys," "degenerates," and "autistic morons."[2]

The WallStreetBets saga took a dramatic turn when they decided to support GameStop, a declining chain of brick-and-mortar video game stores. This unfolded when a Wall Street investment fund bet against GameStop by opening a short position, predicting the company's stock prices would plummet. This strategy involved borrowing GameStop shares to sell them at the current price, then buying them back cheaper after the predicted drop, pocketing the difference as profit. But WallStreetBets disrupted this plan. They started buying GameStop shares in large numbers, which drove the price up dramatically to $380.[3] This sudden rise in price caused huge losses for the investment fund that had bet against GameStop, with estimates of these losses going over $5 billion.[4]

This event sparked a big debate about how powerful Wall Street funds can influence the fate of companies and about market manipulation. However, the impact of WallStreetBets had its limits. When trading platform managers realized what was happening, they stopped the trading of GameStop shares, preventing any further actions like this in the future.[5] With sophisticated tools to monitor market movements and online communication, banks and large institutions could now anticipate and counteract the strategies of smaller, organized groups of investors like WallStreetBets. The significance of WallStreetBets' initiative lies in its uniqueness.[6] It was a rare instance where the collective power of individual, non-professional investors made a noticeable impact. It showed the power of a group of regular people coming together online to take on the big players in finance.

This chapter in financial history reflects a moment of madness and euphoria, marking a unique intersection of finance, social media, and collective action. Following the GameStop incident, WallStreetBets gained a huge number of new users, adding 2.4 million in just a week.[7] Each member shared a common goal: to find the next big play, the next financial adventure. This led them into the volatile world of cryptocurrency speculation or "cryptospeculation."

5.1 THE TRADING GAME

While WallStreetBets was focused on the GameStop stock situation, forum activists started playing the rise of the cryptocurrency Dogecoin (short: DOGE) on the side. Why did the "redditors" choose Dogecoin? Dogecoin was initially created as a kind of joke, inspired by a video game where animals live together in a city and go fishing. Its design featured a Shiba Inu dog, famous from Internet memes.[8] One of the creators of the cryptocurrency, Billy Markus, said he wanted to create a "cryptocurrency for sillies."[9]

The attention from WallStreetBets had an immediate impact: Dogecoin's value jumped by 250%.[10] This was just the beginning of its rise, especially as Elon Musk, the renowned entrepreneur behind Tesla, began to show interest in cryptocurrencies. Musk's actions were pivotal. First, he announced that Tesla would accept Bitcoin for its cars, and then he focused on Dogecoin. His involvement, characterized by sharing numerous Dogecoin memes and openly supporting DOGE, significantly boosted the cryptocurrency's popularity. Notably, even Mark Cuban, a famous American businessman who had previously dismissed cryptocurrencies, started endorsing Dogecoin.[11] Other celebrities, including rapper Snoop Dogg and Kiss guitarist Gene Simmons, also voiced their support.[12] These coordinated expressions of support on Twitter greatly amplified Dogecoin's value and visibility. Despite ongoing discussions about its actual value and usefulness, Dogecoin began to be seen as a major player in the cryptocurrency world.

The founders quickly distanced themselves from the project. When the capitalization of Dogecoin exceeded $90 billion, they withdrew from running the project. Jackson Palmer announced his resignation in very harsh words: "This [everything] is fucked up. I don't want to be the leader of a sect."[13]

As I write this, Dogecoin is the ninth-biggest cryptocurrency in terms of market size, with a whopping value of over $11 billion.[14] It's more volatile than most popular cryptocurrencies, with its price often swinging wildly based on seemingly trivial events. For instance, a tweet from Elon Musk featuring a Shiba Inu dog meme, or a comment from celebrity and adult film star Mia Khalifa about investing in Dogecoin, can send its value soaring.[15] This kind of speculation, fueled by celebrity endorsements, has pushed Dogecoin to incredible heights. Even though it goes against the core principles of Blockchain technology and decentralization (Figure 5.1). Interestingly, about 65% of all Dogecoins are held in just 85 wallets, and the biggest one among them holds 23% of all the tokens.[16]

The story I like most about Dogecoin is that of its project authors. When they launched it, the developers saw it as such a joke that they didn't even keep much for themselves, leaving only a small number of dogecoins worth around $5,000 at the time.[17] Billy Markus, one of the creators, even sold all his tokens to buy a used Honda Civic. Little did he know that years later, Dogecoin would become a sensation, thanks to Elon Musk, Reddit, and a growing fascination with the cryptocurrency. Today, the total value of Dogecoin could buy the entire Honda Motor Company.[18]

In 2023, Dogecoin surged over 30% after Twitter CEO Elon Musk changed the company's logo to a Shiba Inu image, the symbol of Dogecoin. Then, the $258 billion lawsuit appeared accusing Musk of manipulating Dogecoin's price, which skyrocketed over 36,000%.[19] Following the logo

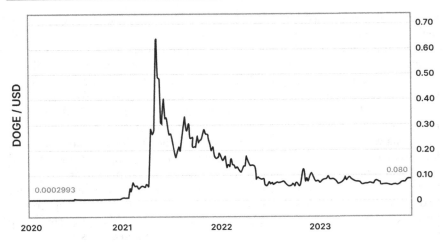

Figure 5.1 DOGE/USD exchange rate.

(*Source:* **Data from coinmarketcap.com.**)

change, Musk tweeted a related meme to his 133.5 million followers. The Shiba Inu image appeared for certain Twitter users, including website visitors. Musk's lawyers have downplayed his tweets as harmless, but his endorsement extends beyond social media. Tesla and the Boring Company, both associated with Musk, also feature in the lawsuit. What's more, Tesla announced in December 2021 that it would accept Dogecoin for some merchandise, leading to significant price increases following Musk's tweets about the decision.

How did a project, initially a mere joke, evolve into a genuine investment avenue for countless people globally? Why does the market support such high valuations for a cryptocurrency when nearly a third of its supply is concentrated in the hands of a single entity? It's evident that Dogecoin stands out as an exception in the crypto universe, which typically features cryptocurrencies with more complex technical foundations and business models. Yet, even considering Dogecoin's unique trajectory, it prompts us to ponder the broader logic of the cryptocurrency ecosystem. Is there a real benefit to the world in having more than 8,800 different cryptocurrencies?[20] Or does it largely boil down to the allure of making a quick profit in the ever-fluctuating world of cryptospeculation?

5.2 CRYPTOCURRENCY SPECULATORS: SAILING THE ROUGH WATERS

Cryptocurrencies, although increasingly more familiar to the general public, are not yet widely used in everyday money transactions. Mostly, people use them for speculation—guessing how their value will change over time.

This speculation involves buying different cryptocurrencies or trading them against regular currencies. The idea is to buy low and sell high, making a profit from these changes in value. This trading happens on platforms called cryptocurrency exchanges.

Today, all tokens and digital coins can be traded freely. On these exchanges, anyone with Internet access can buy any token, using either traditional currency or foundational cryptocurrencies like Bitcoin (BTC) and Ethereum (ETH). However, the journey to this point wasn't always smooth. The first recorded Bitcoin transaction occurred on October 12, 2009, less than a year after Satoshi Nakamoto released the project's code. In this transaction, 5,050 BTC was traded for $5.02 through PayPal, setting the first-ever rate for Bitcoin: 1,010 BTC equaled 1 dollar.

But where does the real-time rate that we see originate? It emerges from the collective decisions of thousands of cryptocurrency holders, as the market continuously assesses the value of these tokens. The price of a cryptocurrency is essentially a speculation on its future worth. Even though it may not be immediately apparent, the valuation of a currency like Bitcoin hinges on crucial questions: will BTC hold long-term value? Will it gain widespread acceptance as a means of exchange and a store of value? The more it is accepted and integrated into financial systems, the more its value will rise, be it against the dollar, euro, or any other traditional currency.

The challenge in assessing the value of cryptocurrencies lies in the uncertainty about their future acceptance. Predictions about their value are often based on past trends and the prevailing mood among investors and speculators. The reason cryptocurrency prices are so volatile is that they're heavily influenced by how much people believe in them as a viable alternative to traditional currencies.[21] Factors like media coverage, political statements, developments within the Blockchain world, and even tweets can significantly sway this belief.

To illustrate, let's revisit a key moment from mid-November 2013. During a US Senate press conference, then-Federal Reserve Chairman Ben Bernanke suggested that Bitcoin might have a bright future.[22] This statement had an immediate impact: within just one day, Bitcoin's value shot up from about $440 to $795. Although there was a correction the next day, with the rate dropping back somewhat, it wasn't long before the price began climbing again. By the end of November and the start of December 2013, Bitcoin had broken the $1,000 mark for the first time ever.

Such extreme fluctuations are uncommon in other forms of investment, bringing with them a high level of risk. This risk is particularly relevant for those investing in cryptocurrencies through speculation and day trading—constantly monitoring the market and making rapid decisions based on the ever-changing rates. I will explore the best strategies for investing in cryptocurrencies in more detail in later parts of this book. For now, it's crucial to grasp the basics of this economic system I'm describing.

5.3 KNOWLEDGE GAP IN THE MARKET

When we look past how emotionally charged the world of cryptocurrency can be, there's something interesting, and a bit sad, happening. Recent stats have shown a funny yet troubling trend. Believe it or not, about one out of every three people who invest in cryptocurrencies like Bitcoin really don't get how it all works. They're putting money into something they don't fully understand. In fact, most investors are in the dark about what actually makes their digital money valuable. It's only a small group, around 17%, who really know what they're doing with crypto and grasp its true potential.[23]

Why is the low level of knowledge about cryptocurrencies among investors such a problem? I'm not talking about the security of their assets; what they do with their money is their private business. I'm looking more broadly at the issue of limited understanding not among ordinary breadwinners of the society but about the main influencers and ambassadors of "crypto" in the economy. The drastic ignorance of these people contrasts with the message that users and leaders of cryptocurrency projects are sending to the world of traditional finance. I know this from my own activity in the Blockchain sector, as well as from the communication I observe among the most ardent cryptocurrency traders, who often have a significant degree of contempt for traditional assets and conventional finance.

This is a shockingly heavy contrast. On one hand, they're supposed to be the experts in this new digital money world, but on the other hand, they're not really showing they know their stuff. It's a problem because they're the ones the rest of the world is looking at to understand cryptocurrencies, and if they don't get it, it's like the blind leading the blind.

In the world of crypto, it's surprising how often the big bosses don't really get what they're doing. That issue often comes down to them not knowing enough about the tech or the money side of things, or sometimes both. A prime example of such disconnect can be seen in the recent developments involving Changpeng Zhao, the former CEO of Binance, the world's largest cryptocurrency exchange. According to Bloomberg Billionaires Index, Zhao was ranked the 69th-richest person in the world, and richest Canadian overall, with a net worth estimated at $23 billion as of November 2023.[24] However, his financial success and industry influence recently took a hit. Zhao and his company, Binance, admitted to breaking money laundering laws. This led to a massive $4.3 billion fine, marking a significant downturn for a key figure in the crypto world. Zhao's case shows that even the top people in crypto can struggle with the complex rules and technology of their industry.

Zhao had previously shown difficulty understanding the field of crypto. In an interview with Bloomberg, Zhang drew a comparison between the fluctuations of cryptocurrencies with the behavior of regular stock markets.

He didn't ignore the ups and downs in the crypto world, but he completely whitewashed it. The CEO said: "Um, and actually Bitcoin is probably less volatile than a similar-sized asset like an Apple stock or even a Tesla stock."[25] But the thing is, that's not really accurate. If you check the facts, Bitcoin is actually way more unstable than most well-known stocks. It's twice as unstable as NASDAQ, the technology sector index. It's also 2.5 times more volatile than the general stock market index SP500 and 10 times more volatile than the EUR/USD rate.[26]

In fact, to assess words like those spoken by the CEO of Binance, you don't even have to conduct advanced financial analysis. Just type into a search engine: "stock AAPL" and "TSLA price." Then, compare those prices to the value of a cryptocurrency, like Bitcoin (BTC/USD). You can't deceive the truth and the laws of economics—trading cryptocurrencies carries enormous risk. But here's the catch: with higher risk, there's a chance for higher rewards. That's why people are drawn to it. It's surprising that not many people question the statements made by the head of the world's biggest crypto exchange. They should, considering how risky that business can be. But the potential for big profits can be tempting, and that's what keeps the game going.

I believe that the lack of understanding of the challenges embedded in the world of Blockchain and cryptocurrencies—both from a technology and economic perspective—is the main barrier that needs to be overcome for these solutions to become more present in our lives. I'm an entrepreneur in the IT industry. I run a venture house specializing in Blockchain solutions. I'm aware of the complexity of software production topics, especially in such a demanding sector. I operate in the Blockchain industry, implementing programming projects for my clients, from banks to startups. On the other hand, I completed economic studies at a university at the top of the global rankings. Approaching the topic of cryptocurrencies from these two sides—economics and technology—I see what a significant part of Blockchain sector participants lack. There should be a synergy between understanding technological solutions and economic impact.

5.3.1 Decentralized finance explained: Blockchain 101

Bitcoin and the early "altcoins" (alternative cryptocurrencies) were essentially digital cash. Think of them as part of a huge, decentralized computer network. They were part of a vast, decentralized computer network, utilizing a technology called the Blockchain. That technology enabled people to transfer money, eliminating the need for banks or intermediaries. Such a system, termed peer-to-peer, involves direct dealings between individuals. Holders of the first cryptocurrencies still use systems that allow them to exchange complex strings of numbers and letters—and that's it. But what does such an exchange look like in practice?

Bitcoin transactions are like messages that are digitally signed using cryptography tools and then sent to the entire Bitcoin network for verification. Transaction information is public and can be found in a digital ledger known as the "Blockchain." The history of each Bitcoin transaction can be traced all the way back to the point where the Bitcoins were first produced or "mined."[27]

Bitcoin transactions are like sending secure digital messages. You use a special online signature, made with cryptography, to prove it's really from you. Those messages go to everyone in the Bitcoin network, like posting on a big public board. Every transaction is visible in a digital ledger called the Blockchain, like a big book that everyone can see. Blockchain shows the history of every Bitcoin from when it was first made (or mined) to now. It's a way to keep track of all the Bitcoin movements.

To send Bitcoin, a user needs access to the public and private keys associated with the amount of Bitcoin they want to send. When we say someone "owns" Bitcoin, what we really mean is that this person has access to a "pair of keys" made up of two elements:

1. The public key (wallet address)—your Bitcoin wallet address works like an email address or a bank account number. It's a unique combination of letters and numbers. You share this with others when you want to receive Bitcoin. Often, it's turned into a QR code, making it easier to share and scan when someone wants to send you Bitcoin.
2. The unique private key (password)—a special password that proves you own the Bitcoin in your wallet. Like a key to a safe, it allows you to send your Bitcoin to others. It's crucial to keep this private and secure to protect your Bitcoin. This is like the key to your Bitcoin safe.

A Bitcoin address is alphanumeric—it contains both letters and numbers.[28] It always starts with 1, 3, or bc1. For example, it might look like this:

3FZbgi29cpjq2GjdwV8eyHuJJnkLtktZc5

Such an address in the form of a QR code would look like this:

Public keys are like an open book on the Internet. They let anyone see how much money a wallet has. Take this example: an address shows it has 0.06525316 BTC in it right now.[29] Since it started, a total of 282 transactions have been made involving that wallet. It has received a total of 2.70421320 BTC and has sent a total of 2.63896004 BTC. You can see all of it on the Blockchain, just by looking it up online with terms like *check Bitcoin address*. But, knowing whose money it is? That's a secret. You'd need to obtain the private key that secures wallets against potential theft.

How can you obtain your own Bitcoin address? I think a good analogy can be found in the world of consumer banking that we're all familiar with. When we decide to open an account, we have to go to a bank. The first question the customer service representative will ask us is about the currency in which the account should be maintained—whether it should be a PLN account, a EUR account, or perhaps a USD account. The same will be true of the software or exchange, which creates a separate wallet address for each cryptocurrency: different for BTC, LTC, ETH, and all other cryptocurrencies. Then, after carrying out the necessary verifications, the bank assigns an account number generated according to a specific algorithm. Today, bank account numbers are assigned according to the International Bank Account Number (IBAN) standard, where the first two letters indicate the country code (e.g., PL for Poland), followed by the individual numbers in the account number. This is similar to how the Bitcoin system works, in which a chosen cryptocurrency exchange or software supporting cryptocurrency wallets automatically generates the user's Bitcoin address. The user can save their public key to share it with other users and receive incoming transfers. However, it's crucial to remember the private key (password) to prevent anyone from breaking into the wallet. It's just like in familiar electronic banking when we send our IBAN number to various institutions or friends whom we lent money to during a night out, while the password for online banking is one of the most closely guarded pieces of information for any responsible person.

When you want to transfer Bitcoin, you have to "log in" to your wallet using your private key. Just like when sending money the usual way, you need to tell your wallet how much Bitcoin you want to send and where it's going—provide the recipient's address (Figure 5.2).

At this point, we're shifting from tech talk to money matters. Bitcoin's way of moving money has two big issues. First, it's quite hard to understand. Second is its singular focus: Bitcoin's network is solely dedicated to transferring money, without any additional functionalities. Is that a problem? Let's use an analogy. Picture a bank charging lots of money for every transfer (regardless of its value). Their electronic banking system only allows you to send transfers to unidentified recipients in the form of complex strings of letters and characters. Besides, it offers nothing: no possibility to top up your phone, no customer services, no extra features. Would it be reasonable to use such a solution?

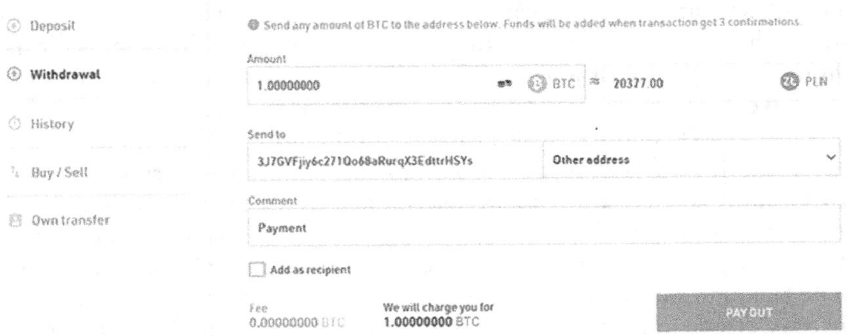

Figure 5.2 The transfer interface of the Zonda cryptocurrency exchange (formerly BitBay).

(Source: Zondacrypto website. Available at: https://zondacrypto.com/en/home. Used with courtesy.)[30]

In addition to the limited functionalities, Bitcoin has a few issues. One big problem is that it takes about 10 minutes to send Bitcoin, and it can cost a lot, even up to $60. The price is way more expensive than what banks usually charge for sending money. People say you shouldn't compare apples to oranges, but let's compare Bitcoin to regular banking anyway. Banks and fintech companies also need time to process transfers. In Poland, where banking services are really good, there's a cheap and popular service called Express Elixir. It costs only 4 to 5 PLN (Polish currency; $1—$2).[31] Poland was one of the first countries in Europe to experiment with such a solution when Bitcoin was getting popular in 2012.[32] Many banks there offer it.

However, nothing and nobody is perfect. As someone who lived in New York and started a business, I saw how US banks work. Transferring money between dollar accounts usually costs $25–30. Some banks also charge about $15 to receive money.[33] That's why many Americans still use checks. In fact, 60% of money transfers in the United States are done with paper checks.[34]

Under such conditions, cryptocurrency transfers seem like the perfect solution and a valuable innovation. But not entirely. But it's not the top choice. Regular banking is pricey, so people are turning to fintech apps like Venmo, Wise, PayPal, and MoneyGram. Why do Americans use fintech applications instead of cryptocurrencies? First, token transfers are just not widespread enough. Aside from cryptocurrency price fluctuations (and thus the unpredictability of transfer fees), I believe that cryptocurrencies haven't yet reached the necessary critical mass in the general population. While 95% of US households have a regular bank account, only 17% have Bitcoin wallets.[35]

Second, let's say you and your friends agree to use Bitcoin to pay for a fun night out. But, in real life, you can't just stop using banks. You need them for many things like paying bills, loans, and taxes. Those places don't accept Bitcoin. Corporations, banks, and the government don't like Bitcoin. They might not trust it, have rules against it, or find it too unpredictable. That's why, even though Bitcoin is cool, we can't use it for everything every day.

5.3.2 If not Bitcoin, then what?

Bitcoin faced some tough challenges right from its early days. It had deep-rooted problems and fixing them wasn't easy. That realization sparked a change in the crypto community. They knew it was time for new solutions. Inspired by Bitcoin's creator, Satoshi Nakamoto, they began creating new projects. The innovations weren't just copies of Bitcoin; they had their own unique ways of working. That led to the birth of altcoins—a new breed of digital currencies. Each altcoin is trying to compete with Bitcoin, aiming to outdo the original in the fast-evolving world of cryptocurrency.

Litecoin, abbreviated as LTC, was a big early effort to improve Bitcoin better. It was founded in 2011 by Charles Lee, a former Google engineer. Lee, who once tried hacking Chrome OS, built Litecoin in his free time. People quickly called it an "improved Bitcoin."[36] For a long time, it was the second-biggest digital currency, until Ethereum (ETH) came along. Litecoin was like Bitcoin's silver to Bitcoin's gold. The idea was Bitcoin would be for saving money and Litecoin for everyday spending.

In technical matters, LTC has significantly surpassed Bitcoin. It uses a different kind of computer puzzle for confirming transactions. Bitcoin really pushes computers hard, but Litecoin is more about using the computer's memory. This makes things faster—a transaction takes only 2.5 minutes with Litecoin, compared to 10 minutes for Bitcoin. The creators of Litecoin wanted it to be useful for everyday people, not just those investing or mining digital currencies. There's also a math side to it. There will be way more Litecoin units than Bitcoin units—84 million versus 21 million.[37] This means there's less rush to buy Litecoin because there are more chances to get some.

Programmers and cryptographers experimented with different types of security, token economy solutions, and transaction mechanisms. For example, PeerCoin was the first to introduce a system of new block verification to be added to the network, which greatly improved the scalability of the cryptocurrency system.[38] Monero provided a higher level of anonymity; unlike the mechanism of pseudonyms assigned to Bitcoin users, the Monero system used a combination of signatures from groups of users that could not be identified as individual persons.[39]

Finally, Ethereum appeared on the cryptocurrency market. The versatile platform for decentralization of money flows, contracts, and databases was created by Vitalik Buterin. The cool thing about Ethereum is it's two things in one: it's a type of digital money (cryptocurrency) and a place where people can make their own apps that are decentralized. Previous Blockchain projects did not have such power.

For example, the basic role of Bitcoin is to serve as a digital currency and store of value. However, it uses a lot of computer power. All those computers work non-stop—they use as much electricity as big countries like Belgium or Finland.[40] Now, what if we could do more with this power? Besides just making e-money, we can add cool things, such as digital contracts, databases, and decentralized apps. And here, in my opinion, lies the greatest value of Ethereum. It's another kind of cryptocurrency, like Bitcoin, but with extra features. Ethereum lets people build a whole new Blockchain ecosystem. Sure, there were some earlier initiatives with Bitcoin, but Ethereum really kicked things off. Vitalik Buterin gave the world a universal platform for—as he himself emphasized—"decentralizing everything."[41] Ethereum's not just about money, it's about changing how we do things online.

Especially after the launch of Ethereum, the number of altcoins began to grow—and there were dozens of them. If it wasn't about technical issues, it was about economic and legal solutions. Looking at the fluctuations in the exchange rates of existing tokens, the Tether cryptocurrency team created the first stable coin—a digital currency linked to the dollar, for example, whose exchange rate was to be stable. Ripple, on the other hand, was trying to create a mechanism similar to Bitcoin, but to completely reverse its assumptions—to provide banks with a safe cryptocurrency XRP for direct exchange between financial institutions.[42]

The introduction of the first altcoins in 2011 and 2012, created a massive speculative market. While some altcoins had real value and purpose, many others didn't offer anything new or useful. The Blockchain community soon started calling those less useful ones "shitcoins."

A lot of tokens are pretty much worthless. Nobody's buying or selling them anymore. That means they lost their trading volume. CoinMarketCap has data on 8,800 different cryptocurrencies. I looked at ones that aren't traded regularly. Guess what? Out of all of them, 1,815, which is 21%, aren't being traded at all. They're just sitting there, not moving. If you have one of these, selling is tough. You have to wait and hope someone wants to buy that kind of ghost token.

In my opinion, people want to make new types of Bitcoin for two main reasons. First, they desire to try out new ideas in the world of Blockchain. Second, the original Bitcoin isn't perfect. It has some technical problems and economic issues. That's why every month, people create new altcoins. As of August 2023, there were more than 9,300 altcoins[43] (Figure 5.3). Many of

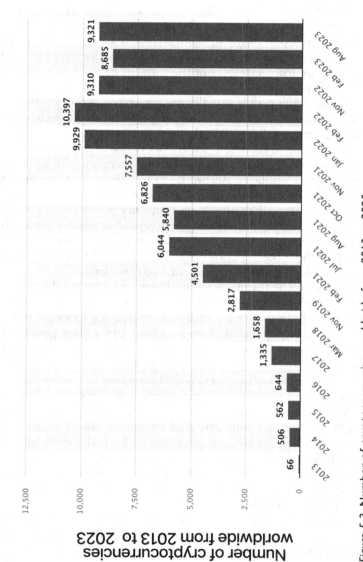

Figure 5.3 Number of cryptocurrencies worldwide from 2013 to 2023.
(Source: Data from Statista).[44]

them arouse either little or zero interest. But some are really popular among investors in them and the Blockchain community.

Tech experiments and their creators deserve recognition. However, the crypto market has too many altcoins and tokens. Most lack solid tech or business reasons. Why do I say so? Because those projects are too convergent. They target the same customer and perform the same tasks. Even big crypto projects usually differ only in small technical aspects or marketing. Unlike startups that get funding from traditional investors (from banks in the form of credit or from investors in the form of capital), many crypto creators skip market research.

They should ask: "Will people actually use my cryptocurrency?" But that step is often missed. I've seen many white papers that make assumptions instead of investigating real demand. Without strong research, those new cryptocurrencies are unlikely to become a "killer" of existing cryptocurrencies.

Let me give you a vivid example that shows the overgrowth of form over content in the "crypto" industry. According to UN statistics, there are 180 traditional currencies in the world.[45] That's a lot for the number of countries on the globe, 195. It seems like almost one currency per country, yet there are regions where multiple currencies are accepted at once—mainly for practical or political reasons. If you do the math, it means around 40 million people use each of those regular currencies. That's a lot of people relying on one currency. So, where do crypto tokens fit into this picture?

When it comes to niche tokens, we don't know an exact number of their user base. However, let's give them a chance and assume that their owners generally believe in the sense of their existence. Now, if we zoom out to look at the entire cryptocurrency world, there are about 295 million people who own some form of cryptocurrency. Bitcoin and Ethereum are the most popular ones, due to their market share. That means that there are only 31,720 users per cryptocurrency. Such a system is unsustainable, as consuming huge amounts of energy for a handful of people simply doesn't pay off. There's no doubt that the majority of token holders bought them for speculation, so someone might consider the comparison of currencies and their users disproportionate. However, cryptocurrencies aim to be real money systems. For some reason, Satoshi Nakamoto wrote in the title of his article: Bitcoin: A Peer-to-Peer Electronic Cash System. Cash system—not a risky object of unlimited speculation. So, we can see a disconnection between how cryptocurrencies are being used now and what they were meant to be.

However, we can refine this analysis. Let's move away from the assumption that cryptocurrencies are an autonomous monetary system. Let's assume (according to the data from 2021) that they should rather be considered a speculative asset. Is there still a justification for there being 6,800 of them on the market? For example, there are 109,000 companies in the world whose shares (equities) can be bought on financial markets. Their total value in dollars is $37.7 trillion.[46] So, we can assume that a public corporation is subject to the same valuation mechanism as tokens of a cryptocurrency project—which is a reasonable assumption, as in both cases we are talking about publicly available markets, which anyone can enter to freely buy the appropriate investment instrument (of course, it's worth remembering that the whole investment process in the case of cryptocurrencies is much simpler). Comparing these two markets, we can see that the average capitalization in the "crypto" market is higher than in the case of stocks. This is not necessarily a good sign, as it may indicate an overvaluation of the market, especially in the context of small, niche, and practically unused tokens bought only for speculative purposes.

Therefore, I see two possible trends: either millions more people will be convinced to use cryptocurrencies, to find a justification for specialized, niche altcoins, or these altcoins will collapse, and a few, maybe a dozen, basic cryptocurrencies will monopolize the market. Of course, this second option seems much more likely. Such a change requires time, though. Currently, the average cryptocurrency user has significantly more projects than the logic of actual utility would justify. That's why I think that niche altcoins are simply a high-risk experiment today. This risk makes the potential gain so large. Cryptocurrencies, especially altcoins, are a great way to speculate. It's true that many of the digital currencies might fail in the short term, maybe in a month, a year, or a few years. However, keeping an eye on the market right now is a smart move. There's still potential to make money, especially in the current period. So, even with the risks, the world of cryptocurrencies remains an exciting and potentially profitable area to explore (Table 5.1).

5.3.3 Cryptocurrencies explained

I talk with clients a lot, and I've noticed they don't really get how cryptocurrencies work. They're familiar with big terms like *decentralization, anonymity*, and *cryptography*—the basic keywords linked to the world of crypto. But I realized how much that basic idea twists what people think about

Table 5.1 Comparison of global stock and cryptocurrency markets

	Global stock market (equities)	Global cryptocurrency market
Number of Available Investment Assets	108,790 publicly available corporations worldwide, according to market data provider Refinitiv (formerly Thomson Reuters)[47]	6,826 cryptocurrency projects according to Statista[48], including 2309 "dead projects" according to Coinopsy[49] 4,517 active projects
Total Value of Investment Assets	$37,700,000,000,000 In 2020 according to Statista[50]	$2,600,000,000,000 as of October 18, 2021[51]
Average Market Capitalization per Asset	$345,966,780	$575,603,277

Blockchain. That hit me during one particular class at college. It was different from the amazing ones I usually had. It was a course about coming up with creative business ideas, but it was taught over at the art department. The professor was trying to teach us about providing new ideas. And he brought up Blockchain as an example. But he didn't talk about it like a computer nerd would. Instead, he called it just a buzzword. He even put a cringeworthy emphasis on the pause between the words—"buzz ... word"—to highlight that it creates a buzz in society.

Presenting a technology with as much potential as Blockchain and "crypto" generally in such a superficial way is not only incorrect but incredibly risky for our pockets. After all, you can't build an investment strategy on ideology and keywords. In my view, it's not the unpredictability of cryptocurrencies that's the problem but the lack of proper theoretical preparation that leads people to make two mistakes. They lose on this market because they either miss out on the opportunities provided by cryptocurrencies (and therefore don't make money, invoking the argument of opportunity cost) or make suboptimal investment decisions that cost them a lot of money. In one case, the mistake is ignoring cryptocurrencies in financial decisions, and in the other, it's impulsive actions in the market.

I've been in the crypto industry for years, and I've seen the whole investment process change substantially. Buying crypto is far more simple now. Back in 2016, when I was in the Emirates, getting Bitcoin was tough. I used a website called LocalBitcoins. First, I had to message someone to buy Bitcoin with dirhams—local currency. Then, I had to withdraw cash from an ATM. After a few messages on WhatsApp, I met up with a guy from Nigeria right in the city. I gave him the cash, and he transferred Bitcoin to my wallet through an app on his phone. Now, the whole process is way easier and safer. You can use big, trusted, and professional exchanges like Coinbase or Gemini. What's cool is they often have bonuses for new users. They add a little money to your Bitcoin wallet when you start. That way starting a crypto journey seems more appealing to the newcomers.

It's much easier to gain knowledge about finance, cryptocurrencies, and the mechanisms behind them. There are lots of resources nowadays. For example, Coursera, a big online learning site, has over 330 courses about finance, which are great for beginners. They cover all sorts of finance topics, even cryptocurrencies. That means anyone can start learning about investing, no matter the regular stocks or digital currencies like Bitcoin. There's also a ton of super helpful videos on YouTube. Both beginners and advanced users often use Twitter and Reddit to follow cryptocurrency and trading experts. I do my own research every day. For instance, I can recommend the VeeFriends group, run by famous entrepreneur and business influencer Gary Vaynerchuk.[52] For those who find certain parts of cryptocurrency a bit tricky, there are tools like trading bots. They can do some of the work for you. Also, there are online communities, like eToro, where people share tips and help each other. With all the available possibilities entering the cryptocurrency market is way easier than—as I experienced—it was a few years back.

Although this basic market knowledge is becoming more widespread, on the principle of "I know what to do on the market, not how it works"—I still believe that basic financial knowledge is necessary for success in speculating on cryptocurrencies. I learned a lot from my studies at New York University and from my own work. That knowledge gives me the confidence to make smart decisions in the fast-moving world of cryptocurrencies. Cryptocurrencies have a lot in common with the traditional Forex market. In Forex, people trade currencies from different countries, as well as special contracts that are linked to the currency trades. Those contracts are kind of like bets on what will happen with the currencies. Most of Forex trading involves what we call fiat currencies. They are just regular money, like dollars or euros, that aren't backed by physical things like gold. Instead, we trust the government that issues them. It's all based on an agreement among people. For example, everyone agrees that the Federal Reserve System is in charge of the USD and gives it its value.

When most countries issue their currencies, they rely on trust in the issuer (the central bank), a fact well-known to the market. The market generally accepts the agreed-upon value of money, acknowledging that one currency can be exchanged for another. For instance, when Poles and Americans engage in a currency transaction, they trust that the National Bank of Poland (NBP) can issue the zloty just as the Federal Reserve (Fed) can issue the dollar.

This trust is not just about the paper or coins; it's about believing that these institutions can back up the value of that money. This system works because everyone agrees on the value of the money and trusts that it can be exchanged. Without this trust, the whole system of money wouldn't work. It's like an unspoken agreement between countries, banks, and people that keeps the economy moving. The trust in money and its value is what makes international trade and currency exchange possible.

People need both currencies because they facilitate important activities such as trading, investing overseas, managing accounting settlements, and conducting further investments. As a result, they create a pair of fiat currencies: the Polish zloty (PLN) and the US dollar (USD), denoted as USD/PLN. Their value against each other is variable, which is defined as the exchange rate. As there are hundreds of such pairs, there are numerous exchange rate combinations that can be used to speculate and make money. For example, if Americans announce strategic partnerships with Poland, American investors will suddenly increase their demand for the zloty. Its exchange rate against the dollar will rise, or in scientific terms, it will appreciate. More dollars will be needed to buy a specific amount in zlotys. If you had a thousand zlotys in your account, you would be able to buy more dollars. But, if Americans stop liking Polish projects, the zloty's value will drop, and the dollar will get stronger against it. In the USD/PLN pair, the zloty becomes less valuable, and the dollar gets more valuable. That's how the money's worth can go up or down, affecting how much you can get when you exchange them.

Cryptocurrencies, like Bitcoin or Ethereum, are made and shared differently than fiat currencies, but the exchange market and rates work the same way. As you know from previous chapters, no institution is behind the cir-culation of Bitcoin or Ethereum, only the Blockchain community. However, the end result is exactly the same as in the traditional Forex market. You can exchange them, just like you would with dollars or euros. What's really interesting is that you can trade cryptocurrencies not only with regular money but also with other digital currencies. Therefore, crypto-crypto, as well as crypto-fiat pairs, are formed. Such a mix of options makes the world of cryptocurrencies full of possibilities for making money, just like in tradi-tional investing and trading.

The similarities between the cryptocurrency market and the standard Forex (FX) market don't end there. Forex has top currency pairs, similar to cryptos. The most traded pair is EUR/USD, making up about 20% of Forex trades.[53] Base currencies are more popular and credible than others, as they account for most international transactions. We're talking about dollars (USD), euros (EUR), Swiss francs (CHF), British pounds (GBP), and Japanese yen (JPY). Why are they so popular? Well, they come from some of the world's largest economies. Plus, they're seen as "safe havens"—really dependable currencies, which will keep your assets safe.

Swiss francs have always attracted investors because they could take advantage of a safe banking sector in Switzerland and even place money earned not necessarily legally. After all, nobody in a Swiss bank would inquire about the origin of the funds. The pound is used as a base cur-rency because it was the primary means of settlement in the 19th and early 20th centuries. It gained immense popularity and a strong reputa-tion because the British Empire covered one-fourth of the Earth's surface, so the pound was needed for large-scale trade in an increasingly global-izing world.[54]

Cryptocurrencies are a new kind of money, similar to the traditional money trading system known as Forex. They've been around for a short time, less than 15 years. In that period, Bitcoin emerged as the leader. It was the very first of its kind, setting the trend for others. Everyone talks about Bitcoin, showing its huge influence, even among those who aren't into Blockchain technology. Bitcoin's market capitalization—total value—which adds up all the bitcoins people have, is enormous. Bitcoin's price in US dollars (BTC/USD) is the most watched number in the crypto world. It's like a bridge between the new crypto money and the regular money we use every day. Following Bitcoin, Ether paired with the US dollar (ETH/USD) is also important. It's the second big player in the crypto market. To under-stand the whole cryptocurrency market, watch two main pairs: Ethereum (ETH) and Bitcoin (BTC). They are the biggest and most important. ETH and BTC are popular and easy to start with. They're great for beginners in digital currency investing—you can start with basic knowledge of the market.

Forex involves the basic currency pairs; however, the unrestricted exchange of currencies between most countries offers the opportunity to trade custom pairs as well. More experienced investors can create their own pairs and speculate on exchange rates even for the most niche, unpopular currencies. The world of cryptocurrencies works in a similar way. If you're up for a challenge, you can start by joining a crypto exchange. The place where you can find not just the usual cryptocurrencies like Bitcoin but also some rare ones. The exciting part is you can buy those unique cryptocurrencies and trade them directly with others. You don't even need to turn them into regular money like dollars first. But remember, that kind of trading is riskier than just sticking with well-known cryptocurrencies like Bitcoin or Ethereum. Why? Because the lesser-known cryptos don't get much attention, which makes them really unpredictable. They might be hard to sell, or "liquidate," because there aren't many people interested in buying or selling them. That's especially true for the smallest cryptos. Sometimes, finding someone to buy them can be really tough.

Let's get back to conventional finance to illustrate how you can introduce custom currency pairs to your portfolio and how that changes your exposure to risk. In setting your positions on the Forex market, imagine combining New Zealand dollars with British pounds. Sounds unusual, right? It's possible, but it's risky. Why? Since very few traders trade such unusual pairs on the Forex market, the transaction volume is much smaller, resulting in lower liquidity and higher risk. However, more risk could mean greater reward. It's like the saying: "No risk, no glory."

The similarities between crypto markets and Forex become clear if you compare pairs of different currencies—traditional and digital (Table 5.2). Let's wrap up our comparison of cryptocurrencies and Forex. The focus is on the way they're managed and the risks for investors. Both markets

Table 5.2 Comparison of forex and cryptocurrency market

	Forex market	Cryptocurrency market
Main pairs	Major world currencies: US dollar, euro, British pound, Swiss franc, yen Major currency pairs: EUR/USD, USD/JPY, GBP/USD, USD/CHF	Major cryptocurrencies: Bitcoin (BTC), Ethereum (ETH) Pairs of major cryptocurrencies with the US dollar: BTC/USD, ETH/USD
Custom pairs	Regional pairs, e.g., the dollar and the euro (USD/DDK) or Swedish krona and Danish krone (SEK/DKK) Any pairs created by Forex traders	Pairs of major cryptocurrencies with local cryptocurrencies (similar to BTC/USD and ETH/USD, as the movement of the cryptocurrency market is usually larger than forex market movement): e.g., BTC/SEK, ETH/DDK "Crypto"—"crypto" pairs, e.g., BTC/ETH

have little regulation. Each country has its rules, but no big international institution watches over them. Even the International Monetary Fund (IMF) doesn't influence the daily fluctuations of the so-called eurodollar (the EUR/USD pair). So, what does affect it? All sorts of global events play a role. Deals between American and European companies, government actions worldwide, even a simple tweet can make an impact. For instance, something as trivial as a tweet from Donald Trump criticizing European Union's economic policies can influence the market. Cryptocurrencies act similarly. Their value can swing based on investor confidence, people's view of the Blockchain industry, and tweets from influential figures. Elon Musk's tweet about Bitcoin caused its value to drop by 5%. But when he said Tesla would accept Bitcoin again, its value shot up by 8%.[55] In July 2017, Trump criticized the strong dollar policy, and the euro weakened against the American currency to its lowest level in two years. In both markets, big names and global events can cause quick and significant changes.[56]

Cryptocurrencies and Forex are similar, but they're not the same. Both are about money, but they work in different ways. If you want to navigate them effectively, you have to know the basic laws governing the money flow between currency systems, investors, traders, and financial institutions. I believe the primary difference between Forex and the "crypto" market lies in the knowledge an efficient trader must possess. The Forex market relies heavily on political situations, the interplay between economies, and the analysis of international business. In the case of cryptocurrencies, it is more about understanding the technological solutions behind them. Each digital coin or token has its own unique setup. Knowing how they work and what makes them different is key. So, if you want to be good at trading cryptocurrencies, you need to understand how Blockchain technology works and how it affects the economy.

Having established that "crypto" and tokens are interconnected and that selected pairs can be created, we need to discuss the final fundamental element of this cryptocurrency puzzle. Since Bitcoin is the largest cryptocurrency, the performance of other cryptocurrencies like Ethereum, Binance Coin, Cardano, or Litecoin depends on the BTC/USD rate. To a large extent, all cryptocurrencies follow Bitcoin, the largest cryptocurrency. This market trend is due to the correlation between all cryptocurrencies. This is easily understood with specific examples.

The crypto world is complex, but it's easier to apprehend when we see how everything is connected. Tokens and cryptocurrencies are the pieces of a larger puzzle. Each piece, or token, can be matched with another, creating pairs. Pairing is a fundamental concept in the crypto world. What's fascinating is how those cryptocurrencies are intertwined with Bitcoin. Their value and market behavior often depend on the BTC/USD rate. Because of its size and influence, Bitcoin's performance is crucial—where Bitcoin goes, others tend to follow. That includes well-known names like Ethereum, Binance

Coin, Cardano, and Litecoin. It's not just a coincidence. It's a market trend driven by the interconnectedness of those digital currencies. By looking at specific examples, this concept becomes even clearer.

Let's take data from a year-long period, starting from mid-October 2020. In Table 5.3, you can see how individual cryptocurrency pairs are linked. The correlation between two financial instruments is measured by a specific coefficient, which can range from −1 to 1. In cryptocurrencies, situations where this coefficient approaches −1 are rare. This would mean that an increase in the value of one cryptocurrency leads to a decrease in another. This usually doesn't happen. People generally buy more cryptocurrencies, rather than exchange one for another. Hence, in the world of Blockchain finance, correlations are positive. If Ethereum gains, Bitcoin probably will follow suit, and vice versa.

All values are relatively high, often exceeding 0.8. In financial theory, such correlations are considered strong. The cryptocurrency market generally moves in the same direction. That's why it's so difficult to spread out your risk by investing in different cryptocurrencies. If one drops in value, others likely will too. It's tough to pick different tokens that don't move the same way. Investing in cryptocurrencies is risky, because you can't easily avoid losses.

The movement of Bitcoin, and all other cryptocurrencies, exhibits a common trend. However, there are deviations in rates, time-shifted corrections, and advanced movements that day traders strive to predict. For example, from January to May 2021, Ethereum grew much faster than Bitcoin. While BTC doubled its value in the first quarter of 2021, Ethereum made an even more impressive charge, from about $700 at the beginning of the year to over $4,000 in early May. In hindsight, it's easy to identify which cryptocurrency should have been bought. The real challenge, however, lies in accurate prediction and the right investment strategy. Speculative success often depends on luck, as evidenced by the stories of many traders and unusual token price movements. But with the right combination of all these factors, cryptocurrencies still offer the potential for significant earnings (Figure 5.4).

Table 5.3 Correlation between pairs of selected leading cryptocurrencies in the period X 2020–X 2021

	Litecoin (LTC)	Cardano (ADA)	Bitcoin (BTC)	Binance Coin (BNB)	Ethereum (ETH)
Ethereum (ETH)	0.71	0.95	0.73	0.90	–
Binance Coin (BNB)	0.80	0.85	0.76	–	0.90
Bitcoin (BTC)	0.87	0.67	–	0.76	0.73
Cardano (ADA)	0.57	–	0.67	0.85	0.95
Litecoin (LTC)	–	0.57	0.87	0.80	0.71

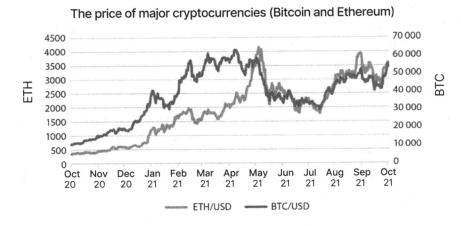

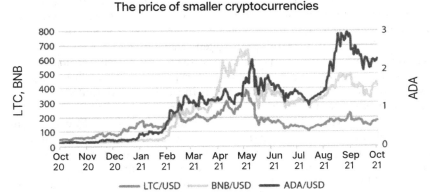

Figure 5.4 The exchange rates of selected cryptocurrencies in the period X 2020–X 2021.

5.4 THE FUTURE OF SPECULATION

5.4.1 New designs, new possibilities

I think that cryptospeculation is a big part of the Blockchain market because it's valuable. Over the years, many new opportunities and token exchange models have popped up. Many of them are still popular, while others have been forgotten.

The first initiatives in the Blockchain environment aimed at bringing investors profit through speculations on emerging projects appeared quite early, in 2013. You guessed it, the project was about improving the Bitcoin mechanism. The aim was to add new functionalities to the Bitcoin protocol so that cryptocurrency exchange would allow sending other encrypted information attached to data blocks in the Blockchain network. In short, a protocol called MasterCoin would use the existing Bitcoin Blockchain, adding smart contract functionality to it.[57] To finance this initiative, the MasterCoin team collected 4,740 BTC, about $500,000 at the time. Investors speculated that they were investing in the project early, hoping for a profit in the future. Although MasterCoin did not catch on (it was too complicated and unintuitive for regular users), it nevertheless gave MSC holders a chance to earn. In 2017, despite the project's expiration, the cryptocurrency's rate increased from $4, reaching then a spectacular value of $123.[58]

In the early days of digital markets, there was a series of exciting developments in the space called DAO, short for Decentralized Autonomous Organizations. Those projects issued tokens, which were supposed to give holders the equivalent of digital shares or voting rights. The first DAO was supposed to be an investment fund run by the cryptocurrency community, without a traditional management structure or supervisory board.[59] In 2016, it managed to gather $150 million—a big achievement at the time. However, by mid-year, a scandal erupted. An anonymous hacker team stole over $50 million in Ether cryptocurrency from the DAO system due to a glitch in the early Ethereum protocol.[60] The DAO's reputation crumbled and lost investor confidence.[61] However, the cryptocurrency community didn't abandon Ethereum itself. People saw potential in it. So, they worked together to fix the problems. It helped the world of digital currencies, also known as the Blockchain ecosystem, to continue growing and evolving—a brilliant example of resilience and determination of the crypto community.

There's always something new happening in the cryptocurrency market. New initiatives are emerging, leading to increasingly perfect ideas not only for the projects themselves but also for fundraising organizations. Over the years, the way cryptocurrency business is managed and risks are mitigated has changed. I remember how big a scandal the DAO-hack was, during the "Wild West" days of cryptocurrency fundraising. The first initiatives were thus exposed not only to business and economic risk but primarily to technological risk. This problem is no longer present today, as the market has evolved enough to solve the technical problems of the most popular Blockchains. The progress in the world of cryptocurrencies has been so great that the intuitiveness of projects is now considered not only from the programmer's perspective but also from that of the regular user. The latest example is NFT (Non-fungible Token) token exchanges, which truly shone in 2021. I'll talk about them in a moment; what's important right now is the example of intuitive and increasingly safe platforms. For example, the OpenSea platform for trading such tokens uses a completely new way of user interaction with technology. On OpenSea, you integrate with another "crypto" wallet, not with a selected nickname, as on traditional forums and social media over the past 20 years.[62] You are identified by the wallet address, which provides not only greater convenience but primarily security (just remind yourself that the likelihood of guessing the private key to the BTC wallet is 2,160). The Web 3.0 paradigm has completely changed, with cryptocurrencies being its central part.

New possibilities concern both ways of allocating resources and the tokens themselves. While the first Blockchain projects were primarily an attempt to improve Bitcoin, the current battle is about something completely different: finding new uses for existing technology. This was the case with the first ICO projects. They sought to implement Blockchain into platforms and digital services used by laypeople. I think in many cases there was a lack of proper technological readiness, sufficient social awareness, or proven market need. Technological experiments with projects, however, pushed the industry forward. An ecosystem has emerged that is increasingly integrating with the world of traditional finance.

What will the future bring? We'll see. I'm most interested in the latest progress associated with NFT tokens, which I mentioned in the context of specialized exchanges. NFT tokens combine cryptocurrency transfers with a unique digital certificate associated with each indivisible token. They represent specific objects, such as works of art, collectibles, game elements, legal contracts, and authenticity certificates. The entire process of issuing an NFT token is about creating an authenticity certificate for an already existing work (e.g., a picture, text, or physical object) and placing it on the Blockchain. Such a certificate cannot be divided, but it can be evaluated and transferred to another person.[63] This means that owning an NFT token would entitle you to confirm: "Yes, I am the owner of this work. I can benefit from it." If we updated our law accordingly, NFT tokens would facilitate the transfer of copyrights. This technology could play such a role today, but current copyright laws are regulated by very outdated law—the Berne Convention, signed in 1886 (the last amendment was made in 1971). How can we properly manage digital reality if we still apply laws, the majority of which were established 138 years ago? Reforming copyright law and opening up to technical achievements could be beneficial for the modern economy, which is so heavily based not on actual production, but on the exchange of knowledge and creative ideas.

Moving authenticity certificates to NFTs could be especially valuable in an era where establishing the origin and authenticity of objects, artworks, and data is so challenging.

This was seen as a potential key benefit of Blockchain technology, even before NFTs existed. The idea was that certificates of authenticity and notarial proofs of possession of valuable assets could be placed in a distributed ledger. Well, this reality is now within reach. The problem is that the sector's immaturity undermines its "here and now" usefulness. But there's a flip side too. Extreme absurdities potentially generate the greatest speculative opportunities.

This reminds me of the infamous story when Laszlo Hanyecz bought two pizzas for 10,000 BTC 14 years ago.[64] Cryptocurrencies prove that the absurdity of economic transactions is a matter of agreement.

I believe what NFTs are currently experiencing is often either valid criticism or misleading generalizations. It was the same with the first cryptocurrencies, which were initially considered financial pyramids, then hailed as a salvation for the financial industry. Jamie Dimon, CEO of JPMorgan Chase, said in 2017 that Bitcoin was a fraud and "will explode at some point."[65] After four years, his bank quietly started investing in Bitcoin funds.[66] What changed during this time? Market participants began to trust each other more. Valuable regulations appeared, several painful cases of actual fraud were worked through, and, above all, people got a better understanding of the value proposition that the Blockchain sector brings to the financial table.

I think a similar future may await NFT tokens. Today, we're talking about extreme cases, like when someone paid 300 ETH (about $1,026,000) for a token representing Nyan Cat—a popular Internet meme featuring a running cat leaving a rainbow trail with annoying music playing in the background, all styled like the early 1980s.[67] It may seem absurd that the holder of those 300 Ether units didn't spend them on a more sensible purpose. However, I have a theory that a person ready for such a risky investment must be an early adopter, or an early cryptocurrency investor. Thanks to an early entry into the industry, such an investor could have accumulated a lot of money in the form of tokens and not converted them all into dollars. So, when a chance for speculation in a new market area appeared, they activated their assets to seize the nascent opportunity and maximize their profits (again). The so-called St. Matthew principle is at play here, which can be adapted to the world of cryptocurrencies from the Bible: "For to everyone who has, more will be given."[68]

NFTs have their undeniable problems, thus repeating the mistakes of previous "cryptos." In a recent sale of six NFTs, the energy cost of creating the NFTs (the energy cost of executing the authentication certificate, not the art itself) was 8.7 megawatt-hours. For comparison, the average American household consumes 893 kilowatt-hours per month.[69] So, in one hour, this sale of six NFTs consumed 10 times more energy than an average American needs in a month.[70] I believe that future NFT projects will try to reduce power consumption and lower that technology's carbon footprint, as at some point, electricity prices will "eat up" the profit that a mass NFT market could expect from speculation.

NFTs are just one example of the dynamic in which the Blockchain industry is developing. Years and years pass; however, new and exciting initiatives continue to emerge in this sector. In the general population, the attitude toward the Blockchain industry is mixed—people either love it or hate it. But one thing is certain—regardless of personal attitudes toward these initiatives, they can be profitable.

5.4.2 How to select tokens for speculation?

Investors are now more interested in putting their money into new altcoin projects. The main reason for that shift is the hope of earning extraordinarily higher returns compared to traditional investments. Regular stock markets can't even match a fraction of the returns offered by new tokens.

A great example here is NEO—a cryptocurrency often referred to as the "Chinese Ethereum." It's a platform for smart contracts and currency exchange. The Chinese government is very strict and doesn't tolerate situations or technologies which it can't fully control. Therefore, it has repeatedly blocked individual Blockchain initiatives and access to certain services for Chinese citizens. Yet in 2017 emerged the opportunity to create a legal cryptocurrency (from the Chinese government's perspective). NEO organized a huge fundraiser. The Chinese government, Microsoft, and several large tech corporations got involved. The result? The starting price of NEO was just over 3 cents. But then it shot up, reaching a high of $180.[71] People who first bought NEO had made a lot of money. Around mid-October 2021, NEO's price was about $40 to $45. That's a massive jump of 133,000%.

NEO did really well. Some might say that "one swallow doesn't make a summer" but I wanted to dig deeper. So, I took a close look at a huge number of cryptocurrency fundraisers—1,344 to be exact.[72] I didn't divide them into technical categories or platforms where the fundraisers were conducted. Instead, I made a list of the ones that made the most money for people who invested in them. I found out NEO isn't the only one. There are projects with several hundred-fold returns on investment. I've listed 4 examples in Table 5.4.

The projects I've mentioned have already ended. However, the real skill for an investor is guessing which new cryptocurrency will do well when it's just starting. It's the sweet spot for making the most money. Often, you can buy the cryptocurrency for less during its early stages than later on. But, how do you find those projects? I don't give out specific advice; that's not my job. I invest for the long term myself. But I do share what I've noticed from watching the market. When looking at different cryptocurrencies or projects to put money into, you should pay attention to a number of factors, presented in Table 5.5.[73]

5.4.3 "Stay but, thou art so fair!!"

Whether we're talking about the first cryptocurrencies or NFTs, all solutions based on Blockchain technology have not just a technical but also a social dimension. It's really about people and how they use it. The idea behind Blockchain was to make dealing with money fair for everyone, but it hasn't worked out the same for all. Some people, especially those who were new to it and jumped in when the hype was at its peak, ended up disappointed.

Table 5.4 Token ICOs

Currency	ICO Date (Start date of collection)	Initial Token Price	Market Price (March, 2024)	Highest Price	Notes
ETH	Jul 22, 2014	2,000 ETH per 1 BTC	$3,496	$4,878.26 (Nov 10, 2021)	Ethereum's native token, used for transactions and collateral.
NEO	Aug 8, 2016	Over $0.03	$14.83	$196.85 (14 Jan 2018)	Supported by the Chinese government and major companies, known as "China's Ethereum".
ARK	Nov 7, 2016	$0.04	$1.12	$10.22 (Jan 10, 2018)	Designed for quick integration of other cryptocurrencies.
STRAX	June 20, 2016	$0.01	$1.50	$22.77 (Jan 08, 2018)	Supported by Microsoft, aims for business application customization.

Table 5.5 Key factors for evaluating cryptocurrency projects

Factor	Explanation	Example
Tokenomics	Factors related to the distribution and flow of tokens in the project should be analyzed: allocation and distribution of tokens, token supply (total, maximum, reissuable, etc.), hard/soft cap—what is the maximum and minimum value that a token collection can reach; the token model (inflationary—when the supply of tokens grows over time, or deflationary—when the supply of tokens is limited to a specific number in advance).	A good project will have a large pool of tokens to ensure their liquidity. The vast majority of the tokens should be in the hands of users, as they are the ones who give them value with their transactions. However, the project team should leave a portion of the token pool for development work in the future. A bad project will allocate a large number of tokens to founders, making a large percentage of the token supply controlled by one entity rather than the cryptocurrency community (as a rule, such a token is riskier).
Innovation	The solutions introduced by the project must represent valuable innovation.	A good project is one that introduces a useful innovation and stands out from the Blockchain competition. A bad project replicates existing models under a new name.
Technology and Blockchain algorytm	For proprietary Blockchains, three factors should be examined: the consensus mechanism, i.e., how new transactions are added to the Blockchain network, the source code, and the pool of developers. For projects put on off-the-shelf platforms (e.g., Ethereum), it is necessary to understand the connection between the project and the platform.	A good proprietary Blockchain project implements the following at the same time: the consensus mechanism must be proven, secure, and effective with minimal impact on the environment, high-quality source code (to be verified with the technical documentation of the project), availability of high-quality developers to develop the project and update it.

Project team	The following questions should be asked: Who is behind the cryptocurrency? Can the expertise of the project leaders be trusted? What ambitions do the leaders have? Do they have a proven track record of success? The involvement of third parties (e.g., technology corporations) will be an added advantage, suggesting that the project team has the right level of technical expertise and business experience.	The project should provide information about the founders or business partners on its website.
Society and ecosystem	All successful "crypto" have vibrant, active communities and, above all, are characterized by a strong commitment by project leaders to communicate with investors and users. All the better if third parties, such as corporations, are involved in communicating and revitalizing the community.	A good project should regularly communicate the progress of development work, animate its community. Channels on Medium, Telegram, Slack, Facebook, Twitter, and YouTube should be checked. A suspicious project will not have the mentioned social channels or such channels will be "dead." This indicates a lack of community around the project, which can cause low token liquidity (if there is no interest, there is also no traffic and no token exchange between users).
Form	Types of cryptocurrency fundraising: ICO, STO, IEO, IDO, NFT token trading.	The chosen collection model should be justified in the project materials (in the white paper or in the project's social media communication).
Market history	Analysis of token history on sites such as CoinMarketCap, Coinranking, Interactivecrypto.com: price, market capitalization, volume of the token in circulation, movements over the past 24 hours, 7 days, 30 days, 90 days, year.	Examples of factors to consider in analyzing past market movements: Is the token value volatile above the overall market picture? When the market falls hard (which happens often)—is the token resilient? When the analysis is done, are the tokens priced at their highest level? If the price has reached its historical peak, it is worth waiting to buy on the so-called dip (decline).

Meanwhile, there are others who've made a fortune with cryptocurrencies. This technology, the Blockchain, isn't just a tool; it's a chance for those who are creative and bold to earn a lot more than what's typical. But figuring out how to be part of that successful group isn't straightforward. There's no one-size-fits-all guide to striking it rich in the crypto world. If it were that simple, everyone would be a millionaire in cryptocurrencies by now. Each person needs to find their own path in this fast-changing and often unpredictable field.

I've been in the crypto industry for a while, and I've learned to be careful about it. It reminds me a lot of what we used to do in school as kids. Do you remember those Yu-Gi-Oh cards and the Pokemon chips you'd find in snack bags? The more you had, the more popular you felt. We used to trade them, trying to collect them all. Sometimes, we'd even use them to "pay" for favors, like getting help in a game or copying homework. But in the end, that's all they were—just fun. Years later, they ended up just sitting in our drawers. They became valuable souvenirs, nothing more. Looking back, I realize that was our first taste of how trading works. We didn't know it then, but we were naturally learning some basics about how exchange and value work, just like in the world of cryptocurrency.

If you're shocked that I'm simplifying the message of cryptocurrencies so much, let me reassure you. I put my own money in crypto. Nevertheless, I don't bet on price changes. I stick to "hodling"—keeping fundamental crypto or well-known altcoins for a long time. I focus on real value, not short-term fluctuations. I trust the basic rules of economics, they convince me. Let's see what the average investor's performance is compared to stock market indices. It's a shock, but they usually do worse! Over 20 years, the SP500 index grew by 6.06% a year. But the average fund investor only saw returns of about 4.25%.[74] Why? People get swayed by feelings, rather than stick to logical, calculated decisions. Crypto prices fluctuate way more than traditional financial products, making it a rollercoaster ride of ups and downs. Investors often react to these sharp swings with emotion, which can lead to less-than-ideal investment decisions.

In this book, I share my observations about the crypto market. I am aware that I'm making bold statements, but I can't ignore certain facts. Over the past decade, 66.5% of analyzed cryptocurrency projects became "dead."[75] What does that mean? That every two of three cryptocurrencies ever created is now completely worthless. Why are these projects considered dead? Some were scams, their websites closed, they had network or wallet issues, they weren't traded much, or they weren't just updated. All this makes investing in cryptocurrencies, whether you're in it for quick trades or holding long-term, really risky. It's like a two-edged sword–high risk but potentially high profit too.

I often think about where Blockchain technology will go in the next decade or so. In 10 or 15 years, I plan to look back at this book. I bet some of my readers will have become crypto millionaires, maybe from smart bets. It's hard to guess how many will strike it rich. Day traders always hope for big wins. However, I think the wild times in crypto trading will slow down eventually. But, as long as it lasts, crypto folks will continue to say like Faust, the main character in Goethe's greatest work. Entranced by the present moment of ultimate happiness for which he had traded his soul, he is urging it to last and not be succeeded by the next moment. In the despair of suffering that is to come, he says: "Stay but [the moment], thou art so fair!"

NOTES

1 https://www.cnbc.com/2021/08/16/sp-500-doubles-from-its-pandemic-bottom-marking-the-fastest-bull-market-rally-since-wwii.html
2 C. Caldwell (2021), Are GameStop's 'Degenerates' Just Getting Started?, "The New York Times", 4.02.2021, access: 8th of February 2021.
3 https://invezz.com/news/2021/01/28/who-are-wallstreetbets-facts/
4 Ibid.
5 https://www.cnet.com/personal-finance/investing/robinhood-backlash-what-you-should-know-about-the-gamestop-stock-controversy/
6 https://www.barrons.com/articles/another-gamestop-trade-might-be-hard-to-pull-off-51612299635
7 J. Murdock (2021), WallStreetBets Subreddit Gains 2 Million Members in a Day Amid Wall Street Siege, "Newsweek", 28.01.2021, access: 28.01.2021.
8 Ibid.
9 https://youtu.be/Z69mKU0W4J4
10 https://finance.yahoo.com/news/story-dogecoin-multi-million-dollar-150000797.html
11 https://www.cnbc.com/2017/06/06/mark-cuban-calls-bitcoin-a-bubble-price-falls.html
12 https://www.cnbc.com/2021/02/08/tweets-from-elon-musk-and-celebrities-send-dogecoin-to-a-record-high.html
13 https://youtu.be/Z69mKU0W4J4
14 https://coinmarketcap.com/currencies/dogecoin/
15 https://decrypt.co/55962/mia-khalifa-invests-in-dogecoin-during-400-extreme-price-rally
16 https://bitinfocharts.com/top-100-richest-dogecoin-addresses.html
17 https://youtu.be/Z69mKU0W4J4
18 https://luxurylaunches.com/other_stuff/billy-markus-founder-of-dogecoin-sold-all-his-coins.php
19 https://www.cnbc.com/2023/04/03/dogecoin-jumps-over-30percent-after-twitter-changes-logo-to-doges-symbol.html
20 CoinMarketCap.
21 https://www.caixabankresearch.com/en/economics-markets/financial-markets/bitcoin-speculative-bubble-or-currency-future
22 https://www.ft.com/content/6c5b941c-5052-11e3-9f0d-00144feabdc0

23 https://www.cnbc.com/2021/03/04/survey-finds-one-third-of-crypto-buyers-dont-know-what-theyre-doing.html

24 https://www.bloomberg.com/billionaires/ "Bloomberg Billionaires Index: Changpeng Zhao".

25 https://markets.businessinsider.com/news/currencies/binance-ceo-founder-bitcoin-crypto-herd-mentality-price-volatility-microstrategy-2021-5

26 The values I provide come from a comparison of a popular measure of volatility in finance—average true range (ATR), which measures the average price change over a selected time frame—https://medium.com/swissquote-education/bitcoin-vs-risk-understanding-volatility-472efe96e439

27 https://www.bitcoin.com/get-started/how-bitcoin-transactions-work/

28 https://btcdirect.eu/en-gb/bitcoin-wallet

29 https://bitref.com/3FZbgi29cpjq2GjdwV8eyHuJJnkLtktZc5

30 https://zondacrypto.com/en/helpdesk/zondacrypto-exchange/payments-and-withdrawals/how-to-transfer-a-digital-currency-to-another-account

31 Ibid.

32 https://www.najlepszekonto.pl/ile-kosztuje-przelew-natychmiastowy

33 https://www.businessinsider.com/personal-finance/wire-transfer-fees?r=US&IR=T

34 https://www.frbsf.org/economic-research/publications/economic-letter/2002/september/why-do-americans-still-write-checks/

35 https://www.newsweek.com/46-million-americans-now-own-bitcoin-crypto-goes-mainstream-1590639

36 R. McMillan (2013), Ex-Googler Gives the World a Better Bitcoin, "Wired", 30.08.2013, access: 25.10.2017.

37 https://www.gemini.com/cryptopedia/litecoin-vs-bitcoin-blockchain

38 http://learningspot.altervista.org/altcoins-history-and-main-features-and-differences-from-bitcoin/

39 Ibid.

40 https://bitcoinist.com/bitcoins-energy-consumption-nears-belgium-finland-figures/

41 https://www.youtube.com/watch?v=WSN5BaCzsbo

42 http://learningspot.altervista.org/altcoins-history-and-main-features-and-differences-from-bitcoin/

43 https://www.statista.com/statistics/863917/number-crypto-coins-tokens/

44 https://www.statista.com/statistics/863917/number-crypto-coins-tokens/

45 Current currency & funds code list, Schweizerische Normen-Vereinigung, 01.07.2016.

46 https://www.statista.com/statistics/242745/volume-of-global-equity-trading/

47 https://www.quora.com/How-many-publicly-traded-companies-are-in-the-world

48 https://www.statista.com/statistics/863917/number-crypto-coins-tokens/

49 https://www.coinopsy.com/dead-coins/

50 https://www.statista.com/statistics/242745/volume-of-global-equity-trading/

51 https://finance.yahoo.com/news/total-crypto-market-cap-hits-062333457.html

52 https://www.garyvaynerchuk.com/meet-the-268-veefriends/

53 https://www.investopedia.com/terms/forex/m/majors.asp

54 C.R. Schenk (2009), The Retirement of Sterling as a Reserve Currency after 1945: Lessons for the US Dollar?, Canadian Network for Economic History conference, October of 2009.

55 https://www.vox.com/recode/2021/5/18/22441831/elon-musk-bitcoin-dogecoin-crypto-prices-tesla

56 https://www.teletrader.com/euro-drops-to-two-year-lows-after-trump-s-tweet/news/details/49341537?ts=1634313260642

57 https://hackernoon.com/a-comprehensive-guide-to-icos-crypto-funding-the-rise-the-boom-the-bust-the-next-b159fdf38010

58 Ibid.

59 E. Rennie (2016), The Radical DAO Experiment, "Swinburne News", 12.05.2016, Swinburne University of Technology, access: 12.05.2016.

60 https://www.gemini.com/cryptopedia/the-dao-hack-makerdao

61 https://hackernoon.com/a-comprehensive-guide-to-icos-crypto-funding-the-rise-the-boom-the-bust-the-next-b159fdf38010

62 https://opensea.io/

63 https://www.theverge.com/22310188/nft-explainer-what-is-blockchain-crypto-art-faq

64 https://www.moneycontrol.com/news/business/cryptocurrency/bitcoin-pizza-day-2021-some-interesting-facts-about-this-special-cryptocurrency-day-6924731.html

65 https://www.cnbc.com/2017/09/12/jpmorgan-ceo-jamie-dimon-raises-flag-on-trading-revenue-sees-20-percent-fall-for-the-third-quarter.html

66 https://www.cnbc.com/2021/08/05/bitcoin-jpmorgan-led-by-jamie-dimon-quietly-unveils-access-to-a-half-dozen-crypto-funds.html

67 https://www.cnet.com/news/nft-bubble-the-craziest-nonfungible-token-sales-so-far/

68 R.K. Merton (1968), The Matthew Effect in Science. The Reward and Communication Systems of Science Are Considered, "Science" 159 (3810), pp. 56–63.

69 https://www.eia.gov/tools/faqs/faq.php?id=97&t=3#:~:text=In%202020%2C%20the%20average%20annual,about%20893%20kWh%20per%20month

70 https://www.ntdaily.com/nfts-are-not-just-bad-for-the-environment-they-are-also-stupid/

71 Top 10 ICOs with the Biggest ROI, Coin Telegraph, dostęp: 27.09.2021.

72 Data from https://cryptorank.io/ico (21.10.2021).

73 Based on: https://gadgets.ndtv.com/cryptocurrency/opinion/how-to-pick-good-cryptos-2545977 i https://kingpassive.com/which-cryptocurrency-to-invest-in/

74 https://www.thebalance.com/why-average-investors-earn-below-average-market-returns-2388519

75 https://www.financialexpress.com/market/rip-cryptocurrencies-number-of-dead-coins-up-35-over-last-year-tally-nears-2000-mark/2226169/

Chapter 6

Crypto entrepreneurs

Picture this scenario: a young student is attending a humanities program at a university in Scotland, living the life of a typical Edinburgh resident and a representative of the now-adult Generation Z. She's looking at several more years of university, followed by the typical path of corporate employment. Her financial situation is currently tied to her parents, with the looming prospect of eventually taking on a hefty mortgage for a small apartment where she'll spend the subsequent years of her life.

But this young woman is driven and full of ideas. She's ambitious and creative, brimming with project plans, yet her business contacts are limited. Coming from a middle-class background, she doesn't have the resources to launch her own company. Under traditional business fundraising paths, she would need to start a project with her own or borrowed funds, secure initial customers, and then seek financing from business angels or Venture Capital (VC) funds. These funds are institutionalized groups of market experts who provide capital to startups in exchange for a stake in the business. However, her idea is still in its nascent stage. Additionally, securing funds from business angels or VCs often requires an extensive network of contacts—a significant hurdle for a new entrepreneur.

However, she doesn't have to give up on her dreams. Keeping up with technical news, she's aware of a newer model of startup financing through cryptocurrency fundraising. Her business idea, with its strong community focus, is ideally suited for implementation on a Blockchain platform. So, she sets to work: conducting in-depth market research, assembling a team of developers and advisors, and carrying out the necessary technological groundwork. They create a white paper, set up a website, and develop a unique token for her project, launching it through an Initial Coin Offering (ICO) procedure.

The token sale led by our Scottish student turned out to be an astounding success. Her well-executed promotional campaign draws in thousands of contributors. Within just a year of beginning her work, she built a project whose token boasts a liquidity of over $50 million. Remarkably, she is the sole shareholder of the company created specifically for tokenization.

DOI: 10.1201/9781032621456-7

From the tokens issued, based on the economic model she authored, she holds over \$120 million. She has, quite astonishingly, become a cryptocurrency millionaire.

Now, it's crucial to emphasize that this narrative isn't a fabricated tale. It's a real-life event that I had the opportunity to witness. The details and the identity of this enterprising individual are confidential, but the essence of her success is a testament to what's possible in the modern world of finance and technology. How did she manage to build such a spectacularly successful project in the world of cryptocurrencies? This is the question that I will explore in this chapter, shedding light on the strategies, challenges, and innovations that marked her journey from a student with an idea to a leader of a multi-million dollar venture.

6.1 THE OLD LAWS OF ECONOMICS IN THE NEW ECONOMY

6.1.1 Cryptocurrency Say's law

Exploring Ethereum and Blockchain projects, we often focus on their speculative aspect. However, that's just one part of a much broader picture. The reality is, without innovative entrepreneurs who believe in their vision and embark on ventures known as tokenization, there wouldn't be any tokens to speculate with on the Ethereum platform. Tokenization is a unique method of raising capital for business development, particularly within the Blockchain industry. Startups often finance their ventures by selling digital tokens that are linked to the platform they're developing. This scenario introduces us to the two key players in this market: the entrepreneurs who issue the tokens, and the speculators who invest in them.

Both of these groups—the creators of the projects and their investors/users—are crucial for the functioning of this economic system. On one side, you have the project initiators, bringing their ideas and expertise to the table. Without them, the creation of new tokenized platforms wouldn't be feasible. On the flip side, launching any business (Blockchain ventures included) requires significant investments of both resources and entrepreneurial energy. Entrepreneurs must not only develop the product but also market it effectively. All of this while channeling the collective enthusiasm towards a singular objective: building a functioning, user-friendly tokenized platform. On these platforms, transactions and access to digital services happen through tokens, forming a unique economic space where users and software product providers can do business.

In this setup, we see a two-way relationship: there's a demand side (the users and investors) and a supply side (the entrepreneurs). Which is more important? I think they are both equally vital. This situation is similar to the age-old question of what came first: the chicken or the egg?

Many years ago, when economics first started as a study, one of the big questions was about the role of demand and supply. This was over 200 years ago. The notion of the "primacy" of demand over supply was articulated by the French entrepreneur and economist Jean-Baptiste Say, who formulated the renowned law of markets, now known as "Say's law." This law posits that "supply creates its own demand." But what does this mean in simple terms? Essentially, it suggests that production is the genesis of demand for a product. The logic follows that someone (here: Apple, Inc.) had to first invent the iPhone for there to be a demand for it in the public. Similarly, a new Blockchain project must be created first for the cryptocurrency community to have something to invest in.

It's especially popular among those who favor a free market without much government intervention. This idea aligns well with the beliefs of the Cypherpunk community and cryptocurrency supporters, who have always been pro-free market. On the other side of this debate is John Maynard Keynes, who believed that government action is essential in fixing economic problems. This ideological tussle between Keynesians and free market advocates began in the 1930s and continues to this day. In this debate, cryptocurrency supporters naturally align with the free market side, placing them in opposition to Keynesians, whose ideas dominate mainstream economics today.

If Jean-Baptiste Say were to witness the evolution of Blockchain startups in our time, he would likely see the tokenization process as a validation of his theory. When startups raise money by selling tokens, they create new markets where people can speculate and make profits. In some cases, these short-term speculations might turn into long-term investments. The success of the Blockchain sector is largely due to the hard work and dedication of entrepreneurs who build these projects and push technological boundaries.

Looking at the leading figures in the crypto millionaire club, it's clear that they are entrepreneurs with diverse business interests. For example, Brian Armstrong, the founder and CEO of Coinbase, has an estimated net worth of $11.4 billion (in March 2024). Matthew Roszak (assets worth $3.1 billion) runs a Blockchain infrastructure company and invests in Blockchain startups. Coinbase is the world's second-largest cryptocurrency exchange, and its market capitalization exceeded $100 billion at its peak. The Winklevoss twins, Tyler and Cameron, each with a net worth of $3 billion, are known for their involvement in the early days of Facebook. In the crypto arena, they established Gemini, a widely recognized cryptocurrency trading exchange. Although Gemini faced financial challenges and went bankrupt in early 2023, the twins continue to be major players in the crypto world. There are also the creators of their own cryptocurrencies, like Vitalik Buterin of Ethereum and Chris Larsen of Ripple. Their success stories are confirmations of Say's law in action. The largest fortunes in the cryptocurrency sector aren't the result of mere speculative chance or random demand for tokens. Success in this field is not about luck—it's primarily the result of relentless effort and strategic vision.

6.1.2 Hope built by the hands of crypto entrepreneurs

All entrepreneurs, particularly in the Blockchain sector, share a fundamental trait: the ability to create new structures to meet specific goals. That can be challenging, especially given the current state of the economy, which is still trying to define its nature and orientation. Key questions arise: should the economy lean toward more centralization or embrace decentralization? Will the influence of global corporations outweigh that of local governments? As we navigate these complex issues in an uncertain future, Blockchain entrepreneurs are playing a pivotal role. Their day-to-day efforts are shaping an ecosystem that might handle a significant portion of the global financial system in the upcoming years, if not decades.[1]

Here, I'm focusing on the broader Blockchain sector, not just on cryptocurrencies, which are often seen as speculative investments. I think many cryptocurrencies are overvalued and don't have solid long-term reasons for their high prices. When you add up the value of all cryptocurrencies, the market says they're worth over $2.65 trillion (on March 2024). On one side, you have a lot of people speculating on cryptocurrencies. On the other side, you have professional VC that carefully evaluates projects based on their business, technical, and social aspects. The difference is huge: cryptocurrencies are valued at $2.65 trillion, but the market for Blockchain startups is only $30.4 billion.[2]

There's a large gap between people's perception of cryptocurrencies' value and their actual worth. Cryptocurrencies are risky but could have a great growth trajectory ahead. How they'll be used in the future digital economy is still unknown. The big difference between their speculative intrinsic values of the technology behind them comes from the market's difficulty in understanding how useful digital currencies really are. Every new technology, from computers in the 1980s to cryptocurrencies now, has risks and big opportunities. Right now, there's a race to find the best technology for a global digital economy.

Blockchain entrepreneurs are working on something much bigger than just making existing financial systems better. They're using Blockchain technology to potentially empower ordinary people, especially those who only have access to basic financial services. This is incredibly important in parts of the world where having a bank account or access to a brokerage is not common. Many citizens of the so-called Western world don't realize how many people globally are excluded from basic financial services, especially in economically underdeveloped countries. In fact, three billion people around the world don't have access to any banking services. Two billion don't even have a basic checking account.[3]

Cryptocurrencies and Blockchain technology aren't just about making it easier for people to get financial services. They can also help traditional banks in many ways. The World Economic Forum points out three areas where Blockchain can really make a difference in finance: making it easier for banks to onboard customers by decentralizing data, cutting fees for transfers and international transactions, and using smart contracts to automate insurance. To borrow a phrase from Neil Armstrong, these might be small steps for the Blockchain sector, but they're huge leaps for countries that are financially excluded.

The progress in expanding banking services is not just theoretical. It's actually happening right now, thanks to crypto entrepreneurs. Interestingly, the countries with the highest reported use of cryptocurrencies are not the world's biggest economies. Surveys show that the most people saying they own or use cryptocurrencies are in Nigeria, Vietnam, the Philippines, Turkey, and Peru (Figure 6.1). Turkey, the wealthiest among these, has a GDP per capita that's only one-fourth of the UK's.[4] In Nigeria, it's 22 times less. This shows that the impact of cryptocurrencies and the Blockchain is being felt strongest in places where financial inclusion is most needed.

Cryptocurrencies, particularly ones like stablecoins that are tied to stable assets (say the US dollar), are becoming a way to keep money safe in developing countries. Consider Nigeria, which has the highest cryptocurrency adoption rate globally. A third of Nigerians surveyed say they use or own digital currencies.[5] This makes sense when you look at their economy: since 2016, the Nigerian Naira has lost half its value, jumping from about 200 to nearly 400 per dollar by the end of 2020. If these assets were converted into a stablecoin like Tether (USDT), they'd be shielded from such dramatic devaluation.[6]

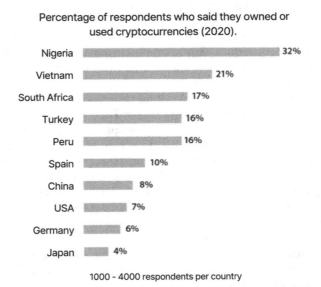

Percentage of respondents who said they owned or used cryptocurrencies (2020).

Country	Percentage
Nigeria	32%
Vietnam	21%
South Africa	17%
Turkey	16%
Peru	16%
Spain	10%
China	8%
USA	7%
Germany	6%
Japan	4%

1000 - 4000 respondents per country

Figure 6.1 Prevalence of cryptocurrencies in the population of top ten countries.

(*Source:* **Data from Statista.**)

The threat of financial exclusion isn't limited to developing countries. It can also hit economies plunged into sudden crises. Take Venezuela, for example, where hyperinflation and economic collapse have made international remittances a lifeline for many families. However, the government's stringent regulations, requiring Venezuelans to use local banks and disclose their financial activities, complicate this lifeline. Transfers from the United States can take weeks and cost up to 56% in fees. Recently, Venezuelan banks, under government pressure, even started blocking online account access from foreign IP addresses. As a result, many Venezuelans have turned to cryptocurrencies for transfers, escaping government control.[7]

Venezuela's situation is alarming, especially considering it was once one of the wealthiest countries per capita just 70 years ago.[8] Economic dynamics shift rapidly, and technical innovations like cryptocurrencies can provide flexible solutions to pressing problems, whether for ordinary banking customers or migrant workers sending money home. Who will deliver these vital fintech solutions? Here come the crypto entrepreneurs.

However, while the potential of cryptocurrencies is immense, it's also true that most cryptocurrency projects fail. The reality is that most cryptocurrency projects don't succeed. This isn't an indictment of the sector—as someone deeply involved in the Blockchain industry, I have a strong belief in the value of cryptocurrencies. However, the success rate of Blockchain startups mirrors that of ventures in other sectors: a staggering 90% of startups fail. The breakdown is telling—about 21.5% shut down within their first year, 30% by their second, half by their fifth, and 70% by their 10th year.[9]

Thousands of crypto entrepreneurs participate in a massive, live experiment. Will their project succeed? Will their cryptocurrencies gain enough popularity to sustain market activity and liquidity? These entrepreneurs are fueled by the hope for sustained demand for their solutions, either to serve as a means of token speculation or to address the needs of those excluded from traditional finance. But launching a cryptocurrency, like any business venture, is fraught with uncertainty. Crypto entrepreneurs face the unknown every day, unsure of what the future holds for their projects. They take risks, and while the majority may not find success, those who do often achieve remarkable results. It's this high-stakes, high-reward nature that defines the essence of entrepreneurship in the crypto sector.

6.1.3 Funding startups 101

The world of finance can be incredibly harsh for inexperienced entrepreneurs. A staggering 82% of young businesses fail due to financial liquidity problems, which is consistently the leading cause of startup bankruptcies.[10] This is where the cryptocurrency sector comes in, offering a unique and valuable opportunity. Cryptocurrency funding is a game-changer for startups. It gives new businesses a chance to survive, perfectly fitting the finance saying, "Cash is life."

Let's take a deep dive into the world of entrepreneurship and explore the different types of startup funding. At first glance, running a business might seem straightforward. You operate in a market, generate revenue, and control the company's growth. However, it's not as simple as it sounds.

In a typical organization, five fundamental roles are crucial:[11]

1. *Management* (for larger organizations): The main role of managers is to oversee the work of others.
2. *Marketing and sales*: This involves promoting products, acquiring sales channels and contacts, attracting customers, and building a company's image to boost sales revenue.
3. *Finance*: This involves planning and securing the company's finances and managing them.
4. *Research and development*: This is all about improving the company's product offerings.
5. *Operations*: This involves coordinating the work of all other areas of the company.

Startups are fundamentally about creating new organizations, often in their infancy, lacking a fully developed product or operating with just a prototype. Entrepreneurs typically hold a vision or an idea and are actively seeking the necessary funding to bring it to life. Given this context, certain functions like marketing and sales become less relevant initially, particularly as there isn't a finished product to market or sell. Similarly, the managerial aspect is often less complex in startups due to their smaller size and lack of intricate organizational structures. Operational tasks in startups tend to be less formalized and often handled "on the fly" by the founders themselves. This improvisational approach underscores the adaptable and dynamic nature of startup operations. In such a setting, the pivotal elements boil down to two key spheres: securing financial backing (the finance domain) and engaging in the research and development required to evolve the idea into a viable product (product development).

In the startup journey, everything initially revolves around developing the Minimum Viable Product (MVP). The MVP serves as a rudimentary yet functional demonstration of the product concept, offering just enough features to attract the first set of users and convince them of its potential value. For early-stage entrepreneurs, particularly those without a strong track record or brand recognition, funding the MVP often hinges on personal finances or contributions from close networks—family and friends. That's colloquially known in startup circles as the "FFF"—family, friends, and fools.[12] This is a common phase, experienced by about 40% of all startups. A notable example is Google, which, in its early days, saw founders Sergey Brin and Larry Page raising $200,000 through such means.[13]

Once the startup successfully creates its MVP and garners initial customer interest, proving its fit and response to market demand, it then moves into a phase of seeking more substantial funding for market expansion. This is where various funding rounds come into play, attracting different types of investors like business angels and VC funds. The stages of funding are often categorized as pre-seed, seed, and then progressing through series A, B, C, and so on, depending on the startup's development stage. The ultimate goal for many is to reach a size and valuation that allows for an initial public offering (IPO). Participation in accelerators and entrepreneurship incubators, such as Y Combinator, can significantly boost a startup's prospects in these rounds. A critical milestone in a startup's valuation journey is achieving "unicorn" status, denoted by a valuation of over $1 billion. This prestigious label is attained by approximately 1% of startups, particularly in the American context, with examples like Uber, Airbnb, and Stripe illustrating this rare success.[14] Unicorns often either go public or become acquisition targets for larger corporations, marking the culmination of their growth and funding cycle.

Historically, entrepreneurs seeking funds for business development have typically followed a well-trodden path, comprising three key stages: (1) relying on funding from FFF; (2) securing investments from business angels; and (3) raising capital through VC fund rounds. These funds have traditionally been obtained through either equity investment or debt financing. In equity investment, entrepreneurs sell company shares to investors, who then expect a return from future profits. Debt financing, on the other hand, involves taking a loan for development, which is repaid from the project's revenues. Both methods are part of traditional finance.

But things are changing with Blockchain technology and the rise of decentralized finance (DeFi), a new area in the fintech world. DeFi is becoming increasingly important for funding because it's growing fast and reaches people all over the world.

This cryptocurrency market keeps getting bigger. Although more projects are competing for funds, the expanding DeFi market means there's more money available for startups. One big advantage of DeFi is its global reach. For example, in the standard VC world, the rule still applies that funds prefer to invest in projects from their markets, rather than looking for even better chances outside their own countries and regions (Figure 6.2).[15]

In DeFi, powered by Blockchain, the focus is on a global approach. This makes it easier to get funding from different countries, unlike traditional finance, which is often limited by regional boundaries. However, it's crucial to navigate the legal intricacies of such international fundraising to ensure compliance and security.

The global reach of cryptocurrency fundraising offers a big advantage for entrepreneurs looking to raise money. But it's not just about location, time

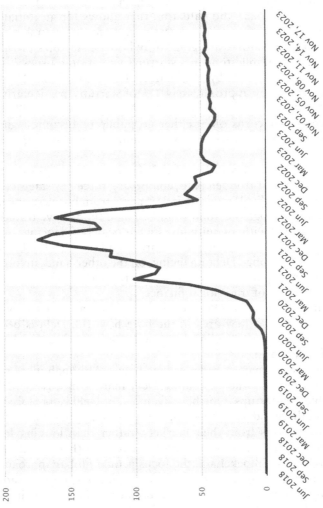

Figure 6.2 The value of cryptocurrencies held in decentralized finance around the world.

(Source: Data from Statista.)

is also a critical factor. The process of tokenization in DeFi significantly streamlines the fundraising journey for entrepreneurs. This method is generally more cost-effective, quicker, and involves fewer complexities than traditional finance routes. Tokenization reduces various financial transaction costs, including those typically associated with brokers and intermediaries.[16] For startups, this means a more straightforward and efficient way to get the funds they need.

With over 8,800 tokens and cryptocurrencies in the market, is there still room and sense in tokenizing new businesses? My view is a resounding yes. We're in the era where the market is actively seeking valuable projects and is ready to back innovative entrepreneurs with the resources they need for their initiatives. While DeFi investments have traditionally targeted private individuals for cryptocurrency fundraising, this trend is gradually changing. It's not due to a lack of funding in Blockchain projects—the sector continues to grow. Leading cryptocurrencies like Bitcoin contain deflationary elements, meaning their value tends to increase over time.

Big investors like banks and investment funds are now showing a lot of interest in DeFi. These groups, with their legal standing and advanced investment capabilities, have much larger resources than individual investors. The increasing involvement of these institutional investors shows how much the industry has matured. BlackRock and Fidelity filed for Bitcoin spot ETFs, showcasing increased financial sector interest in cryptocurrencies. At the same time, a new crypto exchange called EDX Markets, backed by Fidelity Digital Assets, Charles Schwab, and Citadel Securities, started in the United States. In another major move, Goldman Sachs, BNP Paribas, and Deloitte, among others, announced the Canton Network, a new Blockchain network for financial markets.[17] These developments highlight the growing recognition of cryptocurrencies like Bitcoin, which recently reached the $70,000 mark, as it set the new all-time high on March 2024.

The Small Business Optimism Index in the United States has recently reached a 10-year low, leading to an increased focus on technology solutions for small and midsize businesses (SMBs).[18] These businesses are facing funding challenges due to high interest rates and inflation. However, Blockchain and crypto sectors are providing new opportunities, particularly in payments and funding. Blockchain and decentralized technologies are offering SMBs more control and efficiency, reducing reliance on traditional intermediaries. This shift can be transformative for both Main Street and Wall Street economies.

6.2 FUNDING THROUGH BLOCKCHAIN

Currently, the process of issuing a cryptocurrency is relatively simple. Thanks to ready-made Blockchain solutions, commercial implementation is just around the corner. However, it wasn't so straightforward in the early days of the Blockchain ecosystem. Beyond a good idea and market knowledge, making your own cryptocurrency based on Blockchain requires capital, as well as a team of top-notch programmers, cryptographers, and experts. All of this changed, thanks to Ethereum and tokenization.

So, how does tokenization work? An entrepreneur issues and sells a token, which is offered to a wide audience. Almost anyone around the globe can buy these tokens, though sometimes there are rules that might stop certain people from buying, like where they live or other legal reasons. When you, as a potential investor, decide to buy a token, you're stepping into the world of digital investment. You send your money to the entrepreneur. It might be digital currencies like Bitcoin or Ethereum, or it could be in regular, everyday money. Such details depend on the specific project. Once your payment is received, the entrepreneur sends you some of the newly issued tokens. The whole process—token sale—is part of the bigger concept of tokenization. Entrepreneurs are essentially using those sales as a modern-day fundraising tool. They often have their plans and visions outlined in a white paper. That document gives potential investors, like you, an idea of what they're planning to build and how they intend to make it successful. You basically bet on the entrepreneur's idea, hoping that after the final version of the developed platform is released, its course will increase and you'll earn as one of the first investors.

Today, when talking about token sales, we usually mean a few different kinds. Here's a simple breakdown:

- *ICO (Initial Coin Offering)*: The project team creates a utility-type token or cryptocurrency.[19] That method is associated with a big launch event for new digital money. Companies get funds that way, mainly for software projects. People buy new tokens and can use them on the project's platform or conduct transactions within the emerging technological product. Most of those happen on Ethereum, a popular digital currency platform. Most of the offerings happen on the Ethereum platform.[20]
- *STO (Security Token Offering)*: This involves the digitization of financial securities. In return for the payment during the STO collection, the user receives tokens, which simultaneously serve as securities. Platforms that handle STOs make sure everything follows financial laws.[21] It's possible to tokenize many assets: shares in companies, real estate, and even such abstract things as shares in the sale of limited products or artwork.
- *IEO (Initial Exchange Offering)*: It has the same features as ICO, but it all happens on a cryptocurrency exchange. As a result, the exchange takes care of everything, from managing the sale to making the tokens available for trading. IEO is a safer form of tokenization because it reduces the risk associated with market, making for a specific token. The project creators still decide how many tokens to leave on the exchange and how much to use for other purposes or pay out as a security.

- *IDO (Initial DEX Offering)*: The newest generation of collections based on decentralized exchanges (DEX). The issued tokens represent any financial product or cryptocurrencies listed on decentralized exchanges. The whole collection is managed by a smart contract, which transfers part of the collected funds to the project founders and leaves part on the exchange as a liquidity pool—a pool of tokens necessary to always maintain smooth token turnover.[22] That method of investment is often seen as safer because it's easier for investors to sell their tokens whenever they want and exit the investment. That reduces the risk of a drop or lack of token liquidity.

Tokenization launchpads are specialized platforms that provide a comprehensive ecosystem for token issuers to launch their projects and assets on the Blockchain. These platforms act as a bridge between project creators and investors. They facilitate the tokenization process and ensure a smooth and secure launch. Launchpads typically offer a combination of technological infrastructure, smart contract templates, fundraising mechanisms, community support, and token distribution solutions. Moreover, they often provide access to a pool of potential investors, thus increasing the visibility and reach of the project. Launchpads contribute to the overall growth and innovation of the Blockchain ecosystem. They foster collaboration, community engagement, and knowledge sharing. They stimulate the development of new use cases, applications, and solutions built on Blockchain technology.

Tokenization has evolved into a systematic process, greatly advanced by the Ethereum platform, as I already mentioned in Chapter 5 on cryptocurrency speculation. Ethereum, along with its currency ETH, enables the creation of diverse applications using smart contracts. They cater to various market demands and entrepreneurial ideas. Bitcoin mainly serves one purpose: to transfer funds. However, on Ethereum, you can build every type of useful application in the form of decentralized applications (DApps)—from financial products to platforms for digital entertainment. In addition, each DApp can have its unique tokens, creating a specific microeconomic system. Users trade those tokens through the Ethereum protocol. Every crypto entrepreneur can create their own spaces and provide users with needed solutions, thanks to the Ethereum network.

In 2013, some of the first ideas in the world of Blockchain started. Yes, you guessed it, the project was about improving the Bitcoin mechanism. It aimed to add new functionalities to the Bitcoin protocol. Here's the thinking: Bitcoin moves using a complex system called Blockchain. That system could "transport" more than just Bitcoin; it could also carry other important data. So, thanks to Blockchain, the exchange of cryptocurrencies allows the construction of specialized DApps.

I've already mentioned MasterCoin—the first project that built a new Blockchain protocol using the existing Bitcoin mechanism, while adding the functionality of a smart contract to it.[23] Although it didn't catch on, it told others in the field that they should work on similar Blockchain ideas.

Soon, there were several similar initiatives, such as NextCoin, CounterParty, MaidSafeCoin, and Swarm.[24] However, it was Ethereum that really changed the game. It became a milestone for both the development of crypto speculation and the entire Blockchain industry. Ether isn't just a cryptocurrency but also the financial backbone of a platform for building your own Blockchain projects—the whole new playground for creating Blockchain stuff. It was a completely new protocol, written from scratch, with its own programming language (Solidity). Thanks to Ethereum, new Blockchain projects started to emerge on a massive scale. Now, any business person can make their own app or platform. They can even have their own special digital money. Currently, every entrepreneur has the opportunity to build their own application or platform with a custom token, which will differ from other cryptocurrencies in functionality, distribution of funds between users and administrators, and the applied economic solutions.

The most popular standard for building tokens for DApps is ERC-20 (Ethereum Request for Comments 20). With ERC-20, you can easily move tokens from one account to another. The system handles all the details automatically, both for the whole platform and for each user.[25] It works closely with smart contracts, which are fundamental in the Ethereum system. A smart contract is a program built on the Blockchain, which automatically carries out data operations and transactions between users.

Assessing the implementation potential of Blockchain, McKinsey conducted a study on 200 companies. Besides Bitcoin, they found 64 uses for it, like smart contracts, 24 of which related to financial services. In the fintech sector, McKinsey expects that Blockchain will "generate ~$80B to 110B in impact," in the form of higher revenues, lower costs, or capital gains.[26]

Smart contracts and DApps demonstrate their potential through real-world examples. One such instance occurred in 2017 with Idex, a major player in the online trading scene. It was a top decentralized exchange (DEX) known for its high transaction volume, ranked fourth globally. Idex took inspiration from EtherDelta, another exchange, particularly in its smart contract design. However, it was hacked, which weakened its credibility in the trader community. Moreover, EtherDelta faced criticism for its opaque handling of the hack and unfair policies regarding the addition of new digital tokens. In the digital community, especially in forums like Reddit, people tend to take proactive measures. In response to those events, they initiated a "fork"—a fundamental update to a system. They updated EtherDelta's system themselves, making it better from the ground up. Their effort led to ForkDelta, a new version of the exchange. ForkDelta had better tech but still used the core ideas from EtherDelta's smart contract. It's a beautiful blend of innovation and continuity in the world of decentralized exchanges.

Blockchain and smart contracts are really handy. They're like digital building blocks. You can mix and match parts from different projects. EtherDelta is a great example of that. Developers carried out a fork, building a new platform based on the functioning EtherDelta smart contract. They didn't need to obtain permission to carry out the work, since the entire EtherDelta structure was available on Ethereum, that is, on the public Blockchain network.[27] ForkDelta once had the largest number of available ERC-20 tokens: more than 300. Blockchain technology is very flexible. It lets people create new things easily, using already existing components.[28]

In a centralized system, such a scenario would never happen. Imagine you don't like your bank's website, let's call it X-Bank. You have two choices: switch banks or deal with the website's problems. If someone wanted to make a new website using X-Bank's parts, it won't work. X-Bank can cut off access to its API (Application Programming Interface) at any time.[29] An API is like a special key that lets different computer programs talk to each other. It's made up of codes and steps that the people in charge of X-Bank set up. In a world where one company controls it all, like X-Bank does with its website, people who use the service have very little say.[30]

The flexibility of the smart contract mechanism and Blockchain technology is a great field for entrepreneurs. They always come up with new ways to use existing resources for new ideas. Take CryptoKitties, for example. It's a big deal in the mix of Blockchain and digital art. On CryptoKitties, you play with virtual cat pictures.[31] You can breed them, collect them, and even sell them. It's all on a special part of Ethereum called ERC-721. That's where Non-Fungible Tokens, or NFTs, come into play. Each NFT is unique, like a digital snowflake. They're not interchangeable like regular tokens. Instead, they carry distinct characteristics and values. NFTs can be adapted for various uses across different business landscapes. Think of them as versatile digital assets that can appear in video games as special items, in digital art auctions, or as unique collectibles.[32] And as you know from Chapter 5 on crypto speculation, earning opportunities are possible within the framework of collections and investments in NFTs.

Blockchain offers a unique world where every new project presents an opportunity to kickstart a business. By using token collections, individuals can launch their own business initiatives. The world of Blockchain allows anyone to turn their ideas into reality, making it an exciting platform for entrepreneurship.

6.3 HOW TO CONDUCT TOKENIZATION

Tokenization, regardless of the fundraising method, standard, or platform, aims to secure funds for business expansion. This process entails several critical steps:[33]

1. *Evaluation*: Do I really need a tokenization? With over 8,800 tokens in circulation, it's crucial to ensure that a token fundraiser addresses a genuine problem where Blockchain technology adds value. The

primary question is whether there's a real problem that can be effectively solved using Blockchain technology. This step involves a market analysis to identify the target audience for the fundraiser and the nature of the platform being developed.

It's crucial to conduct a competitive landscape analysis, including an assessment of competing projects, their market presence, and technological innovation. This might involve examining their community engagement (e.g., Telegram channel sizes), project inception dates, and growth trajectory.

In addition to Blockchain, it's essential to explore other emerging technologies such as artificial intelligence or Big Data, and how they're integrated into competing projects. Companies like Nextrope specialize in providing detailed market studies to help businesses plan and execute effective tokenization strategies.

The target group profiling helps in deciding whether the fundraiser should be private, targeting a specific group of investors, or public, open to the entire Internet. This decision hinges on the project's nature, goals, and the kind of investors it aims to attract.

2. *Choosing the jurisdiction*: The choice of location is crucial for token projects due to varying legal frameworks across countries. Establishing a legal entity (a company or foundation) is necessary for legal compliance. For instance, offering tokens to US residents brings your project under US regulations. It's crucial to communicate the token's purpose clearly and avoid labeling it as a security or promising high returns to avoid regulatory issues. Some regions, like Estonia or certain Swiss cantons (e.g., Zug), offer specific licenses for token fundraisers.[34] Estonia is often chosen for its low operational costs and the ease of company registration, facilitated by its e-residency program.

   It's important to remember that each entrepreneur has unique needs, requiring tailored strategies and professional legal advice. As a business owner in the technology sector, it's key to understand these nuances. I'm not a lawyer so I don't provide legal advice myself (Table 6.1).

3. *Assemble and Organize the Team*: Building a strong core team is essential. This team should comprise skilled Blockchain programmers, business development experts, and scaling specialists. Additionally, having advisors with diverse expertise—such as former Blockchain project leaders, lawyers, entrepreneurs, and industry influencers—adds immense value. Sometimes, the quality and experience of the team and advisors often weigh more heavily than the technology itself.

4. *Writing a White Paper and Building the Project's Website*: A token fundraiser requires a clear vision and a roadmap that investors can trust.

Table 6.1 Comparison of selected jurisdictions for conducting ICO-type collections

	Estonia	Japan	Singapore	Switzerland	Malta
Regulations related to crypto trading	Legal, license required	Legal, license required	Legal, license not necessary	Legal, license required	Legal, license required
Cost of registration and entry into local ecosystem	Low	Medium	Low	High	Medium
Bank account	Local bank/PsP	Local bank—the process is complicated	Local bank—the process is complicated	Local bank—the process is complicated	Bank offshore/PsP
Capital gains tax	Doesn't apply	Yes (valid up to a maximum of 55% of the amount)	Doesn't apply	Doesn't apply	Doesn't apply
VAT on crypto trading	Doesn't apply	Doesn't apply	Yes (7%)	Doesn't apply	Doesn't apply
ICO registration	Security tokens only	Security and utility tokens	Security tokens only	Security tokens only	Security and utility tokens
Presence of the company's representative in the state	It's not required—e-registration allows to complete most of the registrations online	It's not required—but most often relations with the administration are difficult	It's required	It's required	It's not required—but most often relations with the administration are difficult

(Source: Nextrope. Used with permission.)

This vision is typically encapsulated in a white paper and detailed on the project's website.[35] Key elements to address include:

a. *Problem Definition and Solution*: Clearly articulating the problem the project intends to solve and how it plans to do so.

b. *Market and Competition Analysis*: Understanding both the Blockchain and the broader market context.

c. *Token Economics*: Outlining the flow of funds between users and the platform, explaining how the token will be used, its utility, and its value proposition.

d. *Project Team and Advisors*: Showcasing the experience and expertise of the team and advisors involved.

A white paper in the Blockchain space is distinct from a traditional business plan. It focuses more on the product (e.g., the platform) and its functionalities, especially aspects unique to Blockchain, like token economics. It tends to have a more academic and research-oriented approach, reflecting the industry's roots in the academic sector. This approach traces back to the legacy of Satoshi Nakamoto's original white paper on Bitcoin.

5. *Creating a Token*: The actual creation of tokens involves developing a smart contract on a chosen Blockchain platform (like Ethereum, Binance, and Waves). While the ER-20 token standard is prevalent, newer standards are being adopted for specialized tokens, including NFTs. The smart contract automates the distribution of tokens and ensures adherence to the predefined rules and conditions of the token's use.

6. *Setting the Parameters of the Token Economy*: Designing the token economy is a vital phase in the tokenization process. It involves determining key variables that will dictate how the smart contract distributes funds in the newly created economic ecosystem. When establishing the token economy, several critical factors need to be considered:

a. *Soft Cap and Hard Cap*: The soft cap is the minimum amount of funds needed to make the project viable. If this amount isn't reached, funds are usually returned to investors. The hard cap is the maximum fundraising goal. Once reached, the token sale ends.

b. *Token Exchange Rate*: Setting the exchange rate of the issued token in relation to cryptocurrencies like ETH or BTC is crucial. Some projects opt for a fixed price in relation to the dollar, offering a stable reference point for investors.

c. *Token Distribution*: Deciding the percentage distribution of tokens among different stakeholders is another essential aspect. This includes allocations for platform participants, project initiators, trading platforms, and the budget reserved for technological development.

Given the ever-changing market, consulting experts in this area can be beneficial. The choice of hybrid models or platforms to handle token fundraisers can significantly impact the project's appeal to potential buyers. Implementing the most effective solutions at this stage is key to attracting a larger group of investors.

Designing the token economy is all about finding the right balance. It's important to consider what the project needs, what investors are looking for, and the goals for the future. A good token economy helps raise funds successfully and sets up the project for long-term growth. The aim is to make sure the token is useful and valuable, encouraging people to use and invest in it. This step is crucial for the project's success and sustainability.

7. *Marketing*: Since practically anyone with a cryptocurrency wallet can invest, leveraging all available marketing platforms is key. This involves maintaining active social media accounts (Facebook, Twitter, Telegram, Reddit, BitcoinTalk) and utilizing blogging platforms for broader outreach. General project communication should be consistent, informative, and engaging across these channels. Alongside general communication, it's advisable to introduce diversified modes of token distribution. This typically includes a presale phase offering tokens at preferential terms, followed by a general sale. Each phase requires tailored marketing strategies to appeal to different investor segments.

The promotional aspect of fundraiser marketing has evolved significantly. Platforms like Facebook, which once restricted ads for token fundraisers, now permit and even actively promote them. Utilizing tools like Google AdSense or Facebook Ads has become more common for advertising crypto projects. These campaigns can incorporate affiliate networks, AirDrop campaigns, or multi-level marketing models to incentivize community engagement in promoting the project. Importantly, the cost of marketing in the crypto space has increased dramatically in recent years. This surge in expenses must be factored into the overall budget and fundraising goals. The rising costs can be attributed to the growing competition in the cryptocurrency market and the increased sophistication of marketing techniques required to stand out. This makes it crucial for projects to allocate sufficient resources toward effective marketing strategies that can penetrate the noise and reach potential investors effectively.

Effective marketing not only raises awareness but also builds trust and community around the project. As the landscape of crypto marketing continues to evolve, staying agile and adaptive to new trends and platforms is essential for the success of any token fundraiser.

8. *Technological Work and Launching the Fundraiser*: When starting a token fundraiser, the key technology piece is building a smart contract on a platform like Ethereum. This contract handles all the tokenization aspects. A few years ago, these fundraisers mainly accepted major cryptocurrencies like (ETH and BTC). Now, they've become more accessible, and you can even join in with fiat currency or credit card

payments. When people contribute money to the project, they get new tokens in return. This process marks the beginning of the fundraiser and sets the stage for the project's growth.

After that, the next big step is listing the token on cryptocurrency exchanges. This makes the token available for trading and provides it with market visibility. Listing on an exchange requires meeting specific criteria set by the exchange. Once the token is out there, managing community expectations becomes crucial. Investors and users will look for progress updates, product development news, and strategies for future growth. Regular communication and transparency are key to maintaining trust and engagement.

Another critical aspect of post-fundraiser is ensuring liquidity for the token, which refers to the ease with which token holders can buy and sell the token. This might involve establishing liquidity pools on decentralized exchanges or arrangements with market makers on centralized exchanges. There are associated with additional cost, which need to be considered in the project's financial planning.

The journey of a token fundraiser goes beyond just raising funds. It extends into getting the token listed on exchanges, engaging with the community, and ensuring the token remains liquid and accessible in the market. These steps are essential for the long-term success and stability of the token and the underlying project.

6.4 FORTUNE FAVORS THE BOLD

Business influencers often share stories about chances they missed. Mark Cuban passed on investing in Uber during its early stages. Gary Vaynerchuk also missed out on an early deal, when offered a stake in the angel round of the business. "I could have had 5% percent of Uber for just $200.000," said Vaynerchuk.[36] With Uber's current valuation, that would be worth $8.33 billion.[37]

When we look at businesses—both the ideas behind it and how it's done—we see that making money from an investment often depends on choosing the right time to jump in. The best chances to make a lot of money come when people start a new venture. When it comes to something like a Blockchain project, there are a few things to think about: How good is the team working on it? How well will their product turn out? How much will the token they create be worth? Since there's a lot we don't know, purchasing a token for speculative purposes can feel almost like playing a lottery.

Does it surprise you that as a person deeply involved in the industry, I use such strong words against cryptocurrency fundraisers? Just look at the data. In 2019, the investors who ventured into initial coin offerings (ICOs)faced slim odds—a mere 17% chance—that their tokens would climb above their initial price after six months. That scenario, while slightly better than in

2018 where the likelihood of breaking even was just 8%, paints a stark picture. The reality is that about 90% of those tokens end up selling below their ICO price.[38] That trend reveals a high risk in such investments. However, it's important to note that in the world of cryptocurrencies, success, though rare, can be remarkably profitable.

Looking at the token fundraising market, I see the brutal operation of Pareto's law of distribution. You've likely heard of it as the 80/20 rule. What does this mean? Like the Italian statistician and engineer Vilfredo Pareto, we could set out very complicated mathematical equations to explain the fundamental principle that governs most phenomena in nature, sociology, and economics. However, it boils down to a simple, though very brutal law: 80% of results (outputs) come from 20% of causes (inputs). It means that things like popularity, success, and money are not spread out evenly among everyone.

Inequalities have been a part of human life forever. We can find clear evidence in the form of old stories and archaeological finds. In Varna, a place in modern-day Bulgaria, archeologists looked at old graves from the Neolithic time. They noticed that most people were buried with simple things like beads, knives, and maybe bone bracelets. But, every fifth grave had something special: small items made of gold.[39] And there's more. Just four graves had most of the gold, about three-quarters of all the gold found in that cemetery. Even back then, some small fraction of people had a lot more than others, despite their overwhelming majority.

Originally, Vilfredo Pareto formulated his principle by looking at income and wealth distribution. He first noticed something in Italy: just 20% of people owned most of the money, about 80%. That made him curious. So, he looked at other countries and saw the same pattern.[40] In many places, a small group of people held onto a big chunk of the wealth. Wherever productivity and creativity count, wealth differences appear. As in the Abba song, "the winner takes it all."

In the business world, especially in areas like investment, the distribution of profits isn't always equal. That concept is particularly noticeable in the Blockchain industry, a field that originally aimed to make financial activities fairer for everyone. Instead, Bitcoin itself is a good example of how Pareto's distribution logic works. Bitcoin operates on the network maintained by miners. They use powerful rigs to solve cryptographic problems. That process is crucial for recording Bitcoin transactions on the digital ledger. As a reward for their efforts and the resources they expend, like electricity and hardware, miners receive Bitcoin. However, there's a twist. The mathematical problems in the Bitcoin network have become increasingly difficult over time. Therefore, miners started to form groups, called mining pools, to combine their computing power and stand a better chance at solving the riddles. As a result, a significant portion of the network's power is now concentrated in the hands of a few large mining pools. In fact, statistics show that the eight largest mining pools control about 89% of the total computing power in the Bitcoin network.[41]

The way money is raised in token fundraisers tells us a lot about Pareto's principle. A striking 80% of ICOs attract fewer than 10,000 participants, showing that most of those events don't get much attention. On the other hand, a very small number of fundraisers stand out dramatically, drawing in huge crowds of over 100,000 investors.[42] That disparity is a perfect example of Pareto's rule in action, where a small portion reaps most of the rewards. I looked closely at 860 fundraisers that happened between March 2014 and June 2018. It was a significant period, because the first wave of fascination with cryptocurrencies entered the mainstream. During this timeframe, the EOS project's fundraiser was a standout. It managed to collect a staggering $4.2 billion, which is over 20% of all the funds raised in every campaign during that period. To give a clearer picture of this imbalance EOS raised as much money as the combined total of the lowest 626 fundraisers. It's a vivid illustration of how Pareto's principle operates in the real world, especially in the dynamic and often unpredictable realm of cryptocurrency fundraising (Figure 6.3).

Although tokenization is global, among the most prestigious projects, there is also a Polish thread, which I hold dear due to my own origins. It's the Golem project. It gained significant attention for its unique business concept. Golem's platform allows for the decentralization of computing resources, enabling individuals with powerful, yet underutilized computers or servers to contribute their excess capacity to a network. In return, they earn Golem's cryptocurrency, GNT. It's like an AirBnB, but for computers.[43] That approach revolutionized the way we think about sharing digital resources. The success of Golem's fundraising in the fall of 2016 is a testament to the potential of token sales. They managed to raise a staggering $8.6 million in just 29 minutes, marking it as one of the largest ICOs at the time, just after Ethereum and Waves.[44]

Golem's remarkable achievement highlights the growing interest and confidence in Blockchain technology and its applications. Token fundraisers are

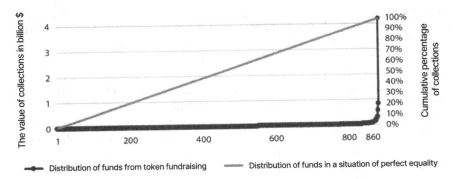

Figure 6.3 Distribution of funds from ICO collections.

(Source: Data from Coindesk.)

a highly flexible form of capital raising. They allow both private individuals and large corporate investors to invest. I've already mentioned how Microsoft supported the NEO project. Similarly, Stratis, another significant Blockchain initiative, gained technological support from Microsoft. Stratis developed a cryptocurrency platform that supports various programming languages, and they managed to raise nearly 1,000 BTC in just five weeks. The initial token price was merely a cent, but its value has since soared to over $2, highlighting the potential of those investments.[45]

Brendan Eich, former CEO of Mozilla, launched his ICO fundraiser for the development of a new browser called Brave. Guess what? He raised $35 million in just 30 seconds.[46] That lightning-fast fundraiser raises some eyebrows. It seems like it wasn't just luck. I'm thinking it was a strategic move by big-time investors. Why do I say that? Well, only about 130 people actually bought Brave's tokens, known as BAT. One major player alone invested a massive $4.6 million and five buyers acquired half of the entire token supply. I think such large projects show the direction in which the biggest cryptocurrency fundraisers are heading. In the future, tokenization will be a big deal in the investment world. It's a game-changer, especially for large institutional investors, because it simplifies the bureaucratic and legal procedures while still maintaining the chance to be a part of developing business.

There's another aspect to consider in the world of token fundraising. While looking at this market, I've noticed some issues. The process isn't always well organized, and there's a lack of clear rules. Also, many people who buy tokens don't fully understand what they're getting into. This confusion can lead to odd demands and mistaken beliefs about how profitable these tokens can be. Plus, there's a general misunderstanding about how crowdfunding really works. This becomes clear when you hear the complaints from people who have donated to these projects. They often express frustration about the direction the projects are taking, showing there's a gap in understanding between the project organizers and the supporters.

Blockchain technology is still a new thing. People who have invested in it really pay attention to every little thing about their projects. They know it's like a test run, full of possibilities. However, the people behind a successful project could go from dreaming of being millionaires to actually being billionaires in the world of crypto. Because it's a world where big risks can lead to big rewards.

NOTES

1 https://www.grandviewresearch.com/industry-analysis/blockchain-technology-market

2 https://www.grandviewresearch.com/industry-analysis/blockchain-technology-market

3 https://www.weforum.org/agenda/2017/06/3-ways-blockchain-can-accelerate-financial-inclusion/

4 https://data.worldbank.org/indicator/NY.GDP.PCAP.CD
5 https://www.statista.com/chart/18345/crypto-currency-adoption/
6 https://www.weforum.org/agenda/2021/01/cryptocurrencies-are-democratising-the-financial-world-heres-how/
7 https://time.com/5486673/bitcoin-venezuela-authoritarian/
8 https://www.nationmaster.com/country-info/stats/Economy/GDP-per-capita-in-1950
9 https://www.nationalbusinesscapital.com/2019-small-business-failure-rate-startup-statistics-industry/
10 https://www.score.org/blog/1-reason-small-businesses-fail-and-how-avoid-it
11 https://courses.lumenlearning.com/wm-introductiontobusiness/chapter/reading-functional-areas-of-business/
12 https://pitchdeckfire.com/resources/what-is-an-fff-round-investor-pitch-101/
13 https://maxpolyakov.com/fff-and-business-angels/
14 https://www.cbinsights.com/research/venture-capital-funnel-2/
15 https://publications.jrc.ec.europa.eu/repository/bitstream/JRC98783/jrc98783.pdf
16 https://link.springer.com/article/10.1007/s11187-020-00337-9
17 https://www.forbes.com/sites/lawrencewintermeyer/2023/07/06/big-financial-institutions-are-adopting-crypto-and-blockchain---what-does-the-technology-offer-smbs/
18 http://www.nfib-sbet.org/
19 https://www.talium-assets.com/ico-sto-ieo-ipo-crowdfunding-how-to-figure-it-out/
20 https://icobench.com/stats
21 Ibid.
22 https://coinmarketcap.com/alexandria/glossary/initial-dex-offering
23 https://hackernoon.com/a-comprehensive-guide-to-icos-crypto-funding-the-rise-the-boom-the-bust-the-next-b159fdf38010
24 https://medium.com/hackernoon/ico-101-history-of-initial-coin-offerings-icos-part-1-from-mastercoin-to-ethereum-4689b7c2326b
25 https://ethereum.org/en/developers/docs/standards/tokens/erc-20/
26 https://bravenewcoin.com/insights/mckinsey-sees-blockchain-technology-reaching-full-potential-in-5-years
27 https://everipedia.org/wiki/lang_en/forkdelta
28 https://www.chainbits.com/exchanges/best-decentralized-exchanges-for-trading-cryptocurrency/
29 https://medium.com/@vikati/ranking-ethereum-smart-contracts-a27e6f622ac6
30 https://www.altexsoft.com/blog/engineering/what-is-api-definition-types-specifications-documentation/
31 http://www.proactiveinvestors.com.au/companies/news/190721/animoca-brands-one-of-the-asx-top-performers-in-2018-190721.html
32 https://medium.com/@vikati/ranking-ethereum-smart-contracts-a27e6f622ac6
33 https://www.velvetech.com/blog/how-to-launch-a-successful-ico/
34 Ibid.
35 https://medium.com/@blockchain101/9-steps-for-launching-an-ico-104b62b34a3c
36 https://www.huffpost.com/entry/this-200k-investment-in-2010-is-worth-33-billion_b_579d8edbe4b00e7e269f99bd
37 https://finance.yahoo.com/quote/UBER/key-statistics/

38 https://papers.ssrn.com/sol3/papers.cfm?abstract_id=3770793
39 https://www.smithsonianmag.com/travel/varna-bulgaria-gold-graves-social-hierarchy-prehistoric-archaelogy-smithsonian-journeys-travel-quarterly-180958733/
40 https://www.getrevue.co/profile/TheWolfDen/issues/the-wolf-den-127-the-pareto-principle-297336
41 https://www.linkedin.com/pulse/paretos-law-crypto-market-r%C3%A9da-berrehili
42 https://medium.com/@cryptoreachco/80-20-principle-for-ico-token-sale-success-f4a7e1552c85
43 https://www.financemagnates.com/cryptocurrency/news/golem-raises-8-6-million-29-minutes-fund-airbnb-computers/
44 https://www.forbes.com/sites/rogeraitken/2016/11/12/fintech-golems-airbnb-for-computing-crowdsale-scores-8-6m-in-minutes/
45 Top 10 ICOs with the Biggest ROI, Coin Telegraph, access: 27.09.2021.
46 https://techcrunch.com/2017/06/01/brave-ico-35-million-30-seconds-brendan-eich/

Chapter 7

Fresh start

7.1 ORWELLIAN CRYPTOCURRENCY

Reflecting on my academic journey, I'm often drawn back to a pivotal book from my school days—George Orwell's *Animal Farm*. This novella had first entered my world during Polish middle school and later resurfaced in my English literature class as part of the international baccalaureate program. The book is about a group of farm animals who kick out their human farmer and try to run the farm themselves. The pigs are the leaders of such rebellion. They wanted to make a place where all animals are equal and happy, but things didn't go as planned.

One of the most striking symbols from *Animal Farm* that has stayed with me is the transformative image of pigs sitting at a table, clothed like humans, drinking alcohol. Initially, these pigs had vowed never to emulate human behaviors or collaborate with them. However, as the story progresses, the stark reality of power dynamics emerges. The revolutionary pigs begin to mirror the very humans they had overthrown. The book's closing line captures this irony: "The creatures outside looked from pig to man, and from man to pig, and from pig to man again; but already it was impossible to say which was which."[1]

Orwell's book isn't just a story about animals on a farm. It conveys a deeper message about political change. It's similar to what happened during the Bolshevik Revolution in 1917. This idea of change and power is something I also see in the world of cryptocurrencies like Bitcoin. They started as a new, different way of thinking about money, separate from traditional banks. But over time, they've become more like the very financial systems they were meant to change.

The creator of Bitcoin, Satoshi Nakamoto, also hinted at his political views. The first-ever Bitcoin block includes a message about the government using taxpayers' money to save banks. This idea of linking politics with finance quickly became popular among Bitcoin users. Here are some quotes that highlight this connection:

DOI: 10.1201/9781032621456-8

Yes, [we will not find a solution to political problems in cryptography,] but we can win a major battle in the arms race and gain a new territory of freedom for several years[2]
—*Satoshi Nakamoto, cryptocurrency community mailing list*

Someone who promotes Bitcoin who is not an anarchist is a crypto-anarchist because Bitcoin is inherently anarchistic[3]
—*Daniel Krawisz, researcher at the Satoshi Nakamoto Institute, panel discussion from 2014*

[Satoshi] just read the morning paper with its continuing news of financial turpitude on the part of elites acting for their own benefit. Aha, there is a perfect snippet about the two agencies responsible for the economic rape of average people: government and the banking system. (...) The digital currency [described in Satoshi's Whitepaper] and payment system to which the message is attached are the antidote to the corruption of governments and banks. From Bitcoin's first words, it returned power to the people
—*Wendy McElroy, publication titled The Satoshi Revolution: A Revolution of Rising Expectations[4]*

The bold statements surrounding cryptocurrencies highlight their dual nature. They were born not just as a technological innovation through Blockchain but also as a spark for a broader revolution, encompassing economic, political, and social spheres. This revolutionary spirit of cryptocurrencies often reminds me of the fervent slogans of the pigs in Orwell's *Animal Farm*, where they proclaim, "Man is the only real enemy we have. Remove Man from the scene, and the root cause of hunger and overwork is abolished forever."[5]

Now, 14 years after the birth of this cryptocurrency revolution, it seems the original spirit of a "worlds-at-war" has faded. The fight between the cryptocurrency world and governments and big finance companies doesn't seem as big anymore. Instead, they're working together. Companies that trade in cryptocurrencies are now big players in financial markets. Investment banks are making a lot of money from things like Bitcoin funds, and even regular banks are trying to make their own types of digital money.

We stand at a critical point for the future of cryptocurrencies. Will they keep being something different in finance, or just become another tool for big banks to make money? Ray Dalio, who started the biggest hedge fund in the world, Bridgewater Associates, has a strong opinion. He says, "I think at the end of the day if it's [about cryptocurrencies] really successful, they [regulators] will kill it."[6] What will happen to cryptocurrencies in the future if he's right?

7.2 CRYPTOCRIMES

7.2.1 Attacks on cryptocurrency exchanges

When you begin trading cryptocurrencies, the common approach is to have two different places to keep them. First, you set up an account on a cryptocurrency exchange. That's where you'll buy and sell your cryptocurrencies. Second, you need a separate wallet. After buying cryptocurrencies, you move them from the exchange to the wallet for safekeeping. Experts in the market advise that method for a good reason. Although exchanges are great for trading, they're not the best for storing your cryptocurrencies. In the past, especially when the cryptocurrency world was just starting, exchanges often faced hacking attacks. These hacks caused traders to lose a lot of money. Hence, having a separate wallet keeps your investment safer.

The story begins with Mt. Gox, the first big cryptocurrency exchange. It started in 2010, around the same time people began using cryptocurrencies. Jed McCaleb, a key person in the Blockchain world, created Mt. Gox. Before, McCaleb helped create Ripple, a system that makes it easy and cheap for banks to send money quickly. Ripple has its own digital money called XRP. By 2018, the value of McCaleb's XRP was about $20 billion, making him one of the richest people in the world, according to *Forbes*.[7] But things changed for McCaleb. He had some disagreements with his team at Ripple, so he decided to leave. He then started a new project called Stellar (XLM).[8] Both XRP and XLM used to be among the top 10 most significant cryptocurrencies on the market.[9]

McCaleb first introduced necessary improvements to the Mt. Gox trading platform and then sold it in 2011—before the major attack and one of the biggest scandals in Blockchain history. Probably for this reason, the problems of earlier projects did not affect McCaleb's business career. After he left, the new management registered a company in Japan for the project and began aggressively promoting the platform. From then on, Mt. Gox was led by Mark Karpelès, a French entrepreneur and Blockchain industry influencer.[10] Before the exchange attack scandal erupted, he was a board member of the Bitcoin Foundation—a non-profit organization dedicated to the development and promotion of cryptocurrencies.

Mt. Gox was once the biggest place in the world for trading cryptocurrencies, handling about 70% of all Bitcoin transactions.[11] It was a really important exchange for cryptocurrencies. But as it got more and more popular, the people running it couldn't keep up. They had a hard time making sure everything was safe and working right. Back in 2013, Mt. Gox already had problems. They weren't following the rules about stopping illegal money activities, known as Anti-Money Laundering (AML) laws.[12] There were also a lot of mistakes happening, like people not being able to trade or take their money out. Because of all those issues, the American government stepped in to keep an eye on Mt. Gox.

It turned out that Mt. Gox's partner did not have the proper licenses for electronic money transfers. In just two months, the US Department of Homeland Security seized over $5 million from the accounts of partner company Dwolla.[13] As these funds ultimately belonged to Mt. Gox users, the popular cryptocurrency exchange began to have liquidity problems. At the same time, the media began to highlight stories of users who could not withdraw funds from their Bitcoin wallets. The average wait time was one to three months, but every fifth respondent waited three months or longer.[14]

That couldn't go on forever. In late February 2014, Mt. Gox stopped all their work and shut down their website. At the same time, a secret company paper got out.[15] It was a plan for handling big problems. The paper revealed some scary news. The company had no money left. They lost over 744,000 Bitcoins because someone stole them. The worst part? They didn't know about the theft for many years.[16]

The company lost a number of Bitcoins equivalent to about 7% of the total global BTC supply. According to the BTC exchange rate in February 2014, the losses of Mt. Gox users amounted to a record-breaking industry sum of $450 million. Despite the passing years, none of the users have received compensation.[17] Legal proceedings against Karpelès and his company are still ongoing in both Japan and the United States. The most important legal and criminal units have been involved in the investigation, including the US Department of Justice. The theft of Bitcoins from the Mt. Gox exchange is suspected to have been carried out by Russian Aleksandr Vinnik, owner of the Bitcoin exchange BTC-e. Vinnik is currently serving a five-year prison sentence. However, he was not convicted for the scandal associated with Mt. Gox, yet for money laundering.[18]

The story of Mt. Gox's fall is both shocking and educational. It's hard to believe that a company could miss the fact that they lost $450 million. The reason for this huge mistake was a problem in the early Bitcoin system, combined with some unusual ways of operation at Mt. Gox. The error, known as transaction malleability, lets people change details in Bitcoin transactions. That flaw had not been fixed until after the big Mt. Gox scandal happened. This whole situation showed how important it is to have good security and careful checks in place, especially when dealing with digital money like Bitcoin. Mt. Gox's mess helped make Bitcoin safer in the end.

When you send Bitcoins, your account confirms the details like who's sending, where it's going, and how much.[19] Those details get a special code called a transaction identifier. But, there's a catch. Part of the info of the code isn't secured. So, someone could change the code without you knowing. Now, it doesn't mess up the important parts of the payment, which are still safe. But it can cause trouble if you expect your Bitcoin transaction to show up with a certain identifier. Let's look at what might have happened with Mt. Gox. They were waiting for transactions to show up with certain codes. But if someone sneaky changed them, Mt. Gox wouldn't see the transactions. The sneaky person could then say, "Hey, my Bitcoin didn't go through." Mt. Gox's system, thinking the transaction failed, would try again and send more Bitcoin.[20] So, a small change in the transaction code can lead to big problems.

The scale of theft in cryptocurrency exchanges surpasses anything we've seen in the analog world. Let's compare it to the greatest robbery that happened in 1997 in the US Six armed men broke into a Dunbar Armored truck, a cash transportation and money transfer company. They made away with $18.9 million, which in real terms (a.k.a. taking inflation into account) corresponds to $42 million now.[21] But even that amount is much smaller than what the hackers took from Mt. Gox back in 2014.

In 2014, Bitcoin developers fixed a major issue, leading to the recovery of 200,000 missing Bitcoins by Mt. Gox administrators.[22] Despite this improvement and ongoing security updates, the risk of cyberattacks in the cryptocurrency world remains high. In contrast, traditional finance has more safety measures. Banks are insured by the Bank Guarantee Fund, so even if they fail, customers and investors are partially (to certain threshold) protected from losing their money. Also, if you forget your online banking password, you can easily recover it by visiting a bank branch.

In the world of cryptocurrencies, people have to take care of their digital money themselves. A big problem is that about 20% of all Bitcoins might be owned by people who lost the passwords to their accounts.[23] For example, there's a programmer named Stefan Thomas in San Francisco. In a 2011 interview with *Wired* magazine, Thomas revealed that he accidentally deleted two backup copies of his cryptocurrencies. He was left with only the third and final copy, which he transferred to an encrypted USB drive named Iron Key. During the interview, he mentioned losing the note with the key to that wallet, resulting in the loss of access to $140,000 in Bitcoins.[24]

Fast forward over a decade, and the Bitcoins remain locked in that wallet, now valued at over $500,000. The Iron Key is designed to wipe its contents entirely if an incorrect password is entered 10 times. Thomas has attempted eight times already. However, a startup named Unciphered approached Thomas. They are a team of hackers specializing in attempts to open such wallets. Their strategy is as follows: they first bought a whole bunch of wallets like Thomas' to recreate its construction. Subjected the wallet to a 3D scanner and then used a precise laser cutting tool to extract the secured chip. The chip was then treated with liquid nitrogen to remove the epoxy protecting it. Subsequently, using an incredibly precise tool, they slowly shaved and polished the chip layer by layer, each time removing material of micron-scale fractions. Every time they removed content from the chip, they took microscopic images and pieced together a model of the processor.

Finally, in July 2023, they successfully bypassed the Iron Key's security, hacking it in a way that allows an infinite number of password attempts, essentially removing the ten-attempt limit. They can now guess the password after approximately 200 trillion attempts, taking around 24 hours. However, there's a significant hitch—Thomas refuses to let this particular company recover his password. He doesn't grant permission to access his cryptocurrencies, and the reasons remain unknown. Is there a motive behind Thomas' reluctance? Could the wallet hold no Bitcoins, or does he seek to avoid the commission demanded by Unciphered?

For sure the story of Stefan Thomas makes for a cool anecdote. I invite you to follow it because with each new answer being given to the public, more and more question marks pop up. However, there is a universal message stemming from such stories. Crypto investors who weren't careful enough now cannot get to their Bitcoin millions. These stories show how important it is to keep track of your digital keys carefully in the world of cryptocurrencies. If you cannot count on anyone else to come and rescue you in moment of panic, you must be proactive and count on yourself before all others.

In the world of crypto, investors must carefully conduct their risk assessment. They must balance risk and the high potential returns offered by cryptocurrencies, which are not typically found in traditional financial products. The cryptocurrency ecosystem, while offering lucrative opportunities, also presents unique risks such as exchange break-ins and various technical challenges. Investors are well aware of the risks, and they factor them into their profitability calculations when deciding to invest in cryptocurrencies. That approach is essential for anyone looking to make money in the fast-paced world of crypto.

In my opinion, when choosing a cryptocurrency exchange, it's most important to look at the operating model, especially for safety reasons. Centralized exchanges, or CEX, work like traditional stock markets. They have a company in the middle of every deal, taking care of the money and making sure everything goes right. On the other hand, decentralized exchanges (DEX), don't have an intermediary. Instead, they use Blockchain technology to record every money move. Some exchanges mix these two types, creating what's called a hybrid exchange or Semi DEX. They try to use the best parts of both centralized and decentralized systems (Table 7.1).

Choosing the right cryptocurrency exchange is about balancing safety and the variety of trading options. Licensed exchanges are safer because they follow stricter rules, but they often have fewer types of tokens to trade and higher prices. That's because they have to meet many legal rules and keep a lot of money in reserve. For example, Coinbase, a big licensed exchange, had to keep $4 billion in cash in 2021 to make sure it followed rules and kept its platform stable.[25] Thanks to the "safety cushion" in the form of cash reserves, the exchange can secure liquidity on its cryptocurrency trading platform. On the other side, unlicensed exchanges don't have to follow as many rules.[26]

Table 7.1 Comparison of centralized and decentralized exchanges

	Centralized exchange (CEX)	Decentralized exchange (DEX)
Controlling party	Platform administrator	User
Security	Risk of hacking	Low chances of hacking due to Blockchain's use at all stages of the user process
Fees	Fees for using the platform in the form of commissions on transactions	Low or minimal fees
Functionality	Provides a variety of functions	Very few functions available
Supervision	High regulatory oversight; licensed activities	Outside regulatory oversight; no license required
Liquidity	High, guaranteed by exchange operator	Dependent on movement of funds on the exchange
Speed	Constant, instantaneous	Lower, dependent on traders' activities

They can offer more types of tokens and lower prices. Additionally, they can change their business practices more easily, which can be good for users who want more trading options and lower costs. So, when you're choosing an exchange, think about what's important for you.

In the world of digital currencies, there are different places, like OpenSea for NFTs (a type of digital collectible) and Uniswap for trading tokens on Ethereum, where people can invest their money. But where those exchanges are located and the rules they follow also matter a lot.[27] Exchanges in Europe, for example, follow European rules and obtain special licenses. Also, in places like the United States, there are even tougher rules for exchanges. Well-known ones like Coinbase and Gemini strictly stick to American standards. Therefore, they are widely considered safer places to trade digital currencies.[28]

We already know how Mt. Gox got hacked. That was a big problem in the world of digital money. Now, compare it to a scandal in 2020 with a German company Wirecard that made systems for online payments and cards. Despite numerous audits by leading corporations such as EY or KPMG, it turned out Wirecard was missing 1.9 billion euros in their accounting entries. The *Financial Times* newspaper found out and looked into how Wirecard worked.[29] The company was doing business in Germany but was moving money through other companies in countries like India, the Philippines, and Singapore. Those countries didn't watch over Wirecard's activities closely, so it was possible to play around with the numbers.[30] A shocking moment came when reporters went to the Philippines. They were looking for the office of one of Wirecard's partners. But instead of finding an office, they found a small hut with a retired fisherman who knew nothing about the situation.[31]

Wirecard was once a big and trusted name in Germany's financial world, listed on the important DAX index. In Germany, financial companies have to be part of the Banking Guarantee Fund (Banking Association—Bankenverband). It gives people a safety net when things go wrong in companies like Wirecard.[32] When we look at Wirecard and compare it to the world of cryptocurrencies, like the Mt. Gox case, we see some similarities as well as differences. Both Wirecard and Mt. Gox were very well-known in their areas—in regular banking and in cryptocurrency exchanges. They started showing small problems at first, but those were often ignored because people trusted them. In the end, journalists and the people who lost money worked hard to uncover the big scandals in both companies.

The main difference between these models is how they protect people from fraud and attacks. In regular banks, there's a rule that they must insure your funds. So, if you become a victim of a scam, you can count on the bank's support and compensation for losses. But in cryptocurrency, like when you use Bitcoin, there's no such protection. If a crypto exchange gets attacked or shuts down, you're on your own. Dealing with cryptocurrencies is risky. You need to be brave and smart because you don't get a second chance or help from anyone if things go wrong.

7.2.2 Crypto in organized crime

The vision of Satoshi Nakamoto in creating Bitcoin was to establish a form of "digital anarchy." Eliminating the central controller of data and money circulation has many advantages: flexibility, freedom, and anonymity. However, human nature also has a dark side. With decentralization, we don't just gain assets—we also encounter significant challenges and problems. What If there is no place for procedures and proper supervision in digital reality? Well, cryptocurrencies can become a tool in the hands of criminals.

Digital money crimes started way before Bitcoin. Let me remind you of e-gold, an early digital money system from the mid-1990s. It had legal and technical gaps that let scammers do illegal stuff, like making fake financial schemes and even funding child pornography.[33] All of it has been proven in court. Fast forward over 20 years and digital money is still sometimes used for crime. But, if you're unsure about cryptocurrencies, hold on before judging. It's not the digital currencies that are the problem, it's how some people choose to use them.

People steal electricity to mine cryptocurrencies. They also use it for illegal gambling, drug dealing, and banned stuff online. Even someone who doesn't know much about crypto or forensic finance gets that. Forensic finance is a new thing. It mixes law, economics, and crime studies. I think there's still little talk about the use of cryptocurrencies in hacker attacks. That's the main point of the crime story I want to share. It's a big deal and it really struck me some time ago.

In May 2021, there was a big cyber-attack on the Colonial Pipeline. The largest pipeline in the United States. It carries a lot of petroleum products—like 2.39 million barrels (or 380 million liters) a day—from Texas to New York. As I'm writing these words at current prices per barrel, that much oil is worth over $186 million. I mentioned the wholesale, not even the retail price.[34] The Colonial Pipeline is a key infrastructure facility for the East Coast. More than 50 million people get their fuel and gas from it.[35] It's really important for businesses, hospitals, firefighters, police, and others who keep the United States safe. But one day, something went wrong. The administrators suddenly couldn't control the pipeline and lost 100 GB of important data. How did that happen?

DarkSide is a group of hackers, likely from Russia. At least that's where they had left first traces of their activity in August 2020. DarkSide is known for ransomware attacks, which have been a big problem online worldwide. "Ransomware" comes from "ransom," meaning demanding money to solve an artificial problem. Hackers put harmful software on a company's computers or lock them out of important files and systems. Then they demand payment for removing the blockade. The attack on Colonial Pipeline cut off fuel supply to many states for 10 days. Initially, they demanded 75 BTC. Hackers like using cryptocurrencies like Bitcoin because it's hard to trace who owns them.

Over the past few years, ransomware attacks have been a huge problem. A situation similar to the blockade of the Colonial Pipeline happened to the Irish health service, and even to a technology giant—Toshiba Corporation.[36] How does a ransomware attack work? The entire chat conversation was recently revealed by an international cybersecurity company, Intel 471.[37] Its team revealed the chat content of one of the American companies that fell victim to the same group of hackers before the attack on Colonial Pipeline. To better understand how a ransomware attack works, it's worth quoting the scenario of a conversation with hackers:

- Your network has been locked! You need pay $30,000,000 now, or $60,000,000 after the amount doubles just tomorrow. After payment we will provide your universal decryptor for all network. Don't worry, we are good decryption specialists.
- How do I know you can decrypt our data?
- We will decrypt some sample file for you.
- When you receive payment, you will not publish the attack or sell exfiltrated data?
- Of course not, you will gain an access to a server with data and will delete it yourself. Also, we can provide to you a pretest report how you have been breached and what need to improve.
- This is a lot of money. My management needs a better understanding of what data you may have taken. Can you provide proof you have our data?

- Yes, will provide a sample for you.
- We are prepared to offer you $2.25 million for the decryption tool for all of our systems and the return of all data that you took.
- You also agree not to post information about this incident and not to sell, share, or retain any copies of our data. We also seek additional detail on how you were able to gain access. Are these terms acceptable to you?
- [We agree to lower the rate, but to 28 million]. The timer it ticking and in in next 8 hours your price tag will go up to 60 million. So, these are your options: either take our generous offer and pay us $28million or invest some monies in quantum computing to expedite a decryption process.
- That isn't much movement. We need additional time. Could you please extend the deadline to Friday?
- I don't think so. You aren't poor and you aren't childen. If you fucked up you have to meet the consequences.[38]

After a few days of negotiation, the company paid the DarkSide hackers $11 million. Colonial Pipeline paid almost $5 million. They used cryptocurrencies, like Bitcoin, for payment. Things ended somewhat well for Colonial Pipeline. In early June, a month after the attack, the US government said they recovered 63.7 BTC ($2.3 million at the time).[39] The FBI found the people responsible. One person they questioned was able to open the digital wallet holding most of the stolen money. They didn't tell how they found the hackers.[40] In a press release[41] they just said that they followed the money transfers between digital wallets using special tools.

What scares me the most about all recent ransomware cases is the trend toward institutionalization. Cybercrime is now organized. Alongside the coordination of ransomware attacks, a new business model has emerged in the hacker community. As early as August 2020, there were posts on Russian forums that DarkSide and similar groups offer an attack platform solution that other criminal organizations can use for a fee. This business model is known as Ransomware-as-a-Service (RaaS). The hackers have created an ethical business as they prohibit their "clients" from attacking key sectors, including education, selected medical services, NGOs, and the public sector.[42] The main targets of the attacks are reputable stock market companies listed on NASDAQ. Anonymous representatives of DarkSide write on their site: "If the company refuses to pay, we are ready to give information before publication so that you can earn on the drop in stock prices. Write to us in the Contact tab, and we will give you detailed information."[43]

People from DarkSide have a bold approach. They promote their illegal services online, just like a regular business. On their website, you'll find a section titled "Why choose us?" where they offer advice and market research. Their business model, known as RaaS, includes a unique "call center" service. This allows DarkSide's clients to force people to pay ransoms through phone calls.[44] They also collaborate with partners to launch distributed denial of service (DDoS) attacks, which are used to shut down websites. That tactic adds extra pressure during ransom negotiations.[45] Tracking down those criminals is difficult. They cover their tracks using both legal methods like the Tor network and illegal ones such as the deep web and dark web.

The Colonial Pipeline attack might turn out to be a good thing. It shows that we can stand up to big ransomware attacks, and there's a chance to get back the money lost. But, it's hard to say if that will always be the case. Will we be able to consistently recover money from hackers in the future? Nowadays, there's a new type of business growing in the Blockchain world. Some companies focus on protecting their clients from cyber threats. They check the safety of computer systems, including the Blockchain-based ones. They do it by simulating attacks. It helps them find weak spots that need fixing.[46] If there's a real attack, modern technology can track the hacker's digital wallet. This way, it's possible to follow the money they stole.

However, identification is only the first step toward recovering funds from a ransomware attack. Currently, criminals use, among other things, split payments and beneficiary identity forging—all techniques that effectively prevent criminal investigation. The ransom for the American pipeline was paid using Bitcoins, although most ransomware-sending hackers demand payment in the cryptocurrency Monero.[47] This is a cryptocurrency that, even more than its predecessors, focuses on solutions that strengthen privacy and complete user anonymity. Currently, it is practically impossible to decrypt the circulation of funds in Monero—although US authorities are already offering high rewards (over $625,000) for software that would break anonymity protections in this system.[48]

Cryptocurrencies, like all tech, are not just good or bad. They're used by people who can be good or bad. Just because some bad guys use crypto doesn't mean it's bad. Blockchain is pretty neat. It adds extra security to financial and legal systems with its complex algorithms. That technology could be a game-changer in many fields. Let's look at the Wirecard incident, where a huge sum of 1.9 billion euros just disappeared. If their accounting had been done on a Blockchain system, that might have been prevented. With Blockchain, it doesn't matter if you're in Germany or the Philippines, everyone sees the same thing. It's beyond national borders. Plus, every transaction made on the Blockchain is registered clearly and permanently. It's like a permanent mark that can't be erased or altered. This level of transparency and security is what makes Blockchain so promising and useful in various sectors. In my opinion, using cryptocurrencies and Blockchain technology can solve many big problems we face today. Perhaps, it would make the world a better place. However, Blockchain isn't perfect. If bad people use it, it can cause harm. Hence, we need good rules and teamwork for projects that use cryptocurrencies and Blockchain.

7.3 EVERY COUNTRY HAS ITS OWN CUSTOMS

Cryptocurrencies were initially envisioned as a system operating independently of government control. However, the reality is more complex. Every Blockchain developer and cryptocurrency entrepreneur holds a citizenship, and when they form companies or foundations, these entities are bound by the laws of the country where they are registered or based. This connection to national legal systems brings varying interpretations of cryptocurrency's legality across the globe. For instance, countries like China have completely banned them, while others have welcomed them with open arms (Figure 7.1).

This variation has led to an international rivalry, as countries compete to attract cryptocurrency investors, Blockchain companies, and technological research. These early divides, formed when cryptocurrencies were just starting, are now shaping the choices and directions of crypto millionaires. The decisions made in these formative years are likely to influence the future trajectory of the cryptocurrency world, determining which nations will lead in this evolving financial landscape.

7.3.1 Reasoned skepticism

Early doubts about cryptocurrencies mainly came from experts in universities. Let's start with the Nobel Prize winners in economics. Paul Krugman called Bitcoin a "more obvious bubble than the housing bubble," an asset without coverage, and a "flashy technological curiosity that no one really understands."[49] Even stronger accusations were made by Nouriel Roubini, a professor at NYU. He called "crypto" the "mother of all bubbles and scams."[50] He said that "cryptocurrencies should not be talked about as currencies" due to their impracticality and fluctuations of around 5–10%. "Even the Flintstones had a better monetary system!"—Roubini thundered.[51]

This academic criticism soon echoed in the financial sector. In the beginning, big banks and investment funds, which could make a lot of money from crypto, kept their distance. For example, in October 2021, even when crypto prices were high, Jamie Dimon, the boss of JPMorgan Chase, said he thought Bitcoin was worthless. But at the same time, his bank was offering crypto-related products and had been using its own crypto coin for bank payments for two years. Dimon later changed his mind a bit, saying he didn't want to be the face of the issue. He pointed out that if customers wanted to buy Bitcoin, the bank would help them do it legally.[52]

Governments and public bodies started paying attention to these expert opinions too. The United States, and California in particular, has always been a leader in digital tech, like online shopping, credit cards, and electronic stock trading. With all this background in digital finance, the United States had rules for digital money even before Bitcoin came around. In my job, I work with lawyers who know all about these rules. They deal with a

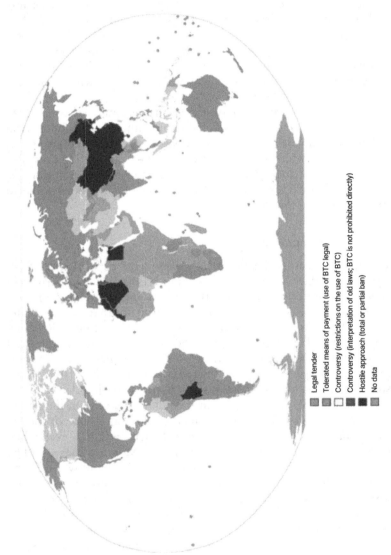

Figure 7.1 Map of Bitcoin's legal status around the world.

(*Source:* **Manabimasu, CC0, via Wikimedia Commons, https://commons.wikimedia.org/wiki/ File:Legal_status_of_bitcoin.svg. Used with courtesy.**)

lot of long, sometimes boring documents about things like how Blockchains talk to each other and check who's using them. However, I would like to share with you what I consider to be the most interesting and useful information.

If you kept an eye on the Blockchain and tokenization market, you should have noticed that it's quite tough for American citizens to get involved. When a crypto project wants to get funding from Americans, it faces a complex and costly set of legal hoops to jump through. This kind of stringent process isn't as common in other countries. So, why is it like this in the United States?

The main reason is the approach of the US Securities and Exchange Commission (SEC). The SEC sets clear rules for all sorts of investments, including stocks, bonds, derivatives, and digital assets like tokens and cryptocurrencies. They use the Howey test to figure out how to handle tokenization. Projects that want to collect tokens have to go through a rigorous registration and monitoring process, as per the SEC's rules. To attract American investors to Initial Coin Offerings (ICOs), following these regulations can be more expensive than creating a system that blocks US investors from participation. But this blocking is a big deal—it means missing out on thousands of potential investors in the States. Over the years, both as someone watching the market and as a service provider in the ICO value chain, I've noticed the costs of this process have been going down. The SEC itself says in their official statements that they look at each case separately.[53] This means that figuring out the value of each project is crucial for entrepreneurs interested in ICOs. It's also a big challenge for the tech service providers involved in these projects. This individualized approach by the SEC has a significant impact on the whole process of launching and managing ICOs, especially when it involves US investors.

Even with the SEC's strict stance on token collections, the United States has stayed at the forefront of Blockchain sector development. An impressive 51% of the world's Blockchain development financing originates from the United States.[54] The Americans have managed to propel cryptocurrencies into the mainstream through strategic licensing, innovative products, and a robust academic sector. Remember, the early cryptographic research that laid the groundwork for commercial applications came from top US universities. This was bound to lead to success.

The blend of high business skills and technical expertise in the United States led to several notable achievements in the cryptocurrency world. Take, for instance, Brian Armstrong and Fred Ehrsam, who previously worked at AirBnB and Goldman Sachs. They elevated investing in the Blockchain industry by founding the cryptocurrency exchange Coinbase. They started with support from the prestigious Y Combinator incubator, moved through several private market investment rounds, and eventually took their company public on the American stock exchange.[55] Coinbase's debut on the New York Stock Exchange was a historical moment, marking the first time a company focused on cryptocurrency operations went public. At the time of its IPO, Coinbase was valued at a staggering $47 billion.[56] These entrepreneurs, who built their exchanges in compliance with existing law rather than against it, not only became crypto millionaires but also billionaires. Getting the balance right between being innovative and following regulations has helped cryptocurrencies grow and become accepted in the United States, setting an example for others in the industry.

Company	Coinbase		Gemini	
Crypto millionaire	Brian Armstrong[57]	Fred Ehrsam[58]	Tyler Winklevoss[59]	Cameron Winklevoss[60]
Completed studies and work experience	William Marsh Rice University (computer science); work at AirBnB	Duke University (computer science and economics); work at Goldman Sachs	Harvard University, Oxford University (economics and business); sports career in rowing and competing Olympic Games at the Beijing IO; experience developing a social media platform social media with Mark Zuckerberg, prior to the creation of Facebook	
Age	40 years	35 years	42 years	42 years
Estimated net assets (XII 2023)	$5.9 B	$1,8 B	$1.4 B	$1.4 B
Position on the global list "Forbes 400" 2023	475	1,633	2,091	2,089

7.3.2 Crypto-islands, crypto-valleys

While many governments were either discouraging investments in cryptocurrencies or setting up tough restrictions (often based on outdated laws), some countries saw a golden opportunity in the emerging Blockchain world. I saw this difference first-hand while living in the United Arab Emirates. I wasn't just observing—I was actively involved in shaping the local distributed ledger technology (DLT) ecosystem. One project I worked on was developing a Blockchain-based notary registry for Dubai's housing market. The UAE government had a big vision with its Smart Dubai strategy, aiming to move key public and infrastructure services to Blockchain technology by 2021.[61] This target year wasn't chosen randomly—it marked the 50th anniversary of the country's foundation.

Dubai didn't meet all its Blockchain goals, but the progress in digitizing the city's Blockchain network is still noteworthy. For example, in 2020, they launched a Blockchain platform for the Emirati customs service, Cross Border e-Commerce. This platform aims to cut the cost of e-commerce transactions by 20%,[62] which is crucial for a country that relies heavily on importing consumer goods like food, clothing, and electronics. Remember, Dubai is home to Jebel Ali, the world's largest commercial seaport.

To the average person, projects like Blockchain platforms for customs or notary offices might not seem thrilling. They're essentially new ways to organize legal and economic data. You won't find viral stories or memes about these IT platforms, unlike the ones the crypto community shares about buying the legendary #Lambo. But maybe that's why Dubai chose to steer clear of the hype around cryptocurrencies. Instead of making crypto-currencies a source of widespread frenzy, they focused on practical, sustainable uses of Blockchain technology in public services and infrastructure. This approach might not be as flashy, but it's a solid, forward-thinking use of Blockchain that can bring real, long-term benefits.

During my time in the Emirates, I experienced the initial surge of excitement around Blockchain technology. The UAE, established in 1971, has always been quick to embrace innovation, interesting economic policies, and new business models. The Emiratis realized that the real value in decentralization wasn't just in flashy projects, but in those that actually work and deliver results.

A friend from Abu Dhabi, the country's capital, once told me about the government's fintech initiatives. The aim was to position the Emirates as the "Switzerland of the Middle East." This meant not only diplomatic efforts and attracting tech investments but also establishing the country as a safe haven for capital, including crypto assets. Dubai has been particularly active in luring technology investors by setting up special economic zones and accelerators like Internet City or the DMCC Crypto Center.[63] The Dubai Multi Commodities Centre (DMCC), UAE's largest free-trade zone, is a significant hub for the crypto industry, hosting over 600 organizations, including 550 local companies.[64] DMCC is known for its extensive use of crypto and DLT, providing a supportive environment with favorable licensing and tax policies for companies in the sector. It also launched the UAE's first dedicated crypto hub, offering co-working spaces, incubation programs, and crypto advisory services. This initiative underlines Dubai's commitment to fostering innovation and growth in the crypto space. In Dubai, there's no resistance to the advancement of technologies due to fear of misuse. Need to chase down a criminal? The Dubai police have got it covered with their fleet of supercars, including the Bugatti Veyron—the world's fastest patrol car.

The Emirates are aiming to be like the "Switzerland of the Middle East," and this goal affects not just how they build their country but also their banking system. Switzerland is famous for keeping bank secrets for over 300 years.[65] Unlike most countries where bank employees may have to share client information with third parties like the government, in Switzerland, breaking this secrecy is a serious crime.[66] This robust privacy is why people from all over the world trust Switzerland with their investments. The numbers speak for themselves: while the global average of bank deposits to GDP is 64%,[67] in Switzerland, it's a staggering 476%.[68] In fact, a quarter of the world's bank deposits are in this small Alpine nation.[69]

Switzerland became a hotspot for Blockchain in the early days. Other countries didn't like cryptocurrencies much, but Switzerland's secret banking laws made it a safe place for new financial technology. This is still true today. Switzerland is home to the majority of big cryptocurrency projects worth over $1 billion. These include famous names like Ethereum, Cardano, Polkadot, Aave, Cosmos, Solana.[70] No other place in the world has so many major crypto projects.

Switzerland is structured as a federation of 26 cantons, each with a significant level of autonomy. Despite all cantons adhering to the same federal banking laws, the canton of Zug swiftly emerged as a frontrunner in the realm of crypto assets. Zug was named the "Crypto Valley," drawing inspiration from California's tech-centric Silicon Valley. What makes Zug special is its very business-friendly laws, which attract lots of entrepreneurs and people interested in cryptocurrencies. In 2021, Zug's government partnered with a company Bitcoin Suisse. They introduced a system where taxes could be paid using Bitcoin or Ethereum, up to an amount of 100,000 Swiss Francs.[71] This modern way of paying taxes is available for everyone living in Zug, whether they're just regular citizens or running a business. The process is super user-friendly—all you have to do is click on the link and go through a simple form that the cantonal authorities themselves send to residents by email.[72]

Zug ranked as the second-richest canton in Switzerland, offers a quality of life comparable to wealthy nations like Qatar. This region's transformation over recent decades is remarkable. Once overshadowed by Zurich, Zug has become a headquarters for major companies, including the commodity giant Glencore.[73] This growth is largely due to Zug's low tax rates and its welcoming stance toward innovation, particularly in the fintech and Blockchain sectors. In 2021 of the 960 Blockchain companies registered across Switzerland and Liechtenstein, almost half, 433 to be exact, were based in Zug. This makes the canton a major hub for Blockchain innovation[74] (Figure 7.2).

Zug is known for its favorable stance toward innovation and low taxation, which has made it an attractive location for businesses. Following a similar path, European Union countries like Cyprus, Malta, and Estonia have also embraced this model, with Malta becoming particularly notable in the Blockchain industry.[75] Malta stands out in this group due to its particularly welcoming stance toward the Blockchain industry. The Maltese government has taken bold steps to attract crypto millionaires by declaring profits from digital tokens and coins tax-free, even for assets located outside

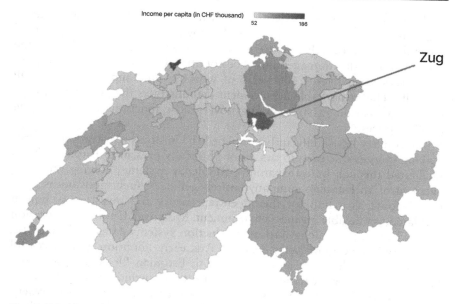

Figure 7.2 Map of Swiss cantons by per capita income in 2017.

(*Source*: Data from Bundesamt für Statistik, Confederation of Switzerland.)

Malta. This forward-thinking approach provided Malta a significant advantage over other countries still deliberating on cryptocurrency regulations.[76]

However, this welcoming policy has its downsides. Malta's openness has also led to significant issues, including corruption, tax evasion, and mafia involvement. The situation was brought into sharper focus following global scandals like the Panama and Pandora Papers. The tragic case of investigative journalist Daphne Caruana Galizia, who was murdered in 2017 following her involvement in exposing corruption, highlights the risks associated with Malta's approach. Her work, especially against government corruption and opposition to cryptocurrency regulations, brought to light the darker aspects of Malta's rapid financial growth. Furthermore, Malta's attractiveness extends beyond its cryptocurrency-friendly policies. The island is also known for granting citizenship relatively easily. With an investment of just under $1 million, individuals can obtain a Maltese passport, offering an attractive tax residence and visa-free access to 170 countries. This policy has drawn attention from various international circles. While the country continues to be known for its beautiful landscapes and pleasant weather, the underlying issues of corruption and crime present a challenging and complex situation.[77]

I think the Maltese model is too extreme, attracting all kinds of investors—including both legitimate cryptocurrency entrepreneurs and those likely engaging in illicit activities. That's why I appreciate the solution introduced by Estonia. As a leader in technological innovation and practical societal applications, Estonians have set an exemplary model with the E-Estonia digitalization agenda.[78] The country's efficient use of digital public services saves over 1,400 years of working time and 2% of its GDP annually. This remarkable achievement demonstrates the potential of digital transformation in streamlining government functions and enhancing public services.[79]

The country has significantly simplified the business registration process, making it accessible even to those not physically present in Estonia. This is facilitated through its transparent e-Residency system, allowing the management of an Estonian company entirely online.[80] Such innovations position Estonia as a hub for digital entrepreneurs and investors seeking a regulated, yet flexible business environment. Moreover, Estonia's integration of Blockchain technology into its production systems dates back to 2012, starting with the inheritance register. This early adoption and successful implementation have set a precedent, with Estonian Blockchain solutions being utilized by other nations and organizations, including NATO and the United States.[81] The Estonian government's approach, akin to how experienced managers run technology companies, has led to a situation where 99% of public services are available digitally.[82]

Estonia's case indeed serves as a valuable benchmark for how governments can promote innovation, particularly in the field of technology. Through a combination of good governance and strategic foresight, Estonia has created an exceptional investment environment, especially in the realm of cryptocurrencies and fintech. The journey of cryptocurrencies there highlights the evolution of investor interest in this sector.[83] Initially, it was the domain of business angels, willing to take risks on a new and unproven market. As cryptocurrencies demonstrated their business value, venture capital funds began to show interest, recognizing the potential in this burgeoning sector (Figure 7.3).

Estonia's leadership extends beyond cryptocurrencies to numerous other sectors within the IT industry. This success story is particularly noteworthy because it was achieved without resorting to ideological extremes, special tax incentives, or allowing a "Wild West" scenario in the cryptocurrency market. Instead, Estonia's approach has been characterized by strong, yet predictable and clear regulations. This regulatory clarity has provided a stable and transparent framework for businesses and investors. This balanced approach may very well be the key to Estonia's success, establishing it as a technological leader not only in Europe but globally. Estonia's model demonstrates that promoting innovation doesn't necessarily require extreme measures. Instead, a combination of clear regulations, a supportive investment environment, and a focus on digital transformation can effectively drive technological advancement and economic growth.

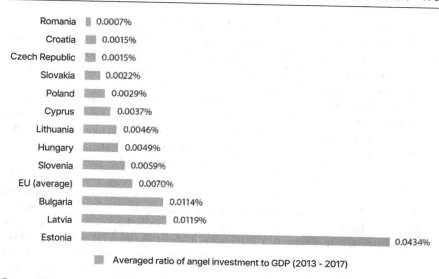

Figure 7.3 Business angels' investments in relation to GDP.

(*Source:* **Data from EBAN—European Business Angels Network.**)

7.4 "DEFEAT THE ENEMY WITH HIS OWN WEAPON"

From its inception, Bitcoin was designed as a technology against government control, promoting a form of digital anarchy. This idea, however, clashed with how real-world economies function, raising questions about the role of central authorities in the world of cryptocurrencies.

Early on, governments and central banks declared either regular war or open conflict on cryptocurrencies. Let's take the United States as an example. The Federal Reserve is responsible for monetary policy (managing the national currency—the dollar). All economic exchange is based on a chain of trust between all economic entities and consumers. Households, companies, associations, and foundations exchange dollars among themselves. Its value is based solely on trust.[84] Bitcoin, introduced by Satoshi Nakamoto, challenged this by proposing a model based on cryptography: "We have proposed a system for electronic transactions without relying on trust."[85]

Especially in the early years of Bitcoin's operation, central banks were not afraid of losing their power but of destabilizing the economic system. In central banking, trust is the foundation of all economic policy. The British learned this perfectly during the so-called Black Wednesday on September 16, 1992. At this time, the UK was a part of the European Monetary System (EMS), which required close cooperation among European central banks and linked their currency rates, all based fundamentally on trust.[86] Meanwhile, George Soros, a charismatic investor and fund manager, started to play against the market rate of the pound, thereby undermining the authority of the British central bank (Exchequer). He built large positions in the pound for a long time and then flooded the market with British currency.[87] In this way, Soros made over £1 billion in one day. The pound weakened by 15% against the German mark and by 25% against the dollar.

The British central bank's intervention to stabilize the situation involved spending over £3 billion.[88] This expenditure meant that each British citizen indirectly contributed around £60 to Soros' profits. Broken trust in the monetary system? The fallout from these events forced the UK to exit the EMS, and this failure in European cooperation fueled a growing wave of Euroscepticism. Within less than a year, the UK Independence Party (UKIP) was formed, which capitalized on criticism of the EU's economic policies and eventually played a significant role in leading the UK toward Brexit.

The significance of "Black Wednesday" extends beyond its immediate financial impact. It serves as a stark reminder of the crucial role trust plays in the monetary system. Recognizing this, central banks quickly understood that Bitcoin, with its decentralized nature, had the potential to disrupt the established economic order. The first major central banking figure to acknowledge Bitcoin's potential was Ben Bernanke, the then-chairman of the Federal Reserve. He suggested that Bitcoin could have value as a transaction and accounting system.[89] That endorsement is particularly noteworthy considering Bernanke's role during the global financial crisis of 2008–2009. Bernanke, who led the Fed during this period, saw the financial system nearly collapse. Yet he managed to maintain market faith in the Fed's control over money.[90] Perhaps this experience informed his openness to Bitcoin, a technology promising innovation in a rapidly digitizing world. In an era of dynamic digital progress, even the Fed recognized that fighting cryptocurrencies was futile. Instead of opposing "crypto," they needed to adapt and possibly even ally with it. The role of the United States in this debate is crucial, as the dollar accounts for 88% of flows in the international exchange market.[91]

Over time, various banks around the world have explored or implemented digital cash systems, reflecting a growing interest in the potential of this technology. A notable example is Russia's initiative to create the CryptoRuble, announced by Vladimir Putin in 2017. The CryptoRuble, designed to have the same value as the regular ruble, entered a pilot phase in June 2021 with 12 banks participating.[92] A key motivation behind Putin's interest in Blockchain technology is its ability to encrypt transactions, allowing Russia to circumvent international sanctions.[93]

The idea of "digital cash" covers various technologies, not just cryptocurrencies like Bitcoin or Ethereum. Central banks might integrate Blockchain technology in their systems, but they usually don't allow public involvement in the creation of money. Central banks have the responsibility to regulate financial markets and maintain stability, which often requires control over the money supply. Globalization has increasingly influenced the role and power of central banks. The global economy is interconnected, with economic policies and market trends in one country, particularly major economies like the United States, impacting others worldwide. Since events like Black Wednesday in 1992, which highlighted the vulnerability of central banks, the global economy has become more integrated, partly due to its increased globalization. However, the basis of this integration has shifted from being predominantly about monetary policy to being driven by technological progress and digitization. This change highlights how advancements in digital currencies and Blockchain technology are transforming global finance, challenging traditional concepts of monetary control and economic stability.

In the public sector, women are currently leading the implementation of public Blockchains. Christine Lagarde, the head of the European Central Bank, and European commissioner Marghrete Verstager, who is responsible for the *Europe Fit for the Digital Age* program in the European Union, are among them.[94] While the earlier narrative around cryptocurrency innovation has centered on men, the involvement and leadership of women could be pivotal. Their role is crucial not just in advancing digital money solutions but also in bridging the gap between various stakeholders: the banking sector, government agencies, private enterprises, and the general public. This trend dovetails with certain findings from psychological research. While most personality traits and interests show no significant differences between men and women, one notable distinction lies in their interests: men often show a preference for things, while women tend to be more people-oriented.[95] That generalization, despite its role in perpetuating wage disparities and labor market segmentation, offers a unique advantage in the context of technology implementation, particularly when it involves social aspects.[96] The ability to understand the diverse needs and perspectives of different social groups is vital for the successful digitization of money. Women's leadership in this sector, with their typically stronger focus on people and relationships, could be instrumental in navigating the complex interplay of interests inherent in the financial world.

China's stance on digital currencies represents a stark contrast to other global approaches, particularly in its treatment of cryptocurrencies. From the beginning of the Blockchain era, China has been openly hostile toward cryptocurrencies, culminating in a ban on cryptocurrency mining, as previously discussed. While the official reason for this ban was environmental protection, many see this as a somewhat ironic justification, given China's significant contribution to global CO_2 emissions, which is the highest in the world at around 30%.[97] The real motive behind China's crackdown on cryptocurrencies like Bitcoin appears to be about asserting control. It's a demonstration of power by the Chinese government and the Chinese Communist Party, as well as the People's Bank of China (PBOC), over the country's financial, economic, and political spheres.

In my view, this is part of a broader strategy where all economic activities must be under the strict supervision of the Chinese authorities. This approach is deeply rooted in the country's Confucian culture, which has been a dominant philosophy in China since the 5th century BC. Confucianism, founded by the philosopher Confucius, emphasizes the ideal of the "noble man" and promotes a hierarchical social structure. This philosophy continues to influence Chinese society and government, shaping their approach to technological progress and digital currencies.

Digital tools, whether cryptocurrencies, e-commerce services, or communication platforms, are designed not to serve individual needs but to uphold and reinforce the prevailing social order. Hence, digital yuan (e-CNY) was created, as China's state-backed virtual currency. The digital yuan is structured to allow the government to monitor all monetary transactions closely.[98] Its distribution follows a two-tier system: initially issued to commercial banks and then to the general public. Commercial banks play a key role in this process, facilitating the conversion of coins and cash into digital yuan. The government desires to integrate technological innovation with its overarching goals of control and societal order. The digital yuan is a clear example of how China views digital finance tools not just as economic instruments but as mechanisms for maintaining governmental oversight and authority.[99]

China's digital yuan system, known as the e-CNY, operates on the concept of "controlled anonymity" (可控匿名).[100] That design theoretically allows the government to have a deeper insight into individual transactions when they're made in digital yuan rather than cash. The primary goal of the digital yuan is to extend governmental influence over the burgeoning e-commerce sector, which currently operates through its own transaction systems like Alipay. However, as noted by Fed Chairman Jerome Powell, the e-CNY essentially functions as a network, enabling the government to monitor every payment.[101]

Setting aside the security implications, one of the most concerning aspects of the digital yuan is its "expiration date" feature. The functionality allows the e-CNY system to be programmed such that the digital currency loses its purchasing power after a certain period, compelling users to spend it within a timeframe determined by the government. This concept mirrors the century-old, yet revolutionary idea proposed by economist Silvio Gesell. Gesell envisioned a form of currency with a government-mandated expiration date, intended to control the velocity of money circulation in the economy.[102] The disturbing aspect of this system lies in its potential to override individual financial decisions. It forces immediate consumption, eliminating the possibility of saving, the backbone of wealth accumulation. In essence, the Chinese version of digital money aligns with the broader social framework of the country, where communal welfare is prioritized over individual economic freedoms. The digital yuan, therefore, is not just a financial tool but a means to achieve cultural objectives in a society where the collective good is placed above personal financial autonomy.

The global landscape of digital money technology reveals interesting trends. Countries like Malta, Estonia, Switzerland's Zug, and El Salvador are becoming early adopters of cryptocurrencies. Those regions have become hubs, or "cryptocurrency valleys," where government adoption has spurred innovation inflows. Significantly, these government-led Blockchain initiatives have cleverly adopted the technological framework initiated by Satoshi Nakamoto, while strategically shedding the associated ideological baggage. That evolution marks a transition of cryptocurrency from a niche, idealistic concept favored by the Cypherpunks to a mainstream technology.

The direction of the global monetary system is now taking a unique turn. In the past, big changes in this system were mostly driven by political decisions. Key moments like the Bretton-Woods conference in 1944 or the United States leaving the gold standard were mainly about politics and economics, without much technology involved. But today, it's different. Technology is now a major force in shaping economic changes. It's a new situation where technology is not just a side note but a central element in the evolution of the global monetary system. It highlights a future where technology and economic policy are closely connected.

We're on the edge of a big economic change, thanks to the growth of the sharing economy, in which assets or services are shared between private individuals (for free or for a fee), usually via the Internet. At the same time, there's the Metaverse, a new digital world that's creating different ways of socializing and doing business. That new reality necessitates a different approach to money. The inevitable move toward the digitization of currency, whether through cryptocurrencies or digital versions of traditional money, is reshaping how economic transactions are conducted. Those initiatives vary, with some being driven by private entities and others by governments, yet each individually contributing to the broader transformation. However, those at the forefront of changes will certainly be the ones benefiting not only financially but also socially. They will not just be making big fortunes but also driving a social and economic revolution. This fits well with what Abraham Lincoln once said: "The best way to predict the future is to create it."

NOTES

1 G. Orwell, Animal Farm, 1945.
2 https://coinjournal.net/news/satoshi-nakamoto-is-clearly-an-anarchist/
3 Ibid.
4 https://news.bitcoin.com/satoshi-revolution-chapter-2-satoshi-libertarian-anarchist-part-4/
5 G. Orwell, Animal Farm, op. cit.

6 https://www.cnbc.com/2021/09/15/ray-dalio-says-if-bitcoin-is-really-successful-regulators-will-kill-it.html

7 N. Popper (2018), Rise of Bitcoin Competitor Ripple Creates Wealth to Rival Zuckerberg, "The New York Times", 4.01.2018, access: 5.05.2018.

8 https://www.forbes.com/profile/jed-mccaleb/?sh=77cde49076bf

9 https://www.businessinsider.in/investment/news/these-are-the-top-ten-most-popular-cryptocurrencies-in-the-world/slidelist/85174407.cms

10 Mt. Gox Resigns from Bitcoin Foundation, Reuters, 23.022014, access: 25.02.2014.

11 P. Vigna (2014), 5 Things About Mt. Gox's Crisis, "The Wall Street Journal", 25.02.2014.

12 J. Blagdon, Technical Problems Cause Bitcoin to Plummet from Record High, Mt. Gox Suspends Deposits, The Verge, access: 12.03.2013.

13 https://techcrunch.com/2013/05/16/mt-gox-dwolla-account-money-seizure/

14 J.I. Wong (2014), 68% of Mt. Gox Users Still Awaiting Their Funds, Survey Reveals, Coin Desk, 15.02.2014.

15 A. Hern, How a Bug in Bitcoin Led to MtGox's Collapse, "The Guardian", 27.02.2014.

16 R. McMillan (2014), Bitcoin Exchange Mt. Gox Implodes Amid Allegations of $350 Million Hack, "Wired", 24.02.2014, access: 25.02.2014.

17 https://www.bbc.com/news/technology-58331959

18 T.B. Lee (2017), Feds Say They Caught a Key Figure in the Massive Mt. Gox Bitcoin Hack, Ars Technica, 27.07.2017.

19 https://www.theguardian.com/technology/2014/feb/27/how-does-a-bug-in-bitcoin-lead-to-mtgoxs-collapse

20 Ibid.

21 D. Rosenzweig (2001), 2 Convicted in $18.9-Million Cash Robbery — via "Los Angeles Times".

22 https://www.welivesecurity.com/2014/03/24/bitcoin-fixes-mt-gox-crash-bug-as-exchange-staff-find-200000-btc-in-forgotten-wallet/

23 https://www.nytimes.com/2021/01/12/technology/bitcoin-passwords-wallets-fortunes.html

24 https://www.wired.com/story/unciphered-ironkey-password-cracking-bitcoin/

25 https://www.businessofapps.com/data/coinbase-statistics/

26 https://www.wsj.com/articles/coinbase-builds-a-4-billion-cash-pile-ahead-of-possible-regulatory-tightening-11629295200

27 https://www.najlepszeplatformyforex.pl/blog/bitbay-informacje-i-opinie-o-polskiej-gieldzie-kryptowalut/

28 https://www.bitdegree.org/crypto/coinbase-vs-gemini

29 Wirecard: Scandal-Hit Firm Files for Insolvency, BBC News, 25.06.2020, access: 25.06.2020.

30 D. McCrum (2019), Wirecard's Singular Approach to Counting Cash, "Financial Times", 9.12.2019, access: 30.06.2020.

31 https://www.ft.com/content/6099ad99-0e3b-4337-b20e-647a166aee6e

32 https://www.finanznachrichten.de/nachrichten-2020-06/50014305-bankenverband-kundengelder-trotz-wirecard-insolvenz-sicher-003.htm

33 e-Gold Security Alerts, e-gold.com, access: 20.09.2013.

34 Considering the retail price (retail price) in the US market, at the very end of the supply chain, customers pay $0.96 per liter of unleaded 95 gasoline at the

stations. This means that the crude oil delivered each day by Colonial Pipeline is converted by refineries into fuel, the total value of which is already $365 million. This is the difference between the cost of wholesale purchases and the revenue from distribution at gas stations.

35 N. Bertrand, E. Perez, Z. Cohen, G. Sands, J. Campbell, Colonial Pipeline Did Pay Ransom to Hackers, Sources Now Say, CNN, access: 23.05.2021.

36 https://raportostanieswiata.pl/raportalia/darkside-i-cyberataki-na-zachodnie-korporacje/

37 https://krebsonsecurity.com/2021/05/a-closer-look-at-the-darkside-ransomware-gang/

38 https://krebsonsecurity.com/2021/05/a-closer-look-at-the-darkside-ransomware-gang/

39 https://abcnews.go.com/Politics/doj-seizes-millions-ransom-paid-colonial-pipeline/story?id=78135821

40 https://www.reuters.com/business/energy/us-announce-recovery-millions-colonial-pipeline-ransomware-attack-2021-06-07/

41 https://www.justice.gov/opa/pr/department-justice-seizes-23-million-cryptocurrency-paid-ransomware-extortionists-darkside

42 https://krebsonsecurity.com/2021/05/a-closer-look-at-the-darkside-ransomware-gang/

43 Ibid.

44 Ibid.

45 Ibid.

46 https://www.esecurityplanet.com/products/best-penetration-testing/

47 K. Rooney (2018), $1.1 Billion in Cryptocurrency Has Been Stolen This Year, and It Was Apparently Easy to Do. CNBC, 6.06.2018, access: 9.06.2018.

48 K. Phillips Erb (2021), IRS Will Pay up to $625,000 If You Can Crack Monero, Other Privacy Coins, "Forbes", access: 11.10.2021.

49 https://www.businessinsider.com/paul-krugman-says-bitcoin-is-a-bubble-2017-12?IR=T

50 https://www.marketwatch.com/story/dont-fall-for-the-bitcoin-bubble-even-the-flintstones-had-a-better-system-warns-economics-professor-nouriel-roubini-11612973303.

51 Ibid.

52 https://www.cnbc.com/2021/10/11/jpmorgan-chase-ceo-jamie-dimon-says-bitcoin-is-worthless.html

53 https://www.sec.gov/news/public-statement/statement-clayton-2017-12-11

54 https://www.statista.com/statistics/1235117/worldwide-blockchain-funding-by-geography/

55 https://www.wired.com/2014/03/what-is-bitcoin/

56 https://www.wired.com/2014/03/what-is-bitcoin/

57 https://www.forbes.com/profile/brian-armstrong/

58 https://www.forbes.com/profile/fred-ehrsam/

59 https://www.forbes.com/profile/tyler-winklevoss/

60 https://www.forbes.com/profile/cameron-winklevoss/

61 https://www.wsj.com/articles/dubai-aims-to-be-a-city-built-on-blockchain-1493086080

62 https://www.unlock-bc.com/news/2020-01-29/dubai-customs-launches-blockchain-powered-e-commerce-platform/?amp

63 https://www.thenationalnews.com/business/cryptocurrencies/2021/10/18/dubai-expects-to-have-more-than-1000-cryptocurrency-businesses-by-2022/
64 https://landing.dmcc.ae/cryptocentre
65 https://fsi.taxjustice.net/PDF/Switzerland.pdf
66 https://www.futurelearn.com/info/courses/switzerland-europe/0/steps/52427
67 https://tradingeconomics.com/switzerland/bank-deposits-to-gdp-percent-wb-data.html
68 https://www.theglobaleconomy.com/rankings/bank_assets_GDP/
69 https://www.swissbanking.ch/_Resources/Persistent/1/9/3/1/1931975d3eae560a669a9139b3d70c52e26a3923/SBA_The_Swiss_banking_sector_EN.pdf.
70 https://rue.ee/crypto-licence-in-switzerland/
71 https://www.coindesk.com/markets/2021/02/18/switzerlands-crypto-valley-has-started-accepting-bitcoin-ether-for-tax-payments/
72 Ibid.
73 https://www.reuters.com/article/us-swiss-fintech-cryptovalley-idUSKCN11E0L9
74 https://www.pwc.ch/en/press/record-growth-in-crypto-valley-despite-corona.html
75 https://www.ibanet.org/article/A26900FC-B3DE-41FE-AC6B-A55CCC2B364A
76 https://www.forbes.com/sites/rogeraitken/2018/10/29/crypto-investors-flocking-to-blockchain-island-malta-in-droves/?sh=35c6f8c45ff9
77 Ibid.
78 https://www.pwc.com/gx/en/services/legal/tech/assets/estonia-the-digital-republic-secured-by-blockchain.pdf
79 https://theconversation.com/estonia-is-a-digital-republic-what-that-means-and-why-it-may-be-everyones-future-145485
80 https://e-resident.gov.ee/
81 Ibid.
82 https://qz.com/1535549/living-on-the-blockchain-is-a-game-changer-for-estonian-citizens/
83 https://investinestonia.com/business-opportunities/blockchain/
84 Saifedean Ammous. 2018. *The Bitcoin Standard: The Decentralized Alternative to Central Banking* (1st. ed.). Wiley Publishing.
85 https://www.wired.com/story/theres-no-good-reason-to-trust-blockchain-technology/
86 G. Alogoskoufis, F. Giavazzi, A. Giovannini (1991), Limiting Exchange Rate Flexibility: The European Monetary System, "Economica", 58 (230): 261.
87 https://www.telegraph.co.uk/finance/2773265/Billionaire-who-broke-the-Bank-of-England.html
88 https://www.youtube.com/watch?v=WBZnau8Px5E
89 https://www.ft.com/content/6c5b941c-5052-11e3-9f0d-00144feabdc0
90 https://www.nytimes.com/2014/02/22/business/federal-reserve-2008-transcripts.html
91 https://www.reuters.com/article/global-forex-reserves-idUSKBN2GQ1O6
92 https://www.cbr.ru/eng/press/event/?id=11003
93 https://www.federalreserve.gov/econres/notes/feds-notes/the-international-role-of-the-u-s-dollar-20211006.htm
94 https://ec.europa.eu/info/strategy/priorities-2019-2024/europe-fit-digital-age_pl
95 https://pubmed.ncbi.nlm.nih.gov/19883140/
96 https://ftp.iza.org/dp13380.pdf

97 https://www.statista.com/statistics/271748/the-largest-emitters-of-co2-in-the-world/

98 https://sanctionscanner.com/blog/china-has-created-its-own-digital-currency-understanding-digital-yuan-387

99 https://www.cnbc.com/2021/03/05/chinas-digital-yuan-what-is-it-and-how-does-it-work.html

100 https://www.industryweek.com/the-economy/trade/article/21174069/chinas-digital-yuan-is-all-about-dataand-perhaps-control

101 https://www.protocol.com/china/digital-yuan-real-worries

102 https://halshs.archives-ouvertes.fr/halshs-00119192/document

Chapter 8

Blockchain governed by corporations

8.1 CORP-EMPIRES

If you've ever had the chance to live in or visit multiple cities, you'll find that each has its own unique heartbeat. For me, New York City was where I truly felt like a part of something spectacular—a cog in a vast and vibrant business, economic, and social machine. While living in other great cities like Miami, Dubai, London, or Hong Kong, you certainly get a sense of being connected to a global economic powerhouse, but there's something about New York that's just unparalleled. It's a city where the pulse of business empires is not just heard but felt in your everyday life.

Imagine walking through New York's streets—even a short stroll becomes a journey through a living museum of business history. You pass by towering landmarks like the Rockefeller Center, the Chrysler Building, or One Vanderbilt. Just hearing these names, you can sense the immense legacy of American business that's built into their very foundations. New York's wealth, primarily built on vast private fortunes, saw its meteoric rise at the turn of the 19th and 20th centuries. Post-Civil War, as the United States rapidly expanded, so too did its need for industry and entrepreneurs, too. This period saw the emergence of influential families, whose initial ventures blossomed into the massive industrial conglomerates and corporations we know today.

When you delve into the history of New York City, you encounter the tales of industrial giants who shaped not just the city but the very fabric of American industry. Figures like Andrew Carnegie, Cornelius Vanderbilt, and John D. Rockefeller were visionaries whose influence is palpable in every corner of the city. Their legacy is etched into New York's skyline, a city that owes much of its distinctive character to the world's first skyscrapers and grand architectural projects. These were bold expressions of ambition and vision. Take, for instance, Carnegie Hall, the world-renowned venue for classical and popular music. It bears the name of Andrew Carnegie, the steel magnate. His contribution to the arts is as significant as his impact on the industrial world.

DOI: 10.1201/9781032621456-9

And who hasn't watched "Home Alone 2: Lost in New York"? Remember the iconic Christmas tree at Rockefeller Center, a symbol of the city's holiday spirit? This beloved landmark is a gift from the Rockefeller brothers, William and John. They built an oil empire with companies like ExxonMobil and Chevron Corporation, ranking just behind Saudi Aramco as the world's largest oil corporation.[1]

The influence of business magnates on contemporary reality is undeniable, and their legacy continues to shape our world today. However, the world of corporations has always been mired in controversy, and this was no different during America's economic boom. Back then, the most influential entrepreneurs were often labeled as *robber barons*,[2] a term coined 150 years ago by *The Atlantic*. This term was used to describe industrialists whose business tactics were seen as ruthless or unethical. They were accused of damaging the environment, underpaying workers, engaging in political lobbying, stifling competition, monopolizing markets, and manipulating stock prices. You might think these critiques sound familiar, echoing modern criticisms of the corporate sector. But this is not a contemporary commentary. It's from a December 1907 article in *The Atlantic Monthly*. This shows that despite technical advancements, certain dynamics remain the same, echoing the sentiment expressed at the beginning of this book: "Everything must change for everything to remain the same."[3]

While corporate strategies have largely stayed consistent, the markets and the nature of lucrative businesses have evolved dramatically. A century ago, corporate wealth was largely derived from heavy industry, like steel or oil. Today, it's the high-tech sector that dominates. The leading tech companies, often referred to by the acronym GAFAM—Google (now Alphabet), Amazon, Facebook, Apple, and Microsoft—are among the world's largest.[4] In 2023, the combined value of these companies exceeded $6 trillion.[5] And then there are companies like Tesla, which in October 2023 had a valuation of almost $800 billion, triple that of the Toyota Motor Company.[6]

Despite the many years that have passed and the shifts in the global economic landscape, today's technology corporations like GAFAM face criticisms reminiscent of those leveled against the industrial magnates of the late 19th and early 20th centuries in the United States. Back then, the economy was driven by resources and mining. Now, it's powered by data.[7] Tech companies understand this shift and are competing not just for technological superiority. Technology is a means to an end—the real prize is control over data, just as control over resources and energy was key during America's industrial boom 150 years ago. This parallel is evident in the modern political discourse as well. US Senator Josh Hawley, during a hearing with Facebook's Mark Zuckerberg, highlighted this issue. He pointed out the monopolistic practices and censorship used by tech giants like Facebook, Twitter, and Google, especially regarding the exchange of sensitive user data. Senator Hawley's remarks, "Mr. Zuckerberg won't answer questions

(...) This is both totally unacceptable and totally predictable because it is exactly what these tech companies have done to the American people and to congress for years now. Which is why it is time we took action against these modern-day robber barons,"[8] and underscore the ongoing concerns about the power and influence of today's tech giants.

In the development of cryptocurrencies, many saw hope for curbing the increasingly bold moves of corporations, in both the financial and tech sectors. The concept of decentralized cash seemed to perfectly align with the fight not only against government control over financial realms but also against the greed of corporations. The Cypherpunk manifesto of the 1990s placed government and corporate power in the same bracket, identifying them as sources of problems.[9] Bitcoin, in this context, was envisioned as a monetary system fully managed by the community, created as an antidote to central authority. Have these ideals been realized?

8.2 BLOCKCHAIN ENTERS THE FINANCIAL WORLD

8.2.1 From haters to adopters

Imagine a world where the way we handle money is completely different from what we've always known. That's the kind of shift Bitcoin and Blockchain technology introduced when they first appeared. They weren't just new technologies; they were a stark challenge to the traditional banking system. Satoshi Nakamoto, the creator of Bitcoin, once said on the forum:

> Banks must be trusted to hold our money and transfer it electronically, but they lend it out in waves of credit bubbles with barely a fraction in reserve. We have to trust them with our privacy, trust them not to let identity thieves drain our accounts.[10]

Bitcoin was born out of a desire to change this system.

So, how exactly does this big shift away from traditional, fiat money work? Let's break it down. To understand it better, we need to look at how money circulates in the economy—the current, centralized one. A centralized system is where the central bank is the only legal issuer of currency and works closely with commercial banks, supplying them with cash, regulating reserves, and stepping in during crises. This monopoly allows central banks to control the total money supply, including the deposits in commercial banks.[11] Although the average person deals mainly with commercial banks (e.g., in account management, card transactions, taking out loans), the policy of the central bank has a huge impact on our lives.

Central banks exert total control over commercial banks, which is beneficial to both parties. The main tool of this control is the system of mandatory cash reserves. These are part of the liabilities (reserve liabilities) that commercial banks must keep in their accounts, instead of lending or investing. For example, in Poland, in 2021 the reserve requirement was 0.5%.[12] What does this mean? I think it's easy to understand with a concrete example.

Let's imagine again that we are the manager of X-Bank and we are creating a loan offer. We manage the cash that X-Bank's customers keep in their accounts. The financial system works in such a way that customers bring cash to the bank because they know they can get it back at any time. I will definitely be waiting for them. But since this cash has been deposited, the bank can turn it around. Let's imagine that X-Bank has 10,000 customers, each of whom has $1,000 in their account. This means that X-Bank manages $10 million. If there were no central bank, all this money would go into the loan action, which is the total loans granted to borrowers. After all, commercial banks make the most money on loans. For example, at JPMorgan Chase, profit from loan interest accounts for as much as 88% of profit from all interest-bearing activities (2019 data).[13] It's certain: commercial banks want to lend as much as possible.

However, at this point, the system of required minimum reserves appears. It works in such a way that the central bank enforces a certain "deal." Because it has a monopoly on money issuance, it tells commercial banks this:

> Due to the system of mandatory reserves, you have to keep 0.5% of all your cash, which your customers keep in the accounts you service, in our accounts. In return for this, we offer you the only available, attractive loan offer liquidity if needed.

Commercial banks agree to such an arrangement. As a result, X-bank collects the entire amount of $10 million from customers. It deposits 0.5% of this amount ($50,000) in the central bank, and the rest—that is $9,950,000—is allocated for loan action.

The circulation of money doesn't end there. The economy is a system of connected vessels. X-bank's credit customers take loans for specific purposes: to buy an apartment, a plot of land, a car, etc. This means that the money granted to customers will eventually end up somewhere. Where? In another bank, let's say Y-Bank. Let's assume that the entire amount from the discussed loan action ends up at Y-Bank. As a result, Y-Bank receives new deposits in the amount of $9,950,000. But since Y-Bank is subject to the same rules as everyone else, it too must transfer 0.5% of the possessed amount to the central bank—that is $49,750. The rest ($9,900,250) is transferred to its own loan action.

In the next stage of this system, funds from Y-Bank will go to Z-Bank, which will again have to deposit the obligatory 0.5% from the acquired sum, that is 0.5% × $9,900,250 = $49,501.25. This system will keep running until the initial amount of $10 million, from which X-Bank started, is exhausted.

These 10 million will eventually end up in the central bank, and $10,000,000 \times 1/(0.5\%) = \$2,000,000,000$[14] will appear on the market in the form of cash. This amount will appear in circulation through money creation. In simplified terms, this means that commercial banks can create 200 times more money than the central bank issued, charging interest on money lent to borrowers, 99.5% of which they never actually had (Table 8.1).

The relationship between central banks and commercial banks is a symbiotic one, where both parties reap significant benefits. Central banks wield power over monetary policy and economic decisions, while commercial banks benefit from this arrangement by being able to extend more loans and, consequently, earn more. There's competition among commercial banks, of course, but they generally prefer to share a larger lending pool, facilitated by central bank policies, than to rely solely on funds from their account holders. The mandatory reserve system multiplies the funds available for lending, making the pool up to 200 times larger than in a free-market scenario without a central bank.

This system, however, was precisely what Satoshi Nakamoto critiqued in the banking sector. He saw the alliance between central and commercial banks as beneficial to them but exploitative toward the general public. Naturally, given this perspective, banks were expected to be hostile to Nakamoto's concept of decentralized electronic cash. This hostility was not surprising, especially after leading economists like Krugman, Roubini, and Stiglitz criticized the idea. Consequently, banks were among the first institutions to dismiss not only the value of cryptocurrencies but also the underlying Blockchain technology.

Banks were initially very resistant to cryptocurrencies. For example, in 2017, Goldman Sachs' then-president Lloyd Blankfein criticized Bitcoin,

Table 8.1 Comparison of monetary systems with reserve requirements and in a free-market system

	Mandatory reserve system	No reserve requirement (no central bank)
Who is the issuer of money?	Central bank	Any entities (commercial banks)
The amount of the reserve rate	Set by the central bank, e.g., 0.5%	None
Who deposits the assets of commercial banks?	Commercial banks (99.5%) + central bank (0.5%). Central bank extends credit to commercial banks for lending action	Commercial banks (100%) - all cash available to the commercial bank
The volume of credit action	Deposits at the central bank × 1/(0.5%) 200 × total deposits from individual customers	Sum of deposits from individual customers to commercial banks

calling it a tool for fraudsters. The main concerns from banks were about Bitcoin's fluctuating value and doubts concerning its market valuation mechanism. Yet interestingly, this attitude changed when it became profitable, all of a sudden. Just four years after Blankfein's comments, Goldman Sachs started offering its top clients cryptocurrency investment opportunities.[15] It's a classic case of the saying *Pecunia non olet* (money doesn't stink)—even if it's in the form of decentralized cryptocurrencies that banks once opposed.

A surprising twist in the story of Bitcoin's acceptance came from the Federal Reserve, the US central bank, not from commercial banks. In November 2013, the then-head of the Fed, Ben Bernanke, said Bitcoin might have a promising future.[16] His statement had a big impact: the value of Bitcoin against the dollar shot up from about $440 to $795 in one day. Although there was a price correction the next day, Bitcoin's value kept rising, breaking the $1,000 mark by the end of November 2013.

As the world of finance evolved, cryptocurrencies slowly but surely began to gain acceptance among top banking executives, despite lingering skepticism. A notable example is JPMorgan Chase, where CEO Jamie Dimon remains a vocal critic of Bitcoin. Yet, paradoxically, JPMorgan has become a frontrunner in adopting Blockchain technology and even venturing into cryptocurrencies. This shift is significant, indicating a broader trend within the banking sector toward embracing these new technologies.

One of JPMorgan's most influential contributions was its extensive research and development of functional Blockchain platforms for the wider banking ecosystem. In 2019, JPMorgan launched the first global banking network that uses its own stablecoin, JPM Coin (pegged 1:1 with the US dollar), to enable instant payments. Additionally, they introduced the Liink initiative, a Blockchain-based financial data exchange network, which now includes over 400 banks.[17]

JPMorgan's involvement goes beyond developing its own projects. The bank actively seeks to be at the center of the cryptocurrency ecosystem. This is the same ecosystem that initially sparked a significant trust deficit toward banks. Despite this, as early as 2017, JPMorgan was among the elite group of finance and technology companies that established the Enterprise Ethereum Alliance.[18]

Whenever I come across such news, I like to "connect the dots," and in this context, the role of ConsenSys is particularly intriguing. This Brooklyn-based software house is a leader in Blockchain solutions, helmed by Joe Lubin, a co-founder of Ethereum.[19] Some might see bringing in an industry influencer like Lubin to a project as a mere prestige boost for a bank, a way to show off its ability to attract top talent. However, I believe figures like Lubin can be game-changers, especially in a traditionally conservative field like investment banking.

The journey of banks from staunch opponents to leaders in implementing Blockchain technology is fascinating. Initially, I think their resistance stemmed from a lack of understanding of the innovation at hand. Bank managers needed to grasp Blockchain and cryptocurrency concepts like "decentralization," "disintermediation," or "distributed ledger." Accounting and transactions have always been the bread and butter of banking, yet there was still a significant knowledge barrier. A key question loomed: who was behind these cryptocurrencies that seemingly "came out of nowhere"? With no traditional issuer to verify or audit, this must have seemed like a complete overhaul of known financial systems to those steeped in conventional banking. It's understandable why they approached the burgeoning crypto sector with distance and skepticism. For them, the whole concept of crypto represented a radical departure from the familiar structures of finance.

Over time, cryptocurrencies and their underlying Blockchain technology reached a "critical mass"—they became widespread enough in society, and banking leaders began to recognize that the tens of millions of cryptocurrency users had valid reasons for embracing this new form of digital money. Managers of financial processes started to understand the entire flow of funds, the process of mining, how value is built, and how transactions are recorded in networks like Bitcoin and other cryptocurrencies. They saw potential in Blockchain for optimizing their own processes.

Working in the fintech industry as a software service provider, I've seen firsthand how the awareness within the banking sector shifted. While American banks were developing their projects, there was a similar movement in Europe, particularly in adapting transaction registers as part of the so-called durable medium. It was here that Blockchain technology found a perfect fit, even in what might be considered a more technical or niche application. My software house was involved in developing one of the first such solutions in Europe for a leading commercial bank. This experience allowed me to witness a significant change in the banking sector's mentality. Instead of just assigning existing technical and process engineers to develop a solution as an add-on, our client formed a separate, dedicated team focused entirely on Blockchain integration and promotion within the organization.

The journey of Blockchain technology in the banking sector mirrors the trajectories of other innovations like cloud products and remote customer onboarding applications. Initially, these technologies primarily offered infrastructure capabilities; however, their practical business applications weren't immediately clear. Nevertheless, as business leaders began to grasp the value these solutions offered, their integration into organizational processes followed naturally.

Reflecting on the widespread adoption of cloud technologies illustrates this point well. Since Microsoft Azure's implementation in 2010, cloud applications have become a staple in the business ecosystem. The tangible outcomes? Significant savings and added value for users of cloud products. And the impact on the providers of these services has been substantial. Take Microsoft as an example. Their revenue model shifted dramatically over the years. While their primary earnings once stemmed from products like MS Office and the Windows operating system, today, their intelligent cloud services, particularly Microsoft Azure, constitute their most significant source of income. In the second quarter of 2021 alone, Azure contributed to 36% of Microsoft's operating profit.

The adoption of Blockchain technology in banking and finance mirrors similar trends seen in the past, such as the widespread acceptance of cloud solutions a few years ago. These optimization solutions, whether related to Blockchain today or the cloud back then, found quick acceptance within the business community. Investments in these mature solutions yielded substantial returns and created value. It's highly likely that well-considered implementations of Blockchain technology have already paid off as process investments. In fact, as early as 2016, McKinsey predicted the widespread adoption of Blockchain technology for commercial purposes within five years.[20] Observing the software solutions market in this sector, I can confirm both the phenomenon and the projected timeframes. Blockchain has seamlessly integrated into the extensive technology portfolios of leading global corporations, particularly in accounting and settlement operations. The primary motivation behind these implementations is cost reduction. Industry reports suggest that up to 70% of the value derived from Blockchain applications stems from their ability to significantly lower the operational costs of businesses in existing processes.[21]

Let's be clear—some Blockchain applications are not very exciting for everyday users. However, their understated nature is what makes them highly profitable. Most customers don't care about the technical details of the bank's backend. They just want it to work smoothly. Technical consultants in top advisory firms understand this value proposition well. They have found a profitable niche in Blockchain applications, benefiting themselves and many corporate clients. Reports indicate that when fully adopted by major banks, Blockchain applications can lead to annual savings of $8 to $12 billion, especially in cash transfer processes.[22] This creates a compelling competition with advantages and positive spillover effects for customers, partners, bank executives, and shareholders.

8.2.2 Financial sector

Let's start with a quick lesson in terminology before diving into specific cases of cryptocurrencies impacting the investment landscape.

I want to make a clear distinction between the terms "banking sector" and "financial sector." The banking sector primarily deals with savings, cash transactions, and loans, while the financial sector encompasses investments, insurance, risk management, and wealth creation.[23] Both sectors heavily rely on fintech, a category of technology solutions tailored to banking and financial businesses. While banks have integrated Blockchain technology into their internal processes for some time, the real cryptocurrency surge is just beginning. Here's another distinction: in banking, we often discuss a range of Blockchain applications, including but not limited to cryptocurrencies. In the financial sector, the primary focus is on cryptocurrencies themselves because they offer opportunities for profit, whether through capital accumulation, speculation, or various investment strategies.

Similar to banks, the financial sector initially approached the topic of cryptocurrencies with skepticism. For financial professionals and analysts, the main concern was not the lack of understanding of new solution's mechanism. After all, stories like mortgage-backed securities (CDOs) and credit default swaps (CDS) were equally incomprehensible to financial managers before, and they eventually led to the major crisis of 2008–2009, which resulted in a loss of trust in the financial sector and the popularization of Bitcoin. Michael Lewis vividly describes this in his book (later adapted into a film) *The Big Short*. Bank employees openly admitted in the industry that the new generation of financial products involved highly complex mathematics, for which they hired statisticians and econometric specialists, even though they had no knowledge of these fields themselves. The movie humorously portrays this with a scene of a financial managers' meeting. The genius hired by the investment bank is stereotypically portrayed as an Asian, presented as a winner of a mathematics Olympiad in China who doesn't speak English. Right after this scene, the supposed genius directly addresses the audience and explains, "Actually, my name is John. I do speak English, but Jared [manager] likes me to say don't because he thinks it makes me seem more authentic. And I got second in that national math competition…"[24]

If cryptocurrencies had already demonstrated their value over the years, why didn't traditional financial institutions invest in Bitcoin when it was just gaining momentum—at least officially? And if the financial world commonly justified supposedly bad (but highly profitable) investments with the argument of speculation, why didn't this apply to the new digital money? Critics, including the Occupy Wall Street movement and early cryptocurrency enthusiasts, pointed out that the financial sector had mastered the art of justifying risky instruments with previous crises. It wasn't a matter of assessing risk, as proper modeling and pricing could handle that. Experimental cryptocurrency investments could have been integrated with greater diversification in the existing portfolios of banks and funds. However, I have a theory that it was about something else: the certainty that funds wouldn't be defrauded and lost in a new, untested system. After all, cryptocurrencies are unregulated, making them inherently riskier in the eyes of traditional financial institutions.

The Winklevoss brothers, known for their legal battle with Mark Zuckerberg over the creation of Facebook, were one of the first entrepreneurs to recognize the need for regulated financial products in the cryptocurrency space. Their story became widely known through their HarvardConnection project, which Mark Zuckerberg initially agreed to work on but later failed to deliver the promised technological solutions.[25]

After years of legal disputes, both parties settled for a total of $65 million. With the funds obtained from the legal settlement, the brothers made a bold decision in April 2013. At that time, the price of Bitcoin (BTC) was around $130, and Cameron and Tyler Winklevoss used part of their settlement money to purchase approximately 1% of the total Bitcoin supply.[26] This strategic move allowed them to establish their own cryptocurrency exchange, known as Gemini. Right from the beginning, the Winklevoss brothers adopted a strategy of bringing order and regulation to the cryptocurrency "Wild West." They introduced structured rules and practices to cryptocurrency trading, aligning it with the well-established standards of the traditional financial sector.

Gemini's strategic advantage lies in becoming the first cryptocurrency exchange to operate under the regulatory framework of banking laws. This savvy move reflected the business acumen of the Winklevoss brothers, who launched their exchange with a strong commitment to obtaining the necessary licenses. This approach not only earned them the trust of financial regulators but also garnered respect within the cryptocurrency community. In May 2016, Gemini achieved a significant milestone when it was granted a custodian license by the governor of New York. This license allowed Gemini to act as a custodian, holding client assets in the form of cryptocurrencies. It marked the first time in history that digital currency resources were entrusted to a custodian. Under this license, Gemini is required to uphold the same standards for safeguarding digital assets as traditional banks and funds do for customer funds held in cash reserves. Gemini goes the extra mile to ensure the security of client funds by storing them in the State Street fund based in New York.[27] This practice has made Gemini, despite being a centralized exchange primarily owned by the Winklevoss brothers, widely regarded as a secure platform.

Adhering to traditional banking standards proved equally effective for another major cryptocurrency exchange, Coinbase. Both Gemini and Coinbase are highly popular platforms for cryptocurrency trading, with Coinbase also holding a financial services operator license. What set Coinbase apart was its historic listing on the stock exchange, making it the first company exclusively dedicated to cryptocurrency operations to achieve this milestone. Coinbase's debut on the New York Stock Exchange marked a significant milestone for the industry, signaling the integration of cryptocurrencies into the broader financial sector. This listing served as a strong indicator of the maturity of the cryptocurrency business.[28]

Further evidence of cryptocurrencies' integration into the financial sector comes from specialized products introduced by investment banks and funds. Notably, there are Bitcoin-based instruments, known as Bitcoin ETFs (Exchange-Traded Funds), which are investment funds traded on stock exchanges designed to track various market indices.[29] Historically, ETFs were associated with traditional indices like the German DAX, but now they include Bitcoin as well.

For years, there were efforts to introduce ETF indices tied to cryptocurrencies like Bitcoin, but regulatory hurdles prevented their launch. The market took thus a different approach by creating a conventional financial product known as Bitcoin futures contracts. These futures contracts enable speculation on Bitcoin's future price movements. It's crucial to distinguish between BTC (Bitcoin) and Bitcoin futures contracts. In the case of futures contracts, an investor agrees to buy or sell Bitcoin at a predetermined price in the future. When the contract matures, the agreed-upon transaction occurs regardless of the current daily BTC price. If the contract anticipates a larger increase in BTC price than what actually occurs, the investor profits, referred to as trading at a premium.[30] Conversely, if the BTC price is lower than the contract rate, the investor incurs a loss, known as trading at a discount. Futures contracts are a well-known tool in traditional finance, making their adoption for Bitcoin a significant development.

The creation of futures contracts was a key starting point; thanks to them, since October 2021, cryptocurrency investments are compatible with the traditional financial sector. The ProShares Bitcoin Strategy ETF, abbreviated as BITO, was created based on futures contracts.[31] The fund grew to over $1 billion in assets in two days; it reached this threshold faster than any other ETF before it.

On Wednesday, Jan. 10, the Securities and Exchange Commission (SEC) approved the first-ever spot Bitcoin ETFs, including those from Fidelity, BlackRock and Invesco. In total, the SEC approved 11 spot Bitcoin ETFs, and 10 of them started trading on Thursday, Jan. 11.

"Investors today can already buy and sell or otherwise gain exposure to bitcoin at a number of brokerage houses, through mutual funds, on national securities exchanges, through peer-to peer payment apps, on non-compliant crypto trading platforms [...] While we approved the listing and trading of certain spot bitcoin ETP shares today, we did not approve or endorse bitcoin. Investors should remain cautious about the myriad risks associated with bitcoin and products whose value is tied to crypto."[32]

The chief investment officer of California-based crypto investment firm Castle Funds, Peter Eberle, said in an interview that the approval would have a positive impact on the price of bitcoin. What do the approvals mean for other crypto investments? "Crypto tokens are highly correlated. If BTC does make a big price move, then other tokens will also participate to some degree. It will also make it likely that we will see an ETH ETF, which could provide significant tailwinds for ETH," Eberle said.[33]

Recent developments in the traditional financial sector highlight the significant progress made in bridging the gap between conventional finance and cryptocurrencies. Despite initial skepticism, cryptocurrencies have been integrated into traditional trading using terms that are familiar and widely accepted in the world of investors and financiers. These products have now entered the financial mainstream, with even renowned institutions like

NASDAQ offering crypto indices.[34] From my own observation and experience working with clients in the traditional financial sector, I've noticed that many of them may not fully grasp the broader economic and social context. They tend to focus on the immediate perspective of financial operations. However, when we take a step back and consider history, we see that financial engineering has driven numerous projects and economic systems that have left a lasting legacy. Just think of the achievements of the Renaissance Florentines in areas like accounting and banking or the innovations of Dutch merchants with their corporations and futures contracts. I believe we are currently experiencing an equally transformative moment in terms of the widespread adoption of cryptocurrencies. They are no longer just a technical curiosity but also a compelling avenue for capital investment. Digital assets in the hands of established financial institutions have the potential to reshape both the cryptocurrency and traditional finance industries.

8.3 BLOCKCHAIN CONQUERS THE CORPORATE WORLD

Blockchain and cryptocurrencies are often mentioned together, but they are not the same thing. It's crucial to understand this distinction to grasp how tech corporations have discovered another valuable aspect of the technology that underpins decentralized finance (DeFi). Cryptocurrencies are digital assets that enable users to exchange value in a decentralized manner, thanks to cryptographic mechanisms. This exchange of value occurs through the use of Blockchain technology. Now, let's talk about the Blockchain. Think of it as a type of data recording system, but with a twist—it's a distributed ledger.[35] In simpler terms, Blockchain serves as a decentralized database. Instead of storing data on a central server that's connected to all network users, information can be shared directly among users within a decentralized protocol. So, in essence, Blockchain provides the infrastructure for cryptocurrencies and many other decentralized applications. Understanding this relationship is key to appreciating how these technologies are reshaping various industries, including finance.

Among the world's 100 largest corporations, a substantial 81 have integrated Blockchain solutions into their operations.[36] This adoption isn't limited to tech giants; it spans various industries. Leading software companies like Microsoft, IT consulting firms such as Accenture and TCS, advisory companies, banks, and e-commerce platforms are part of this wave. But what's noteworthy is that even sectors seemingly unrelated to digital tech are onboard. Take Nestlé, for example. They've embraced Blockchain through the OpenSC platform, allowing consumers to trace the history and origins of food ingredients. It empowers consumers to make informed purchase decisions based on their preferences, dietary requirements, or ethical considerations.[37] In the fuel industry, Shell has followed suit, offering LO3

Exergy fuel with transparent information on blend composition and origin for station operators.[38] Beyond that, luxury brands like LMVH, Prada, and Cartier have formed a consortium to introduce the Aura platform. This platform enables their esteemed customers to verify product origins and digital certificates of authenticity—a testament to how Blockchain technology is making waves in unexpected sectors.[39]

Lately, I've been observing an intriguing trend where corporations are forging direct partnerships with Blockchain entities. In my line of work, we offer corporate client's guidance and develop platforms and products tailored for various applications within large organizations. These applications often involve technologies like HyperLedger Fabric or IPFS protocols, which might sound mundane, but they deliver tangible value to corporations. The current landscape of Blockchain technology is unique; it's no longer about peddling rudimentary Blockchain products. Instead, we're witnessing the emergence of groundbreaking applications, epitomized by the concept of the Metaverse, which I'll delve into in Chapter 9. Given this landscape, I believe it's an opportune moment for corporations to embrace Blockchain technology in their operations.

Blockchain has reached a point of widespread acceptance, enabling the creation of various business-oriented applications. This normalization of Blockchain technology mirrors past tech revolutions, such as the advent of personal computers in the 1980s or the integration of the early Internet into business operations in the 1990s. Similar to the skepticism that surrounded the Internet during the dotcom bubble, cryptocurrencies and speculative investor activity today face criticism, which also extends to Blockchain as a technology underpinning DeFi.

I foresee the next remarkable advancements in Blockchain technology emerging not solely from startups but also through collaborations involving corporations or purposeful partnerships. Large entities will rely on intrapreneurship, internal projects within corporate teams to drive innovation. Alternatively, partnerships of multiple entities will work collectively to develop pivotal components of the future Blockchain ecosystem. With corporations leading these implementations, we can expect economies of scale and instances of innovation influencing other "non-Blockchain" sectors. DeFi solutions and Blockchain technology, in general, have the potential to revolutionize various industries, including digital art, where major tech corporations could leverage Non-fungible Token (NFT) token solutions.

However, there's another aspect to consider, one that raises some concerns about the role of corporations in the development of the Blockchain sector. While leveraging distributed ledger technology, corporations can potentially solidify their position as economic giants. Despite the concept of empowering users, Blockchain has the potential to reinforce corporate dominance. The risk in such a model is the creation of a world where apparent decentralization brings people closer to technological advancements, but this may not necessarily be a positive development. It's easy to envision a scenario in which irrevocable user data stored on the Blockchain strengthens the market power of corporate Blockchain developers, potentially at the expense of individual users. This is why I emphasize the importance of establishing mechanisms for societal oversight over corporations. In a decentralized world, accommodating diverse interests is paramount, and Blockchain technology exemplifies the complexity of achieving this balance.

NOTES

1 https://www.visualcapitalist.com/ranked-the-largest-oil-and-gas-companies-in-the-world/
2 F. Baldwin Lida (1907), Unbound Old Atlantics, "The Atlantic Monthly", C: 683, access: 16.10.2015.
3 https://www.unz.com/print/AtlanticMonthly-1907dec-00812
4 https://archive.ph/20200127180010/https://fxssi.com/top-10-most-valuable-companies-in-the-world
5 https://www.statista.com/topics/4213/google-apple-facebook-amazon-and-microsoft-gafam/
6 https://finance.yahoo.com/news/tesla-worth-3-times-more-021127064.html
7 https://blog.s4rb.com/data-is-the-oil-of-the-21st-century
8 https://youtu.be/SnBrkwqwO-8
9 Hughes Eric (1993), A Cypherpunk's Manifesto.
10 https://satoshi.nakamotoinstitute.org/quotes/banks/
11 https://www.britannica.com/topic/bank/Influence-of-central-banks
12 https://www.nbp.pl/home.aspx?f=/o_nbp/informacje/polityka_pieniezna.html
13 https://www.mx.com/moneysummit/top-us-retail-banks-income-revenue/
14 This value results from the money multiplier. The money multiplier refers to how an initial deposit can lead to a larger final increase in the total money supply. This bank credit will, in turn, be re-deposited in banks, allowing lending to continue to expand and the money supply to expand further. For the required reserve rate of 0.5% in Poland, the money creation multiplier is 200. This results from the multiplier formula and the theory of economic mathematics—https://www.economicshelp.org/blog/67/money/money-multiplier-and-reserve-ratio-in-us/
15 https://www.bloomberg.com/news/articles/2021-07-21/bitcoin-btc-where-rich-family-offices-are-investing-goldman-survey-shows
16 https://www.ft.com/content/6c5b941c-5052-11e3-9f0d-00144feabdc0
17 https://forkast.news/video-audio/jpmorgan-onyx-jpm-coin-banking-blockchain/
18 The co-founders' companies included brands such as Accenture, Banco Santander, Bloc-kApps, BNY Mellon, CME Group, ConsenSys, IC3, Intel, J.P. Morgan, Microsoft or Nuco—https://entethalliance.org/enterprise-ethereum-alliance-launches/
19 Ibid.
20 https://bravenewcoin.com/insights/mckinsey-sees-blockchain-technology-reaching-full-potential-in-5-years
21 https://softtek.eu/en/tech-magazine-en/cybersecurity-en/70-of-the-value-of-the-blockchain-lies-in-the-reduction-of-costs/

22 https://builtin.com/blockchain/blockchain-applications
23 https://www.differencebetween.com/difference-between-banking-and-vs-finance/
24 https://www.youtube.com/watch?v=FoYC_8cutb0
25 *The Facebook, Inc. v. Connectu, LLC et al*, California Northern District Court, 9.03.2007 — via Justia.
26 https://www.ft.com/content/a9d4b73a-abdd-11e6-ba7d-76378e4fef24
27 https://www.gemini.com/blog/welcome-to-gemini
28 https://finance.yahoo.com/news/biggest-ipo-history-experts-weigh-103553733.html
29 https://www.gpw.pl/etfy
30 https://time.com/nextadvisor/investing/cryptocurrency/bitcoin-etf-approved/
31 Ibid.
32 Securities and Exchange Commission. Statement on the Approval of Spot Bitcoin Exchange-Traded Products. Accessed 10 sty 2024. https://www.sec.gov/news/statement/gensler-statement-spot-bitcoin-011023
33 https://www.nerdwallet.com/article/investing/spot-bitcoin-etf
34 https://www.nasdaq.com/crypto-Index
35 https://bernardmarr.com/what-is-the-difference-between-blockchain-and-bitcoin/
36 https://www.blockdata.tech/blog/general/81-of-the-top-100-public-companies-are-using-blockchain-technology
37 https://techhq.com/2020/07/nestle-why-the-worlds-biggest-food-company-uses-blockchain/
38 https://www.coindesk.com/markets/2019/07/11/oil-giant-shell-invests-in-startup-that-uses-blockchain-tech-for-energy-tracking/
39 https://www.lvmh.com/news-documents/news/lvmh-partners-with-other-major-luxury-companies-on-aura-the-first-global-luxury-blockchain/

Chapter 9

Metaverse

9.1 THE NEW REALITY

Picture this: It's the year 2061, and the world has undergone a remarkable transformation, thanks to rapid advancements in technology. The rules and economic landscapes we once knew have been reshaped entirely. The days of a clear divide between the IT sector and conventional industries are gone. Imagine you're working in spaces specially adapted for this digital age, or you're utilizing cutting-edge AR (Augmented Reality) and VR (Virtual Reality) tools. Through special goggles or immersive holograms, you effortlessly connect with your company's team and collaborators. The need for physical travel to attend meetings or interact with others is a relic of the past. Now, you can transport yourself to the perfect meeting spot or join your friends on a virtual trip to Bali with just a few clicks. These digital spaces offer hyper-realistic experiences, allowing you to engage in activities reminiscent of the analog world but without the limitations of time and space. In this parallel universe, you can seamlessly switch between work, socializing with friends, attending events, or even exploring a vibrant romantic life—all within the confines of the Metaverse. The Metaverse has become a digital oasis, offering a limitless range of possibilities. It's a world where the boundaries of reality and fiction have blurred, and where the only constant is change. Welcome to the Metaverse of 2061.

9.1.1 Science fiction becomes fact

Reading the description above, it may sound like science fiction, but it's not too far from what we've seen in movies like Steven Spielberg's *Ready Player One*. In that film, set in 2045, people enter a parallel reality called the OASIS using special VR goggles. Their mission? To find a hidden "Easter egg" left by the late OASIS founder, James Halliday, which promises a massive inheritance of his $500-billion fortune and control over the game.[1]

DOI: 10.1201/9781032621456-10

The OASIS is an irresistible space, engaging not just the eyes but all the senses. It's a stark contrast to the drab and ruined real world where the characters reside. People flock to the OASIS for new experiences, and they stay to fulfill their dreams and create a better version of themselves. In this digital realm, they have real influence, a stark departure from the limitations of the analog world. They navigate it through customizable avatars, and it's worth noting that the main character, Wade Watts, drives a DeLorean from *Back to the Future* in the game—a fun touch for fans.

However, science fiction films are one thing, and assessing the future of the IT sector is another. Science fiction often presents extreme visions of the digital world as cold and calculated, pitted against the warm, idyllic analog reality. In my view, this portrayal is somewhat naive. The role of cinema and literature is to tell captivating tales, fuel the imagination, and offer entertainment, even if it sometimes paints a stark contrast between the real and digital worlds.

Despite its flaws, Spielberg's vision of a future where the digital and real worlds blend has some good points. Notably, the film aligns with the likely visions of the Metaverse that may materialize in the future. Some of these elements are already within our grasp. In *Ready Player One*, characters engage in a game using VR goggles—a technology we're familiar with today. They create incredibly lifelike avatars, a feat that's certainly achievable even now. Moreover, the Oasis in Spielberg's film operates on the gamification principle, where participants strive to obtain a unique digital egg with a specific monetary value—a clear analogy to Non-fungible Tokens (NFTs). It appears that the new digital reality is closer than both science fiction enthusiasts and authors might have anticipated.

To understand how the Metaverse works today, look at two big players:

- social platform Facebook,
- video game Fortnite.

Mark Zuckerberg, who runs Facebook, and Tim Sweeney, who leads Fortnite's company—the leaders of these endeavors frequently express their intentions to create components of a larger interconnected metaworld, akin to the social networks we're familiar with in today's Internet landscape. When Mark Zuckerberg announced his company's rebranding as Meta, his goal was to offer users a platform for collective exploration of virtual spaces, irrespective of their physical locations.[2] Once again, Fortnite's vision of the Metaverse goes beyond mere gaming, as Sweeney himself articulated, "The Metaverse is 'a real-time, computer-powered 3D entertainment and social medium in which real people would go into a 3D simulation together and have experiences of all sorts.'"[3]

9.1.2 Connection to the analog reality

The concept of the Metaverse, though becoming increasingly familiar today, remains a profound mystery. As a result, speculating about its relationship with the analog reality is a challenging task. Deciding whether a user should dedicate their time to the analog or digital world will be a complex decision. Factors like the prevalence of the Metaverse will play a pivotal role. How many individuals will inhabit this cyber reality? What activities will be possible there? Will the Metaverse serve as a space for work, entertainment, socialization, or perhaps all of these simultaneously—reshaping our perception of leisure time and how we spend it? These are all open-ended questions. To make any predictions, it's vital to understand the pertinent concepts. I'll guide you through them step by step.

So, what does the term *Metaverse* signify? To capture its meaning accurately, we need to recall some facts from Latin lesson. While Latin may not be in everyday use today, it served as the universal, and often exclusive, means of communication for the intellectual elite for centuries. From the days of ancient Rome to the emergence of modern Europe, with France at the forefront, Latin facilitated discussions on the most profound topics among scientists, astronomers, and philosophers. It's no surprise that Latin, along with French, holds a prominent place in influencing present-day English, with 29% of English words having Latin or French roots.[4]

In Latin, the cosmos (*universum*) was described, and this term has endured in its current form (universe) in English. *Universe* denotes the entire reality—the world, the cosmos. This word comprises two components: the Latin prefix *uni-* literally means "one," and *-verse* originates from *vertere*, meaning "to turn, convert, transform." Consequently, the Latin word *universum* signifies "the whole world, the cosmos, the entirety of existing things."[5] Until the notion of crafting and describing a parallel reality surfaced, this universe was the extent of our comprehension. Until the era of technological revolution and the advent of the new Internet, the analog world was our well-understood, universal point of reference. Could this word, intended to encompass all the reality we knew, encounter competition?

As it turns out, the word *universe* no longer encapsulates our entire understanding of reality. This revelation, which might have seemed impossible during the 3,000-year history of the Latin language and the several hundred years of English alone, finally occurred in 1992. This breakthrough was ushered in by Neal Stephenson when he published his science fiction novel *Snow Crash*, introducing the term *Metaverse* for the first time. In the novel, he depicted a virtual 3D world populated by avatars representing real people.[6] What sets this word apart is its prefix—not *uni-* but *meta-*. *Meta* signifies something that goes beyond existing categories and definitions. It means "above" or "beyond." The Metaverse transcends the confines of the analog universe; it is a parallel reality coexisting with the known universe, fundamentally altering the rules of the game.

Among all the objective definitions of the Metaverse, free from marketing or ideology, one that resonates most with me is the one formulated by Matthew Ball, an American technology investor and analyst:

> A massively scaled and interoperable network of real-time rendered 3D virtual worlds that can be experienced synchronously and persistently by an effectively unlimited number of users with an individual sense of presence and with continuity of data, such as identity, history, entitlements, objects, communications and payments.[7]

In a simplified view, the Metaverse, or its various iterations, can be seen as an evolution of the mobile Internet—a successor to the stationary Internet era when connections were initially delivered via rudimentary telephone lines and billed in minute packets. Back then, access to the Internet was a novelty, something we could only sporadically enjoy. Utilizing Internet resources was not only expensive (costing as much as a minute of telephone conversation) but also quite cumbersome. Universal computer mobility was inconceivable; most of us had old PCs stationed in our rooms. Laptops were significantly pricier than already-not-so-cheap desktop computers. The idea of carrying the Internet in your backpack was a tantalizing vision for tech-savvy youngsters but remained financially out of reach for their parents. However, this was about to change rapidly.

The widespread adoption of smartphones and mobile Internet provided virtually everyone with constant access to computing resources and online connectivity via mobile networks, all at a fraction of the previous cost of PC computers. This paved the way for a more profound integration of Internet services into our daily lives. The days of using communicators intermittently (for instance, when we were in a specific location with access to a PC, like our rooms) were replaced by continuous communication. We used to set statuses on ICQ, and about a decade later, we began sharing snaps and Insta Stories. Thanks to mobile Internet, not only did communication solutions transform: our interactions with technology and the people around us also evolved as well.

Now, you might wonder, how does the Metaverse promise to be an improved version of the mobile Internet? To grasp the leap in our current understanding of the Internet brought about by the Metaverse, we should examine seven criteria that technology analysts consider necessary for the emergence and popularization of this new digital reality. Prominent analysts like Matthew Ball have explored these criteria. However, it's worth noting that the current mobile Internet already possesses some of these functionalities. Yet, we cannot label the present reality as the Metaverse; there's still a long journey ahead (Table 9.1).

Table 9.1 Features of the Metaverse and relevance to the now Internet

Criteria[8]	Description	Is it present in the modern Internet?
Continuity	Metaverse never resets or stops; it just continues indefinitely	Yes
Synchronization with the real world	Even with pre-planned and self-contained events, just like in "real life," the Metaverse will be an authentic experience that exists consistently for everyone in real time	Very limited
No restrictions on access	Anyone can be part of the Metaverse and participate in a specific event/place/activity together, at the same time and potentially with the same effect	Yes, however, centralized online platforms employ tactics that allow selected users access to a better category of services, thereby segregating users
Autonomous economy	In the Metaverse, individual users, teams, and companies will be able to create, own, invest, sell, and be paid for a wide range of "work" that produces "value" recognized by others	No autonomous economy; the modern Internet carries over economic realities from the analog world
Comprehensive experience	The Metaverse will be an experience that includes both the digital and physical worlds, private and public networks and experiences, and open and closed platforms	No. Currently, there is a clear divide between the analog and digital worlds; a Facebook event, for example, may include live coverage, but the experience of interacting with such content leaves the user feeling that he or she is merely an observer of the phenomena, not a part of it
Connections data and resources	The Metaverse will offer unprecedented interoperability, i.e., complex connections between data, digital objects, resources, content, and so on. In each of these experiences—for example—a character or avatar from one game will be able to seamlessly transition to another; a car designed for Rocket League (or even for the Porsche website) can be brought to work in Roblox	Very limited interoperability, present only within the centralized services of individual providers
Universality of open-source content, fairness in its distribution	The Metaverse will be filled with content and experiences created and supported by an extremely broad spectrum and a large number of contributors, some of whom will be independent creators, informal groups, or commercially oriented businesses. The authenticity of the origin of data in the digital economy will be overseen by the NFT circuit	Unfair circulation of content; in the modern Internet, either content is paid content (paywall access blockers), or there is an unlawful transfer of content, without adequate compensation to creators

9.2 FROM WEB 1.0 TO WEB 3.0

9.2.1 Where do we come from?

The rise of mobile Internet was a big step toward the Web we use today, known as Web 2.0. But what happened before that? Since we're talking about the future of digital tech in this chapter, let's first understand its past, at least the part that matters most to us. So, let's take a quick trip through Internet history.

The initial significant phase was the popularization of web pages. The network we've come to know and use on our PCs began to take shape in 1990 with the establishment of the "hypertext" protocol, also known as WorldWideWeb (originally referred to as W3). While this mechanism has undergone numerous enhancements over time, the fundamental logic of the WWW system has remained unaltered for three decades. It operates as a network of "hypertext documents" navigated using specialized software (browsers) following a client–server architecture.

Remarkably, the first webpage ever shared using the WWW protocol is still operational today. It belongs to the Swiss research center CERN, and you can visit it at http://info.cern.ch/hypertext/. These early years of the Internet, which I refer to as Web 1.0, can be observed through these initial web pages. They were static, unable to adapt their appearance or functionality to the user's preferences.[9] The webmaster decided how users could interact with the page based on their own ideas and convictions of how things should be. These pages were built in a basic way (usually using tables and just the objects created in the HTML programming language), which made it tough to view them on devices with different screen sizes. Files were mainly stored on central servers without advanced ways to share content. So, from a technical viewpoint, Web 1.0 was quite basic. But those were just the early days; more Internet changes were still to come.

Let's shift our focus away from the technical details and programming solutions. In my view, what truly defined Web 1.0 was the way information was distributed. In the initial version of the Internet, there were only a handful of content creators, and the majority of users were consumers. This meant that in Web 1.0, information flowed in one direction: from content creators to consumers. Information was tightly controlled, and users relied heavily on the site administrators. There was much less competition in content delivery compared to today.

The Internet primarily served as a "read-only" tool. Users were essentially just receivers of content, and they were quite scattered. Social media, as we know them today, didn't exist in Web 1.0. The first genuine social networking site, SixDegrees.com, launched in 1997, allowing users to create profiles and connect with friends. However, platforms like SixDegrees didn't completely address the one-way communication issue of Web 1.0. First, these services made it easier to communicate with friends and family, but they didn't facilitate sharing more advanced content. Second, social media platforms were still relatively niche. For instance, at the height of SixDegrees' popularity, it had 3.5 million registered users, representing just over 1% of all Internet users. In comparison, more than 62% of Internet users are on Facebook today.[10]

Significant advancements occurred when websites that allowed users to freely create content gained popularity. Web 2.0 brought about the common practice of average Internet users, without programming knowledge, to establish profiles on social networks (like Myspace and Facebook) or personal blogs (using services like Blogger, Tumblr, and LiveJournal).[11] Content could now be easily shared, commented on, and rated. Consequently, the flow of information on the Internet underwent a transformation. Web 1.0 was static, while Web 2.0 was dynamic, where every user played a dual role as both content recipient and creator.[12]

I've noticed that discussions about the emergence of Web 2.0 often emphasize progress and the democratization of content access. Indeed, as regular Internet users, we gained powerful tools through mobile Internet and social networks. Thanks to these tools, anyone can report news or even create their own piece of the digital landscape. The vast reach of platforms like Facebook or X enables a broad audience, resulting in strong network effects that lead to economies of scale and an overall improvement in the efficiency of communication systems.

However, there's another aspect of this transformation that often goes overlooked. In the current Web 2.0 model, network traffic heavily relies on a few services that control the entire flow of information on the Internet. For instance, in 2000, there were approximately 361 million Internet users worldwide,[13] with just over 17 million web pages. Today, it's estimated that 4.66 billion people have Internet access, but there are only around 1.9 billion web pages.[14] This means that at the start of the Millennium, there were roughly 212 web pages per average user, while today there are only about 2.4 pages per user.

We witnessed how risky it can be for the global Internet community to rely on a few centralized providers during the issues Facebook encountered in October 2021. For about six to seven hours, Facebook's services worldwide, including WhatsApp, Messenger, and Instagram, were unavailable due to a configuration error with domains. Users flocked to alternative services like Twitter, Discord, Signal, or Telegram, causing server overloads and crashes.[15] Internet service disruptions are a tangible phenomenon. Cisco, a prominent corporation specializing in telecommunications and cybersecurity, operates a project called "The Thousand Eyes," monitoring server attacks and error events. Short but financially painful outages don't affect small service providers or small and medium-sized businesses, but they have a significant impact on technological giants like Microsoft, Oracle, or Facebook. These giants manage critical network infrastructure and are responsible for delivering digital services within the Web 2.0 paradigm, upon which the modern world relies heavily.

I think we'll see more frequent service disruptions like the one Facebook faced in 2021. I previously wrote about ransomware attacks aimed at leading technology corporations such as Toshiba and Olympus.[16] Dozens of incidents have already occurred in various corporations using various technologies. For example, back in 2011, there was a big problem called the PSN Hack. Hackers got their hands on credit card info from 77 million PlayStation users. Some of these cards had important security codes recorded too. This led to a lot of people in the United States getting charged for stuff they didn't buy, like plane tickets from German airlines and things from Japanese online stores. PlayStation Network (PSN) was down for 24 days, and Sony had to settle lawsuits by paying $15 million to the affected users.[17]

One fundamental aspect of Web 2.0 is its centralized and deterministic nature. We might believe that by building our audience on platforms like Facebook or Twitter, we become influencers, giving us a false sense of control over the communication process. But here's the thing: in Web 2.0, the people who run these platforms not only decide what shows up in your feed but also what info gets shared. In September 2021, someone named Frances Haugen, who worked at Facebook, leaked some inside documents. These papers show that Facebook intentionally uses strategies to push content that divides people and makes them angry, even if it means spreading hate.[18] Why? Because it keeps people using Facebook for longer, especially to look at ads. Therefore, not only does the platform allow harmful content, but it also encourages it.

On the other hand, when centralized services apply "community protection standards," there's a lot of room for discretion. Content monitoring often lacks a clear and transparent appeals process. For instance, a whopping 99.3% of videos flagged for alleged standard violations are reviewed solely by an algorithm.[19] This algorithm doesn't consider the context in which specific statements are made. Consequently, even neutral creators on platforms like YouTube, such as history teachers, lawyers, social activists, or independent journalists, have faced numerous instances of their videos being removed, and sometimes their entire channels wiped out.[20] Interestingly, investigations have revealed that the platform made exceptions for popular creators like Logan Paul, Steven Crowder, and PewDiePie.

Finally, the most controversial topic must be addressed: banning in the centralized network. Just as individual content faces censorship on current social media platforms, this problem extends to specific individuals being denied access to these services for political or economic reasons. As someone who observes and participates in the tech world, I can't ignore the controversial and arbitrary rules for blocking certain users. It's perplexing how X (Twitter) blocked Donald Trump's account. At the same time, Taliban, Islamic fundamentalist leaders who came to power in Afghanistan through terror, have amassed hundreds of thousands of followers through social media. The Taliban use social media to spread their propaganda, thus violating all human rights and democratic values.[21]

So, what can we infer about Web 2.0 from these stories? In my view, three main takeaways highlight that the current network model can't keep evolving as it is. Changes are imperative, and users need more empowerment. First, the current network has grown organically, thanks to users' trust in service providers who handle our data and money. Yet, numerous instances involving leading Internet platforms demonstrate that these providers have eroded our trust through their actions. Second, the current system amplifies the power of network service operators at the expense of individual users. It seems that neither money nor political authority can fundamentally change this paradigm. Third, the current financial system in Web 2.0 relies on centralized cash mechanisms based on trust, which users have progressively lost in service providers. The straightforward conclusion is that the Web 2.0 model, built on trust, conventional bank transactions, and arbitrary access to digital services, is reaching its limits. A new deal is needed.

9.2.2 Where are we heading?

Moving beyond Web 1.0 and 2.0, it's time for a new network model, one that departs from the current static and centralized system. The upcoming revolution can be boldly described as a breakthrough, which we call Web 3.0. The Metaverse will be part of it.

Web 3.0's defining feature will be how we handle data. In this new paradigm, data won't be stored as proprietary assets on centralized servers controlled by tech giants and made available to users on their terms. Instead, data will be distributed among the entities that use it. This shift will rebalance the power dynamic between service providers and users. Through a combination of private and public keys, individual users will have control over what information they keep private and what they share with the wider network. This change isn't just about empowering users; it also enables service providers to craft more compelling business offerings. Without the ability to arbitrarily manipulate or restrict access to Internet resources, innovation, rather than monopolistic practices, will become the primary source of competitive advantage.

So, what defines Web 3.0? It's a concept that's still evolving, an uncharted territory for us. However, I believe that we can outline four critical factors that characterize Web 3.0 as follows:

1. *Openness*: Web 3.0 services will be constructed using open-source software. Even if profit-oriented corporations are the driving force behind their development, they'll have to rely on an open and accessible community of developers throughout the value chain.[22] While Google, for instance, currently follows a similar model for developing its software, it still places control in the hands of the corporation rather than the user community. Shifting this paradigm will make technical progress truly grassroots and organic. Instead of serving the

imposed business strategies of tech giants, it will be responsive to specific demands from the user community.

2. *Trustless Mechanism*: In Web 3.0, the network itself will enable participants to interact publicly or privately without the need for intermediaries.[23] Today, this role is fulfilled by operators and administrators of Internet platforms, requiring users to place trust in them for safeguarding their data and interests adequately. While data security is enforced by regulations to prevent corporations from losing profits, numerous actions within the current Web 2.0 network indicate that intermediaries in information and value exchange are sometimes abused, to the detriment of individual users.

3. *No Access Barriers*: In Web 3.0, anyone, be it users or service providers, can participate in the network without having to seek permission from a governing body.[24] This return to the network's roots will restore it as a space where ideas collide, and the community decides what content is accepted and promoted. This will align with the idea that communication technologies should facilitate the free exchange of thoughts in a marketplace of ideas.

4. *Protocol Flexibility and Content Portability*: Web 3.0, along with its core component, the Metaverse, will demand a broader, more intricate, and resilient set of standards and technological protocols. To ensure system interoperability and synchronize live experiences, we will have to refine and "standardize" many existing protocols, classifying them based on individual functions rather than just file formats. For instance, current graphic standards (GIF, JPEG, PNG, BMP, TIFF, WEBP, etc.) will need standardization because most existing protocols are closed, preventing users from transferring content across different systems. Amazon, Facebook, and Google use similar technologies, but they are not designed to work seamlessly with each other. Changing this paradigm, made possible through open development of open-source software, will elevate the overall value of the digital economy.

One of the natural outcomes of these fundamental principles will be the shift to decentralized digital currencies—cryptocurrencies—for value exchange in Web 3.0. The driving force behind this revolution will predominantly be Blockchain technology. While other peer-to-peer technologies could be utilized to some extent, they might not scale as effectively. In my view, Blockchain stands out as the most suitable technology for realizing the four core principles outlined here, while simultaneously delivering the essential elements of Web 3.0: openness, flexibility, a trustless mechanism, and unrestricted access to digital services. Various forms of Blockchain technology facilitate decentralized data exchange (such as the InterPlanetary File System), value exchange (cryptocurrencies), and even copyright management (NFTs).

Just like the shift from Web 1.0 to 2.0 brought significant changes to business and society, we are now on the edge of a revolution that will impact our economy and laws. Web 3.0, including the Metaverse, will require entirely new rules for managing communication, enforcing regulations, and handling taxes and copyrights for digital content through NFTs.[25] But the big question is: who will create these rules? In the past, Web 1.0 and 2.0 were largely under the control of national governments. However, the structure of Web 3.0 will make it incredibly challenging for current nation-states to regulate effectively. Instead, Web 3.0 will be a mix of social and corporate technology. Depending on the path chosen, oversight of Web 3.0 may be in the hands of corporations, which could take on various forms, such as being social, decentralized, or partially controlled by supranational corporations. This shift in control and governance is a critical aspect of the upcoming Web 3.0 era, and it's something we need to navigate carefully and thoughtfully.

The evolution of Web 3.0 and the Metaverse is marked by significant challenges and conflicts, as seen in the legal battle between Apple and Epic Games, the creators of Fortnite. This confrontation began in April 2020 when Apple removed Fortnite from its App Store. Epic Games had introduced its own payment system within the app, circumventing Apple's 30% fee.[26] Fortnite, the leader in the online gaming world, serves as a preliminary glimpse into the potential of the Metaverse, though it represents only a part of its vast possibilities.

A year after Fortnite's removal, Epic Games initiated legal proceedings against Apple, accusing it of monopolistic practices and antitrust law violations. During the hearings, Tim Sweeney, Epic Games' CEO, portrayed Fortnite as more than just a game. He suggested it was a pioneering force in digital experiences, transcending traditional gaming boundaries.[27] Conversely, Apple's defense compelled Sweeney to admit that Epic Games had intentionally flouted Apple's guidelines through "Project Liberty," an initiative designed to sidestep Apple's App Store fees.

This legal saga between Fortnite and Apple underscores two pivotal trends shaping the Metaverse's evolution. First, the emergence of a new digital realm is likely to incite friction between established Internet frameworks and novel paradigms. Looking ahead, a clash of ideologies is imminent: the current centralized model, which relies on trust and established corporate policies, will face off against a decentralized approach driven by smart contracts and open-source protocols.

Second, Fortnite's trajectory illustrates a foundational approach to building the Metaverse, showcasing the integration of broad technology platforms, user communities, and diverse digital experiences. This integration evolves to such a degree that it forms an alternate reality parallel to the physical world. Fortnite stands at the forefront of this evolution. Epic Games has not only cultivated an active community of over 350 million users[28] but has also innovated a new genre of digital entertainment, combining gaming, concerts, and communal digital experiences. This strategy predated the digitization trend accelerated by the COVID-19 pandemic.

A landmark event in this journey was the inaugural music concert held on Fortnite's virtual Pleasant Park stage, drawing an audience of about 10.7 million players in-game, with an additional 2 million tuning in via Twitch, Mixer, and YouTube streams.[29] This concept was further popularized by leading rappers and pop artists. For instance, Travis Scott's concert within Fortnite attracted 12.3 million live viewers on the game's island, with 45 million more watching replays on Epic Games' platform.[30] Such events are significant achievements, especially considering that 53% of Fortnite's players are aged between 10 and 25.[31] This demographic is just beginning to gain economic influence, increasing their value in the emerging market for Metaverse reality services. As these young users mature, their preferences and spending power will shape the digital service landscape, reinforcing the importance of platforms like Fortnite in the burgeoning digital world of the Metaverse.

In my opinion, the journey toward a fully realized Metaverse, as exemplified by Fortnite, is not just a technological leap but a cultural and societal shift. Fortnite, as a "mega app," offers a glimpse into this future, integrating community engagement, identity creation through avatars and spaces, and digital entertainment.[32] However, the transition to a genuine parallel reality requires more than just these features; it necessitates the development of a sophisticated economic ecosystem that supports digital financial assets like NFTs.

Looking ahead, I believe the Metaverse will eventually reach the level of technical sophistication that will not only appeal to early adopters, such as gamers and tech enthusiasts, but also attract mainstream users. This will mark a significant turning point, as the Metaverse becomes an integral part of daily life, much like the Internet today. However, predicting when this transformation will occur is challenging. The development of the Metaverse will likely be a mix of organic growth driven by user needs and strategic technological advancements. As this evolution unfolds, it will be shaped by various factors, including user experience, economic models, and cultural trends, ultimately leading to a rich, multifaceted digital world parallel to our physical reality.

9.3 PRIESTS OF THE DIGITAL METAWORLD

As we look at the big changes happening with the Metaverse, it's important to ask: who will benefit the most from this revolutionary digital shift? Will the world where we interact a lot in digital spaces be better or worse than the one we now know?

The idea of a fully working Metaverse is still pretty new and futuristic, so it's hard to give clear answers right now. But let's think about where the Metaverse might go. There are three main ways it could develop: led by big companies, by communities, or a mix of both. No matter if the Metaverse is built by companies looking to make money or by groups of developers with a mission, the real leaders will be people. Ultimately, both a corporation and an independent developer group are social constructs, backed by individuals with their own motivations and goals. So, what guides these leaders? Is it profit, the pursuit of innovation, a desire to reshape social interactions, or a combination of these? The answer to this might shape the character of the Metaverse and its impact on society. As you think about this, consider the human element at the core of this digital revolution. What do you think drives the architects of our digital future?

Reflecting on Stanley Milgram's psychological experiments from the 1960s can offer us valuable insights, especially as we think about the future of the Metaverse. Milgram's work explored how far people would go in obeying an authority figure, even if it meant going against their own moral principles. In his experiments, he asked men between 20 and 50 years old to administer what they thought were electric shocks to a "learner" for every wrong answer given. These shocks, which were actually fake, increased in intensity to levels that would be considered lethal if they were real.[33] Milgram's findings were eye-opening: people could be driven to inflict harm on others, under the influence of authority, even if it went against their personal beliefs.

In the Metaverse, like in any community, there might be a social hierarchy with leaders and followers. This leads us to wonder about the influence these digital leaders will have. What kind of behaviors and attitudes will they promote? What will motivate users in the Metaverse? Will there be initiatives to encourage good behavior among all users? Think about it: will the Metaverse push people toward positive actions, or could it bring out negative traits? It's an interesting question, especially if the Metaverse becomes a place where leaders exercise a lot of power over what's considered right or wrong. It seems crucial then to figure out what behaviors should be encouraged and what should be discouraged in the Metaverse. It's a bit like in the real world, where society rewards behaviors that are seen as good and punishes harmful ones. This discussion opens up many questions about the future of the Metaverse. How will it shape our actions and decisions? What role will the leaders play, and how will they influence the community? It's a lot to think about, especially as the Metaverse continues to grow and evolve.

In the analog world, good and evil evolved organically over centuries. Now, we're at a pivotal moment where these moral compasses can be redefined at the technological level. This is a unique opportunity to guide the digital metaworld toward positive ends, ensuring that it contributes to building a better, more ethical world. However, the path ahead isn't without its challenges. The darker aspects of this digital frontier, often depicted by science fiction authors, serve as a cautionary tale. It raises the question: what if we fail to steer this digital evolution toward good? I often wonder how a great mind from the past, like the German philosopher Friedrich Nietzsche, would perceive and analyze the Metaverse. Imagine Nietzsche today, equipped with a VR headset, delving into the intricacies of this digital universe:

- What's the most beautiful thing about the development of a parallel digital reality?
- My hopes…

NOTES

1 https://www.empik.com/player-one-cline-ernest,p1180782953,ksiazka-p*l*
2 https://www.theverge.com/22701104/Metaverse-explained-fortnite-roblox-facebook-horizon
3 https://www.theverge.com/2021/5/3/22417697/apple-epic-fortnite-app-store-antitrust-trial-day-1
4 T. Finkenstaedt, D. Wolff (1973), *Ordered Profusion; Studies in Dictionaries and the English Lexicon*, C. Winter.
5 https://www.etymonline.com/word/universe
6 https://www.theverge.com/22701104/Metaverse-explained-fortnite-roblox-facebook-horizon
7 https://www.matthewball.vc/all/forwardtotheMetaverseprimer
8 https://www.matthewball.vc/all/theMetaverse
9 https://www.geeksforgeeks.org/web-1-0-web-2-0-and-web-3-0-with-their-difference/
10 https://www.statista.com/statistics/264810/number-of-monthly-active-facebook-users-worldwide/
11 https://www.twilo.net/blog/web-1-0-to-web-3-0/
12 https://firstmonday.org/article/view/2125/1972
13 https://www.pingdom.com/blog/incredible-growth-of-the-internet-since-2000/
14 https://www.internetlivestats.com/total-number-of-websites/
15 https://www.nytimes.com/2021/10/04/technology/facebook-down.html
16 https://techcrunch.com/2021/09/12/technology-giant-olympus-hit-by-blackmatter-ransomware/
17 https://www.gamesindustry.biz/articles/2021-04-14-playstation-networks-24-days-of-downtime-10-years-ago-this-month
18 https://www.wsj.com/articles/the-facebook-files-11631713039
19 https://www.theverge.com/2019/6/7/18657112/youtube-hate-policies-educators-journalists-activists-crossfire-takedown-demonetization
20 https://www.theguardian.com/technology/blog/2011/apr/29/playstation-network-hackers-credit-cards
21 https://www.politifact.com/factchecks/2021/aug/23/instagram-posts/twitter-hasnt-suspended-afghanistans-president-the/
22 https://medium.com/fabric-ventures/what-is-web-3-0-why-it-matters-934eb07f3d2b
23 Ibid.
24 Ibid.

25 https://www.matthewball.vc/all/themetaverse
26 https://www.theverge.com/2020/8/13/21366438/apple-fortnite-ios-app-store-violations-epic-payments
27 https://www.theverge.com/2021/5/3/22417697/apple-epic-fortnite-app-store-antitrust-trial-day-1
28 https://www.statista.com/statistics/746230/fortnite-players/
29 https://www.knowyourmobile.com/consoles/are-fortnite-concerts-live/
30 Ibid.
31 https://boardgamestips.com/destiny-2/what-is-the-average-age-of-fortnite-players-2020/
32 https://www.knowyourmobile.com/consoles/are-fortnite-concerts-live/
33 https://onlinelibrary.wiley.com/doi/10.1111/j.1559-1816.1999.tb00134.x

Chapter 10

Is it possible to change the world of finance once again?

10.1 DI LAMPEDUSA LOOKS AT TODAY'S WORLD

When I look at the banking sector on one hand and cryptocurrencies on the other, I'm confident that we're living in times of a breakthrough. At the beginning of this book, I mentioned the historic achievements in financial engineering and the great inventions that propelled the economic development of societies. These advancements once took literally thousands of years to materialize. But what about today? Well, a cryptographic innovation called "Bitcoin," introduced in 2009 by Satoshi Nakamoto, has accelerated the pace of events. It went from being just a theory among cryptographers to a significant financial instrument. Those against whom Bitcoin was directed initially, tried to combat it, yet they eventually changed tactics and started using cryptocurrencies to their advantage.

Where are cryptocurrencies and the whole Blockchain sector heading? I find a quote from Giuseppe Tomasi di Lampedusa especially relevant in answering this. His words are the guiding theme of my book, reflecting the profound insight of this Italian author. Di Lampedusa, famed for his novel *The Leopard*, provides a compelling parallel. "If we want things to stay as they are, things will have to change," declares Tancredi, an aristocrat aware of the inevitable demise of his world of privilege. He symbolizes the old guard, *the ancien régime*, forced to evolve or risk losing their standing.[1]

This echoes the stance of modern bankers toward cryptocurrencies and Blockchain technology. Initially resistant, they've now largely embraced these innovations, much like how the Kingdom of the Two Sicilies grappled with maintaining relevance in a unified Italy. Di Lampedusa portrayed a pan-European shift toward nation-states, resisted by entrenched local powers. And what's happening in the financial industry? A similarly consequential change—namely, decentralization and elimination of intermediaries in economic exchange.

Observing Jamie Dimon, CEO of JPMorgan Chase, as he criticizes Bitcoin, while simultaneously offering products related to it, I'm reminded of Tancredi from *The Leopard*. It's a similar mixed bag when governments battle existing cryptocurrencies yet develop their own ones. It's somewhat

DOI: 10.1201/9781032621456-11

ironic. On the one hand, I find it amusing how the banking sector and governments create their own versions of the tools that the early Cypherpunk movement tried to use to destroy this central authority. On the other hand, I see how the principle that "If we want things to stay as they are, things will have to change" works in practice.

But why this shift? Why have banks joined a revolution seemingly against their dominance? The answer is straightforward: it's profitable. Blockchain has become a technology just like other fintech solutions that streamline a range of financial processes. It's in these improvements wherein lies the key to the great fortunes that will be built on cryptocurrency applications and Blockchain technology. These decentralized and distributed ledger technology (DLT) solutions are exactly what banks and financial institutions need. They provide robust, secure, and importantly, global platforms for data and value transfer. This is where the future of finance is heading, reshaping the essence of the industry.

Could Satoshi Nakamoto have ever envisioned his creation being used in such a transformative way? Bitcoin's journey has been nothing short of extraordinary—from a niche interest among cryptographers to making headlines on Bloomberg. It transitioned to a cornerstone of financial engineering, not by conquering the banking sector but by being assimilated into it.

This shift in cryptocurrencies' role is really put into perspective by Jackson Palmer, the co-creator of Dogecoin. Dogecoin began as a joke, combining cryptocurrency with the popular Doge meme featuring a surprised Shiba Inu. It was a meme-turned-cryptocurrency, capturing the community's imagination. Beyond its initial gimmick, Dogecoin funded remarkable initiatives, like supporting the Jamaican bobsled team's Olympic bid, funding wells in Kenya, or assisting dog training for autistic children.[2]

So why would its creators, Jackson Palmer and Billy Markus, step away from such a successful project? The reasons were twofold: scale and ideology. Dogecoin's soaring to a $90 billion capitalization was alarming for them. They criticized the project's trajectory, where speculation transformed a meme token into a lucrative venture. Palmer's move away from Dogecoin and his critique of the crypto world really highlighted the huge gap between Dogecoin's original joke status and the wild speculation it sparked. Jackson Palmer later wrote on Twitter:[3]

> After years of studying it, I believe that cryptocurrency is an inherently right-wing, hyper-capitalistic technology built primarily to amplify the wealth of its proponents through a combination of tax avoidance, diminished regulatory oversight and artificially enforced scarcity.

Despite claims of 'decentralization', he continued:

> the cryptocurrency industry is controlled by a powerful cartel of wealthy figures who, with time, have evolved to incorporate many of the same institutions tied to the existing centralized financial system they supposedly set out to replace.

The Dogecoin saga is indeed a standout story. It's a bit tricky to assess the whole crypto sector based on a project that started as a joke, but Jackson Palmer's perspective is quite insightful. His comments shed light on the disillusionment within parts of the cryptocurrency community, especially among those who were ideologically committed to the Blockchain movement. Figures like Palmer feel betrayed by the unfulfilled promise of cryptocurrencies offering equal wealth opportunities. This disillusionment echoes the sentiments of the early Cypherpunks. They laid the groundwork for the development of cryptocurrencies. They were around at a time when Bitcoin and its kin were either unknown or actively opposed. Their vision of a transformative, egalitarian financial system contrasts with the speculative and commercialized reality that some projects, like Dogecoin, have come to represent.

In addition to those like Palmer, there are other notable figures who found themselves on the losing end of the crypto revolution. Take Mike Hearn, a Bitcoin project developer, for example. He believed that the cryptocurrency community's ambition to transform cryptocurrencies into a global financial system would drive acceptance of crucial changes in early-stage projects like Bitcoin. However, the sector displayed its contradictory nature. It was overly permissive, allowing, as Palmer described, a "powerful cartel of wealthy people" to exploit Blockchain technology for personal gain. At the same time, the governance of projects like Bitcoin proved too inflexible, with a developer community often resistant to meaningful development and crucial updates in a system that was supposed to be a collaborative effort.

Ironically, a few years ago, cryptocurrencies were stuck in a peculiar spot—they were too significant to be ignored but still too niche, unexplored, and misunderstood to fully captivate the business plans of traditional bankers. Initially, crypto enthusiasts and speculators could rightly view themselves as part of a digital and financial counterculture. However, as with any movement that gains momentum, a shift toward mainstream acceptance and commercialization was inevitable.

The journey toward the acceptance of cryptocurrencies within the banking sector was a gradual process, marked by strategic milestones that showcased the business utility of digital assets. The initial hurdle lay in gaining regulatory acceptance, as cryptocurrencies faced skepticism and even hostility from regulators. Over time, this sentiment evolved, with key figures in traditional finance, such as the chairman of the Federal Reserve, Ben Bernanke, recognizing the potential of cryptocurrencies. As the regulatory landscape shifted, the next crucial step was the development of a robust infrastructure that would facilitate the seamless buying and trading of cryptocurrencies. This development was spearheaded by prominent exchanges like Coinbase, Gemini, Kraken, and Binance, which played a pivotal role in simplifying the crypto market for average users. These platforms provided user-friendly interfaces, making it possible for individuals without in-depth knowledge of crypto mechanisms to participate in the market effectively.

As cryptocurrencies gained regulatory and infrastructural support, they began to be seen as attractive assets for diversifying investments.

If you're reading this quickly, take a moment to slow down. We're in the middle of a big change, and it's worth paying attention to. A mere 15 years ago, Bitcoin emerged as a programming curiosity, captivating a group of enthusiasts exchanging ideas on digital anarchy in mailing lists.

In a world where becoming a regular millionaire is tough, the idea of becoming a crypto millionaire is pretty tempting. But is it too good to be true? That's the question we're facing as we watch this digital experiment go from a nerdy project to a serious contender for the top spot in storing wealth.

10.2 WOULD HAVE KARL MARX INVESTED IN CRYPTOCURRENCIES?

The years 2020 and 2021 brought about a profound global transformation. The COVID-19 pandemic disrupted long-standing economic norms, shifting desires from urban living to a newfound yearning for homes with gardens in rural or mountainous settings. In London, for example, rents have begun to fall significantly, with suburban house rental prices rising by 11%.[4] Our lifestyles also underwent a significant change. Many individuals, rebelling against traditional consumerism, abandoned common supermarkets in favor of eco-friendly stores or direct purchases from local farmers. For millennials and Generation Z, conscious consumer choices and awareness of environmental issues became central. It appeared as though people were adopting slower, healthier, and more fulfilling lives. Despite the pandemic's widespread economic impact, various business support programs and global anti-crisis measures mitigated the effects for many companies and their employees. However, amid this relatively optimistic outlook, a concerning issue emerged—income inequality, spotlighted particularly by progressive left-wing observers.

In 2020, the number of ultra-high net-worth individuals saw a staggering 24% increase, marking the fastest growth in 18 years.[5] Furthermore, the combined profits of the 10 wealthiest individuals during the pandemic were sufficient to fund COVID-19 vaccines for the entire global population.[6] Notably, Democratic activist Alexandria Ocasio-Cortez gained social media popularity for making a bold statement at a high-profile gala in New York's Metropolitan Museum of Art. In an event where tickets cost up to $30,000, AOC appeared in a white dress bearing the bold message: "Tax the rich."[7] What was once considered a private matter—the wealth of the affluent—had evolved into a significant social issue, bringing attention to the pressing need for addressing wealth disparities.

As the gap between the rich and the middle class widened at an alarming pace, one of the most scrutinized publications in mainstream economics became

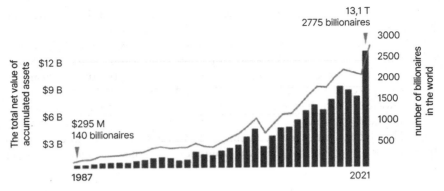

Figure 10.1   Number of billionaires around the world and the total net value of their assets.

(*Source*: Data from https://www.forbesmiddleeast.com/billionaires/world-billionaires/2021-vs-1987-how-forbes-billionaires-list-changed-in-35-years)

Forbes' flagship list—the compilation of the world's richest people. This exclusive group expanded rapidly in 2020, with 660 ultra-wealthy individuals added, bringing the total to 2,775 people, each boasting an average fortune exceeding $4.7 billion.[8] While most entrepreneurs so far made their fortunes either in conventional business or in simple IT services, recent years have created a new category of wealthy people: crypto millionaires. (Figure 10.1).

While most entrepreneurs amassed their fortunes in conventional business or straightforward IT services, recent years have created a new category of rich people: crypto millionaires. In 2021, nine new entrepreneurs who owe their fortune to Blockchain technology appeared on the *Forbes* list.[9] The prestigious magazine also maintains a separate, very interesting list of "The Richest People in Cryptocurrencies."[10] *Forbes* sets the lower wealth limit for recognizing someone as a crypto millionaire at $350 million. What can we learn about them? Comparing both lists, we primarily see that crypto millionaires are young people. While the average age on the large list of all the richest people is 67, for crypto entrepreneurs, it's only 42.[11]

Beyond age, another defining trait is their inclination toward risk-taking. This is vividly illustrated by the daily fluctuations in cryptocurrency rates, showcasing a marked difference when compared to traditional financial instruments. In financial parlance, this volatility is a key metric. Unlike most entrepreneurs from the broader *Forbes* list, who typically list their companies on stable stock exchanges like those in New York or London, crypto millionaires navigate a world of substantial daily fluctuations. While traditional investments, such as the American SP500 index, are considered relatively safe, the cryptocurrency landscape presents significant daily swings compensated by the promise of high profits. A clear illustration is found in the comparison of the results of SP500 and the Bitcoin rate (Figure 10.2). In

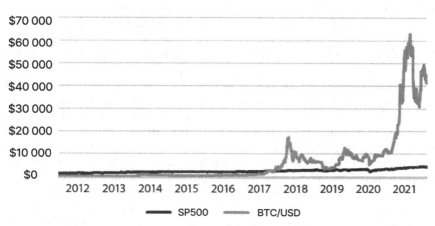

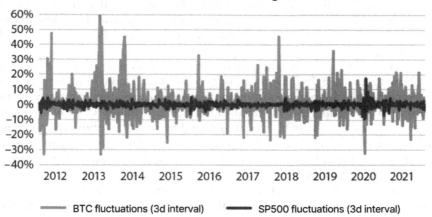

Figure 10.2 Comparison of cryptocurrency market movements and the American Stock Exchange.

essence, fortunes built on cryptocurrency businesses carry a higher degree of risk, but this risk has allowed the most astute investors to become highly successful crypto-specialists. The contrast in risk appetite and investment dynamics paints a vivid picture of the evolving landscape where the allure of crypto assets is reshaping traditional notions of wealth accumulation.

Third, the entry of crypto millionaires into the exclusive league of the rich has shed light on an important question about the future of finance and the sociology of wealth. Is Blockchain technology truly paving the way to wealth for everyone in the world? The underlying assumption was that cryptocurrencies, operating beyond government control, would provide equal access to financial services for people irrespective of their origin or economic status. However, has this vision materialized? In my perspective, not quite.

On one side, Blockchain was meant to be a global technology, breaking down barriers for regular people to use financial services. On the other hand, there was a loud assurance in the global public debate that a model of diversity, globalization, democracy, and capitalism—all these social solutions—would gradually include those previously excluded into the high-tech culture community and developing countries into developed ones. This idea was put forward by one of the most important analysts of the modern world, Francis Fukuyama. He wrote about the "end of history"—a situation where technical and civilizational achievements would enable all countries to advance socially.[12] Of course, Fukuyama wrote in the context of broad global considerations, but this logic should also work on a micro scale. This approach makes sense; there are about 400,000–800,000 people in the world who own at least 1 BTC.[13] That's a large amount at today's rate, and there are even smaller investors. According to estimates from leading cryptocurrency companies, there are about 75 million registered Bitcoin wallets worldwide.[14] In June 2023, the number of users of all cryptocurrencies exceeded 425 million.[15] This means that Blockchain, thanks to its key implementation in the form of cryptocurrencies, has become a global technology.

As cryptocurrencies reached more people, a multitude of ideas emerged on how to leverage this new technology for financial gain. In theory, cryptocurrencies held the potential to empower societies economically, a particularly alluring prospect for financially excluded individuals. Cryptocurrencies became so widely accessible that they found favor among those from underprivileged backgrounds, including people in developing countries and ethnic minorities. This, at least theoretically, offered hope for addressing complex socio-economic issues.

Cryptocurrencies challenged established norms, breaking free from painful correlations present in traditional financial systems. For instance, in the United States, areas with lower percentages of residents holding bank accounts tended to be hotspots for organized crime.[16] In Italy, regions under the influence of the mafia often experienced higher costs for obtaining credit by companies compared to other areas.[17] Cryptocurrencies disrupted these patterns because their decentralized structure didn't factor in the elements that traditional financial models would deem as higher credit risks, such as residing in an "inappropriate" neighborhood or having an "undesirable" skin color. What took years of advocacy for equal rights for customers in centralized finance was inherent in the "crypto" sector from the start. During the Civil Rights Movement, insurers in the United States were offering black clients only two-thirds the value of policies compared to whites, with higher premiums. In the world of cryptocurrencies, such discriminatory practices would be impossible due to the openness of the system. Access to financial services isn't based on arbitrary profiling but on the user's own will—all that's needed to be part of the cryptocurrency environment is access to the Internet.

It's essential to recognize that while some may enjoy comfortable conditions reading these words in a cafe, the world is not uniformly beautiful everywhere. Utilizing a bank account and paying substantial transfer fees is still an aspiration for Mexican immigrants at the border crossing in El Paso, Texas. For millions in Sub-Saharan Africa or South America, located far from the nearest city or bank branch, it's an unattainable dream.[18]

While cryptocurrency optimists argue that the surge of projects in the decentralized finance (DeFi) sector paves the way for wealth accumulation for an average person, regardless of socio-economic status, origin, skin color, or residential address, a crucial question looms: does this revolution truly benefit everyone equally? Is the dream of becoming a crypto millionaire as attainable as the access to the benefits that cryptocurrencies promise? After years I spent navigating in this sector, my conviction is that it is not. Blockchain technology, with its primary application in cryptocurrencies, has undoubtedly opened doors for creative, innovative, risk-taking individuals to earn, as evidenced by the stories I've shared in this book. However, these success stories are more of an exception than a rule. The realization of the dream of crypto-millions remains a rare scenario, echoing the inexorable laws of economics, such as the Pareto distribution, which assert that wealth tends to concentrate.

This principle applies across various financial domains, be it investing in the stock market (with leaders like Warren Buffet), the Forex market (where George Soros made a fortune), or cryptocurrencies. However, what about the broader cryptocurrency community? Media narratives abound with stories of individuals who, driven by conviction in the potential of cryptocurrencies, risked their life savings, only to lose them during significant market corrections.

Another concerning aspect is the observed addiction to trading cryptocurrencies, mirroring the behavioral patterns of compulsive gamblers.[19] The irrational behaviors of participants in this sector accentuate a series of problems, leading to a scenario where, even in the "crypto" world, the adage "the rich get richer, and the poor get poorer" holds true, echoing the sentiments of Percy Bysshe Shelley, an English Romantic poet.

In the world of crypto speculation, traders' irrational behavior is more visible than on the traditional stock market, leading to an inability to effectively build wealth through cryptocurrencies. For instance, fans of technical analysis in cryptocurrencies often fall into the habit of judging reality from a time perspective. In English, this is called hindsight bias, a tendency to think that one knew all along what would happen. Technical analysts might draw specific lines on candlestick charts, suggesting a cryptocurrency's directional movement. This might be taken as gospel truth, akin to a revealed word from a favored trading influencer. Given that a considerable number of active day traders follow such influencers' advice, these words can turn into a self-fulfilling prophecy. Furthermore, there's the confirmation bias trap, where individuals tend to notice or seek information that aligns with their existing beliefs.[20]

The challenges faced by new crypto-financiers mirror those portrayed in movies like *The Big Short* or *The Wolf of Wall Street*. Much like Jordan Belfort promising his subordinates that they would have become "the greatest CEOs in the United States of America," crypto enthusiasts often envision themselves owning a mythical #Lambo financed by their Bitcoin investment profits. While such success stories do occur—whether after years in corporate roles, investment banking, or long nights monitoring crypto charts on a computer screen—they are not the norm. There needs to be a school of smaller fish swimming around the big fish, highlighting the rarity of these exceptional stories.

In my classes at NYU, where we delved into the sociology of entrepreneurship, wealth, and capitalism, one of the key figures we studied about was Karl Marx. While the assumption in a free market suggests equal access to wealth opportunities for everyone, Marx challenged this notion by dividing society into distinct classes: farmers, proletariat, and bourgeoisie—the ruling class and owners of capital.[21] According to Marx, the private ownership of the means of production enriched capital owners at the expense of workers.[22] While his predictions of the fall of capitalism and its self-destruction mechanisms didn't fully materialize and often led to the establishment of bloody communist regimes, some of his ideas remain relevant, even when analyzing the potential of becoming a crypto millionaire in a modern, digital economy.

It's essential to recognize that Karl Marx lived in the latter half of the 19th century when economic realities were heavily shaped by the division of people into categories—more related to their aspirations than formal distinctions. During Marx's time, widespread industrialization was unfolding, marked by the mechanization and automation of production. Cities were rapidly growing, absorbing villagers who transitioned from farming to factory work. The capital owners were those who constructed the factories—owners of buildings and machines that facilitated production. In contemporary sociology, traditional social classes like proletariat and capitalists are no longer the focal points. Instead, we grapple with a three-level division: the upper class comprising wealthy individuals, the middle class encompassing managers and salaried employees, and the lower class—sometimes referred to as the "precariat," engaged in precarious jobs that offer uncertain and basic livelihoods. This shift in societal structure reflects the evolution from the industrial era Marx lived in to the complex dynamics of the present digital economy.

Over the years, numerous concepts have surfaced regarding the traditional trajectory of social advancement—moving up the class ladder from lower to middle and from middle to upper class. A manifestation of such aspirations is encapsulated in the American dream, a collection of ideals where economic freedom offers opportunities for prosperity, success, and social mobility achieved through hard work. Despite a growing perception that the American Dream is becoming more challenging to realize, a significant portion of US residents (51% of those surveyed) still believe in its feasibility. However, statistical trends reveal a shift—while around 90% of children born in 1940 found themselves in higher income positions than their parents, only 40% of those born in the 1980s can anticipate similar socio-economic advancement.[23]

Inspired by Marx's ideas, sociologists like Thomas Piketty highlight that contemporary society doesn't offer equal opportunities for getting rich. Piketty's research indicates that capital owners, particularly entrepreneurs, accumulate wealth faster than those providing physical labor.[24] The question arises: were cryptocurrencies designed to challenge this rule and level out the playing field? Unfortunately, data reveals that 2% of entities on the Bitcoin network control 71.5% of all available BTC units. This concentration of wealth raises concerns about cryptocurrencies' transformative potential in addressing historical economic inequalities.[25]

For the majority navigating the elusive path to wealth, cryptocurrencies have proven to be a tool akin to other elements in the business ecosystem—a technology simplifying the journey to millionaire status but not eradicating existing barriers. While cryptocurrencies facilitate capital raising through token collections, achieving financial success still demands substantial self-denial, responsibility, and hard work, as is the case in any economic pursuit. Decentralized finance has enabled active speculation, but success requires learning from mistakes or delving into advanced analytical work encompassing economics, finance, and technology theory. The allure of easy money with minimal effort fueled dreams within the Blockchain sector, resulting in both notable successes and equally spectacular failures. Consequently, cryptocurrencies affirm an age-old yet perennial truth: wealth and poverty are not states of possession but states of thinking.

What can you gather from these thoughts? You're encouraged to analyze them yourself. This book intentionally goes beyond stories of people who became extremely rich with cryptocurrency, delving into market functioning, economic mechanisms, and innovative ideas. Since the time of Vilfredo Pareto, statistical laws have remained unwavering, indicating that the colossal majority of readers will likely not become crypto millionaires. Assertions to the contrary either ignore the sector's rules or peddle visions of easy money through coaching services, which is often baseless. In examining cryptocurrencies and business aspirations individually, it becomes evident that true fortunes are not shaped by chance or the capricious sway of fate dictating the direction of the BTC/USD chart.

In any sector, including the dynamic world of Blockchain, authentic crypto fortunes emerge from carefully considered business decisions.

The right foundation enables a select few entrepreneurs to surpass the realm of crypto millionaires and even ascend to crypto billionaires. However, these individuals are exceptions, the chosen few—the whales in the crypto-currency ocean, around which plankton, minnows, and smaller and medium fish navigate. In the Blockchain world, each entrepreneur must decide their role based on their dreams, abilities, and, importantly, their intentions.

10.3 IS BLOCKCHAIN A CHANCE FOR YOU?

If you dream of becoming a crypto millionaire, it's important to think about whether you have the right qualities for success in any business, not just in the crypto world. There are two main psychological qualities that greatly predict individual success: intelligence (IQ) and openness, which means being open to new ideas and experiences. These traits are part of our personality, and we don't have much control over them as we grow older. This might be disappointing for those who believe they can switch careers easily with just the right attitude. Starting and running a business is not for everyone. It requires a specific kind of personality.[26]

I'm talking about a creative mindset, not just doing the same tasks over and over in your business. This creativity is crucial, especially in new industries like cryptocurrencies and Blockchain technology. Research shows that successful entrepreneurs share similar traits with artists. Both entrepreneurs and creators take risks, and while many try their luck, only a small group succeeds. However, those who do succeed often achieve remarkable success. To emphasize this point, think about a Spotify project called Forgotify in 2017. They created a playlist with 4 million songs that had never been played out of the 20 million available on Spotify. This means that one in every four songs had zero plays. On the other hand, the most popular artist on Spotify at that time, Drake, had his songs played 4.7 billion times.[27] This illustrates how success in creative fields, including entrepreneurship, often comes to a select few while many others face challenges.

But there is also a broader dimension of reflections on cryptocurrencies and Blockchain. In the analysis of technical progress operate Kranzberg's laws. These are six principles that also perfectly describe the "crypto" sector and how to approach it. I will quote all of them here:[28]

1. Technology is neither bad nor good, nor is it neutral.
2. Every technical innovation requires additional progress to be fully effective.
3. Technical progress comes in waves, large and small.
4. Although technology can be a major factor in many social issues, non-technical factors take precedence in decisions related to policy in this area.
5. All history is important, but the history of technology is the most important.

6. Technology is a field of human activity. Therefore, the history of technology is also a matter related to human action.

As we close our discussion, let's consider Kranzberg's first law. This law perfectly illustrates how, in my view, we should approach evaluating the cryptocurrency sector. The Blockchain technology that makes cryptocurrencies work isn't inherently good or bad. We shouldn't see it as a savior or a threat to the modern banking sector. Instead, it's a space for promising innovation that can address many problems in today's globalized world. It's crucial to understand that the value coming from using Blockchain goes beyond what digital money alone offers, especially in today's economically unstable environment. Blockchain technology isn't neutral because it has the potential to bring about significant changes. These changes will impact not only financial operations but also how we think about exchanging value in various markets, including finance, law, and even art.

Considering their enormous potential, cryptocurrencies and Blockchain can meet a specific societal need: the need for a tool that is scalable, open, doesn't rely on physical cash, is fast, and is universal. It should be accessible to every individual and company that traditional banking currently limits. Because of the many advantages I've discussed in this book, Blockchain and cryptocurrencies can't be seen as neutral. We can't be indifferent to this major revolution in the world of finance. I believe that only a rational approach to the phenomenon of decentralization will enable society to truly benefit from the opportunity in front of all entities. These entities will make Blockchain their genuine, calm ally rather than seeing it as an enemy or a false friend.

NOTES

1 https://www.radici-press.net/gattopardo/
2 Ibid.
3 https://www.independent.co.uk/life-style/gadgets-and-tech/dogecoin-crypto-cult-founder-jackson-palmer-bitcoin-b1884531.html
4 https://www.standard.co.uk/homesandproperty/renting/london-rents-fall-suburban-and-countryside-rentals-rise
5 https://www.bbc.com/news/business-57575077
6 https://www.bbc.com/news/world-55793575
7 https://www.newsweek.com/met-gala-ticket-cost-money-raised-1627921
8 https://www.livemint.com/market/cryptocurrency/bitcoin-boom-minted-nine-new-cryptocurrency-billionaires-last
9 https://www.forbes.com/sites/johnhyatt/2021/04/06/the-cryptocurrency-tycoons-on-forbes-2021-billionaires
10 https://www.forbes.com/richest-in-cryptocurrency/#90bcee81d496
11 Ibid.

12 https://fukuyama.stanford.edu/
13 https://bitcoinist.com/how-many-people-actually-have-at-least-1-bitcoin/
14 https://www.buybitcoinworldwide.com/how-many-bitcoin-users/
15 https://www.statista.com/statistics/1202503/global-cryptocurrency-user-base
16 https://digitalcommons.odu.edu/cgi/viewcontent.cgi?article=1032&context=sociology_criminaljustice_etds
17 E. Bonaccorsi di Patti (2009), Weak Institutions and Credit Availability: The Impact of Crime on Bank Loans, Bank of Italy Occasional Paper No. 52.
18 https://data.worldbank.org/indicator/FB.CBK.BRCH.P5?most_recent_value_desc=false
19 https://www.bbc.com/news/uk-scotland-57268024
20 https://www.businessinsider.com/what-is-behavioral-finance?
21 https://www.ocr.org.uk/Images/170204-marxism.pdf
22 https://courses.lumenlearning.com/boundless-sociology/chapter/economic-systems/
23 https://www.theguardian.com/inequality/2017/jun/20/is-the-american-dream-really-dead
24 https://newrepublic.com/article/117429/capital-twenty-first-century-thomas-piketty-reviewed
25 https://news.bitcoin.com/analysis-shows-bitcoin-whales-are-stockpiling-but-btc-ownership-is-not-highly-concentrated/
26 https://blog.maskys.com/jordan-peterson-on-entrepreneurship-selling-and-matching-your-job-to-your-temperament/#how-does-psychological-temperament-link-with-entrepreneurship-what-predicts-success
27 https://www.billboard.com/pro/drake-rihanna-top-spotify-year-end-lists/
28 M. Kranzberg (1986), Technology and History: Kranzberg's Laws, "Technology and Culture", 27 (3), pp. 544–560.

Printed in the United States
by Baker & Taylor Publisher Services